Astrology, Science and Culture

Astrology, Science and Culture

Pulling Down the Moon

Roy Willis and Patrick Curry

Oxford • New York

First published in 2004 by
Berg
Editorial offices:
1st Floor, Angel Court, 81 St Clements Street, Oxford OX4 1AW, UK
838 Broadway, Third Floor, New York, NY 10003-4812, USA

Berg is an imprint of Oxford International Publishers Ltd.

Library of Congress Cataloging-in-Publication Data
A catalogue record for this book is available from the Library of Congress.

British Library Cataloguing-in-Publication Data
A catalogue record for this book is available from the British Library.

ISBN 1 85973 682 3 (Cloth)
1 85973 687 4 (Paper)

Typeset by JS Typesetting Ltd, Wellingborough, Northants.
Printed in the United Kingdom by Biddles Ltd, King's Lynn.

www.bergpublishers.com

Contents

Introduction   1

1   Astral Science before History   15

2   The Sky as Mirror   25

3   Actors on the Celestial Stage   39

4   The Astrological Story   49

5   Divination and the Stars   55

6   Varieties of Astrological Experience   65

7   Disenchantment – and Re-enchantment   77

8   Science and Astrology   93

9   Divination Today   109

10   Minding the Heavens   127

11   Conversing with the Stars   135

Appendix   151

Bibliography   153

Index   167

Introduction

A philosophy that does not include the possibility of soothsaying from coffee-grounds, and cannot explicate it, cannot be a true philosophy.

Walter Benjamin

Our subtitle comes from a passage by Plutarch (*c.* 46–120 BCE). In *de genio Socratis*, 590a, he mentions the divinatory practices of the women of Thessaly, 'who are supposed to be able to pull down the moon'. But the tone of his remarks is not admiring but scandalized. Very little in the debate about astrology is entirely new. The word itself means the 'word' (*logos*) or 'language' of the stars, and is now customarily contrasted, as a pathetic remnant of primitive superstition, with the academically respectable science of *astronomy*. This latter term means 'measurement of the stars', and accurately reflects Galileo's famous contention that only that which can be measured is truly real. Quantity is primary, quality secondary. This book maintains the converse proposition, daring to privilege sensory quality over a row of digits, and is devoted to investigating and recovering a stellar language of apparently immemorial antiquity; a mode of communication that is part of our common heritage as human beings, and evident, albeit at the most mundane level, every time we say 'Good morning!' to our neighbour. This is a primal faculty that seems to be embedded in our genes, ironically the very entities now commonly presented, in the current version of reductive materialism, as the sole and invisible masters of our personal and collective destinies (cf. Dawkins 1989).

This, then, is a study of a social phenomenon that attracts enormous popular interest and virulent scientific contempt in roughly equal measures. Our central argument is that astrology is best understood as a divinatory technique: a dialogue with the divine in a postmodern, post-Christian, and newly reanimated, universe.

Theoretical Orientations

Our key term *dialogical* is, of course, shamelessly appropriated from the seminal work of Mikhail Bakhtin (1990), and endowed with a carnal dimension not readily apparent in the Russian master. For us, the drive to communicate is inscribed in our flesh, part of our innate human heritage along with a seemingly unique species ability to put ourselves imaginatively in the place of our dialogical other. This idea is already implicit in Husserl's notion of 'inter-subjectivity', though the father of philo-sophical phenomenology still clung to the ghost of the isolated Cartesian *Cogito* in the guise of a posited 'transcendental ego'. It was left to Husserl's brilliant disciple Maurice Merleau-Ponty to finally liberate the phenomenological project from the last vestiges of Cartesian and Platonic dualism by recognizing the perceiving and communicating body as the very ground of all human knowledge and experience (Merleau-Ponty 1962). The Dialogical Imperative, if we may so call it with a passing nod to Kant, immerses us from the beginning in perpetual conversation with an environment perceived as pervaded with life and intelligence. As the philosopher David Abram observes in his inspired exegesis of Merleau-Ponty, 'perception always involves, at its most intimate level, the experience of an active interplay, or coupling, between the perceiving body and that which it perceives':

> Prior to all our verbal reflections, at the level of our spontaneous, sensorial engagement with the world around us, we are *all* animists (1996: 57)

Our innately motivated bodily participation in the world opens, as we shall see, on to an arena of cosmic scope in the human dialogical engagement with divinity, and the prospect of an astrology newly conscious of its ancient roots in the carnally grounded astral science of prehistoric humanity (see Chapter 1).

Here let us note certain fundamental consequences of our dialogical reading of human nature. In its essential, necessary openness – the inherent duality of dialogue which is also, and most fundamentally, a many-voiced plurality – this reading permanently guarantees us against any possibility of collapse into monolithic solip-sism. However, it also means we must perforce abandon for ever all ambition to theoretical closure, the dream – or nightmare – of a final, all-embracing theory of everything, the breathtakingly arrogant project so dear to materialist and reductionist science. Being ourselves part of a Nature in a permanent flux of becoming entails that we are always in a state of being adventurously, and dangerously, open and vulnerable in a universe we are ourselves responsible for constructing as co-creators with divinity. Such a condition is inherently subversive of our socially conditioned sense of personal identity, insofar as we are willing to participate consciously in the work of the heterogenous and polymorphous deities. Knowing nothing of god or goddess, modern science has nevertheless recognized almighty power and wisdom in the gene. As James Watson, co-decipherer with Francis Crick of the natural script embodied in the DNA chain, has observed: 'We used to think that our fate was in the stars. Now we know that, in large measure, our fate is in our genes' (see Davis 1998: 130).

There speaks the voice of materialist and objectivist science. Yet, as we shall see, in the moment of ritual divination the exclusive dualisms of subject and object, mind and matter, what is outside and up there (including stars) and what is down here and inside (including genes), partially dissolve in awareness of cosmic connection. Multiplicity remains, separation remains, but there is also relatedness, there is participation. Bringing an anthropological perspective to bear on the topic of astrological divination, we see the true business of astrology as participation in the greatest dialogue of all, the grand conversation of earth and heaven.

Conversation, whether mundane or cosmic, is a learned technique. As individuals, we may well, and profitably, spend a lifetime developing and perfecting our ability to communicate with our fellows in everyday life. As for the cosmic dimension, for countless millennia humankind has employed the species-level language of myth to construct a trans-personal and trans-cultural world of the collective imagination. In that perduring enterprise, it appears that women may well have played a pioneering role (see Chapter 1).

Compelling Attraction

It is a safe assumption that human beings have always found the heavens a source of wonder, meaning and guidance. The particular tradition of doing so that we know as astrology originated in ancient Mesopotamia about 4000 years ago, but is now virtually global.[1] Notwithstanding all the subsequent changes and refinements, most recently computerization and mass marketing, its ancient intuitions, and the craft of their explication, seem to have lost none of their compelling attraction in the twenty-first century CE. Having survived sweeping indictments by various political and intellectual authorities of the day, from the Christian Church to secular scientists, there is no reason to think astrology will not continue to exist, perhaps even flourish, in the future. In other words, there are good grounds for supposing that astrology is, or at least involves, a relatively fundamental human experience. And that in turn is surely a good reason to take it seriously as a phenomenon and therefore a subject in its own right. The words of Terence from the first century BCE – 'nothing human is alien to me' – are the still unshakeable defence of its study. (It actually needs only an observation of Hazlitt's, though: 'Whatever interests is interesting'.) Yet in the academy the partisan intentions of its critics have largely succeeded, because even when astrology has been addressed, all too often it has been as merely a failed version of something else: a primitive or incomplete magical religion, or else a pitiable or contemptible pseudo-science. As a result, not only has an integral dimension of human experience been systematically ignored by intellectuals whenever and wherever it might apply to us, but so has an enormous resource for human self-understanding. There is astrology itself: what exactly unites the experience of a Babylonian priest, a seventeenth-century almanac-writer and a postmodern astrological consultant? In addition, there is the phenomenon of its opposition: what is it about astrology that equally

– 3 –

provokes a Cicero, a St Augustine, and (although their grasp of the subject vastly exceeded his) a Richard Dawkins?

In what follows, the scientific attack on astrology will be addressed in detail, especially the way in which it exceeds what can be justified in strictly scientific terms. That excess will be analysed as the scientism – essentially, science as a rationalist cult – which drives astrology's most influential contemporary critics. If that lobby deigns to notice our critique, they will probably hold it up as a demonstration that denying the ultimate truth of modern science leads to defending astrology, of all things. But what such a charge really amounts to is that we dare to assert the right to existence of other forms of life than those offically approved by a Committee of Scientific Experts, and the current Witchfinder General. To this, we plead guilty.

Among the least culpable professional intellectuals are historians, who have produced some excellent studies in recent decades which go some way to overcoming this prejudice. Even here, though, the gestures denying the fact of studying a living and continuing tradition are unmistakeable; and their work suffers for it (for example Grafton 1999). Much more problematically, however, psychologists' tests of astrology have almost all consisted of crude attempts to demonstrate that astrological effects are attributable to something else (usually forms of cognitive error) that psychologists are more comfortable with. And many who would baulk at Adorno's idiosyncratic blend of psychoanalysis and Marxism still accept without a second thought his view that belief in astrology is a pathological indicator of authoritarian irrationalism (Adorno 1994).[2] Sadly, most anthropologists who are perhaps best-placed of all to do astrology justice have yet to perceive this exoticism on their own cultural doorstep, while the absence of their grasp of ritual and religion has too often left the few sociological surveys of astrology thin and banal. Serious philosophical studies of astrology are almost non-existent (but see Guinard). Our book is intended to help remedy this situation.

The tendency to vehement condemnation of astrology while remaining proudly ignorant of it is only part of a greater and more complex process, of course, which is partly the subject of this book. But let us also appreciate a simple, clear expression of that problematic, like a beautiful and rare flower, when we come across it. 'The ancient magical ceremonial quality of art', wrote the Orkney poet George MacKay Brown, 'makes it profoundly suspect to all puritans, hedonists, humanists, democrats, pragmatists, rationalists, progressives; and nowadays nearly everyone fits into one or other of these categories' (Brown 1969: 130).[3] Detected by the keen noses of the true believers in modernity, that quality is also what ultimately makes astrology so objectionable. But it is equally why we appreciate it, and would like to see it readmitted to civilized cultural conversation, beyond as well as within the academy. Both parties stand to benefit.

Apprehensions of Wonder

How did we, social historian and social anthropologist, separately arrive at our engagement with astrology?

Roy Willis writes: As a child I was soon made aware of an environing culture that saw no call to find symbolic meaning in Nature, whether on the earthly or celestial planes. Indeed, any suggestion of mysticism was frowned on in our upwardly mobile middle-class household. I did, however, pick up the exciting idea that there might be intelligent life out there. In the 1930s the planet Mars with its reported 'channels' that might be canals was the favourite locale for an extra-terrestrial civilization, a possibility brilliantly exploited by the writer H.G. Wells in *War of the Worlds*. His novel captivated my infant imagination. Then came a deeper and more unsettling apprehension of wonder, when I chanced on Sir James Jeans's *The Mysterious Universe* in my father's modest library. He had, I think, been given the book as a school prize, and whether he'd ever read it I didn't discover. But I'll never forget the strangely disturbing thrill, combining ecstasy and terror, provoked by a photograph in it of the Andromeda galaxy, imaging billions of stars caught in a swirling tidal race. I never told anyone about this odd experience. As for astrology as such, I didn't encounter it until I became a school drop-out before the term was invented, and, at the early age of sixteen, enrolled as a trainee journalist with a local newspaper. One of my apprentice assignments there was to fabricate horoscopes for the weekly column 'What the Stars Foretell', and I like to think I made a reasonable job of it, being an imaginative kind of chap. How long this presumably harmless exercise in deception had been going on, I had no idea, but it seemed like a well established journalistic practice, similar to the weekly 'fiddling' of expenses I was taught to manage with the jocularly-styled 'wangle sheet'.[4] The attitude to the ancient, once-royal craft of astrology I learned then was a good-humoured contempt for a popular belief presented as little more than a quaint survival from a pre-scientific age.

And now, half a lifetime later, after admission to Oxford University at the age of 33 to study anthropology under the legendary Edward Evans-Pritchard, with various ethnographic field trips and an array of publications in animal symbolism, structural analysis of oral tradition, mythology and spirit healing under my academic belt, I embark on the investigation of what was initially for me a virtually unknown subculture. The quest has led to unexpected insights and a fresh and integrative perspective on the anthropological project in the current free-floating epoch of postmodernity (cf. Bauman 1992). My first interview in this new line of research was with John Henry, a colleague in Edinburgh University and author of an academically respected study showing how modern science emerged from the 'Natural Magic' of the Renaissance period (Henry 2002 [1997]).

I met Dr Henry aware that astrology, a systematized body of knowledge with roots in remote prehistory, is almost uniformly dismissed by present-day scientists and scholars as a relic of an unenlightened past, an absurd pseudo-science with no place in the intellectual furniture of rational people. I was also aware that, despite the contempt and hostility of the official guardians of truth, astrology today still exerts a powerful influence on the public at large. As Professor Richard Dawkins notes with distaste, books promoting astrology easily outsell texts on astronomy (Dawkins 1998: 115). I went to John Henry in the hope that he could clarify what was going on. Is it, as Dawkins supposes, simply a matter of people clinging on to infantile delusions of faith in a magical universe, or are there deeper, possibly darker, reasons for the current vitality of a system of knowing that should, by rational criteria, have become extinct with the dawn of the age of scientific understanding in eighteenth-century Europe?

War over 'the Mars Effect'

Commonly in anthropology, the questions posed by the field investigator in the beginning come to seem absurdly naive before the end, and so it has proved with this particular piece of research. The first issue I raised with John Henry was the possible objective truth of astrological theory, and the works I drew to his attention in this context were the extensive publications of French psychologists Michel and Françoise Gauquelin. This scholarly couple caused an academic furore lasting more than two decades by purporting to prove, using a vast mass of statistical evidence, that – as astrology has long held – planetary positions at the time of birth correlate with specific personality traits. In particular, the Gauquelins' data appeared to prove conclusively that people born with the planet Mars rising above the horizon were highly likely to achieve prominence in the military or athletic fields (Gauquelin, M. 1969/1996)

There was a similar close correlation between those born with the planet Saturn rising and subsequent brilliant scientific careers. These surprising – for scientific orthodoxy – results have withstood numerous determined attempts by sceptical scientists to prove them false. So well founded do the Gauquelins' data appear to be that the eminent psychologist Hans Eysenck, not otherwise known for his liberal opinions, felt able to conclude that these 'inexplicable' findings 'cannot just be wished away because they are unpalatable or not in accord with the laws of present-day science' (Eysenck and Nias 1982: 208).[5]

In retrospect, I find interesting in itself my choice of the Gauquelin case to open an academic discussion with Dr Henry. For here, in Gauquelin, was a man with apparently impeccable scholarly credentials (his scientific qualifications were in psychology and statistics) producing solid evidence of cosmic connectedness in the face of a dominant scientific paradigm that sees the wonders of human being as no more than the chance outcome of a series of evolutionary accidents. Now, however, I can see that Michel Gauquelin's thinking (he has been the main exponent), notwithstanding the scandalous nature of his conclusions, remains solidly within the mechanistic worldview inherited from the Enlightenment. Gauquelin rejects virtually the whole wonderfully intricate conceptual apparatus of traditional astrology: the 'houses' (twelve divisions of the zodiac), 'aspects' (degrees of arc between any two planets in the zodiac) and the myth-laden zodiacal signs them-selves, all repositories of astrological meaning in the ancient craft. In place of these hallowed concepts, Gauquelin advocates a frugal 'neo-astrology' (his own term for his work), which is exclusively concerned with the terrestrial effects of the Moon and just four planets: Venus, Mars, Jupiter and Saturn (Gauquelin 1988). As I now see it, Gauquelin's 'neo-astrology' has little or nothing to do with the 'reading' of astrology as a way of knowing which we develop in this book.

Back then, however, it seemed an agreeably 'middle of the road' issue with which to open the discussion and, sure enough, Dr Henry was acquainted with the controversy and, like Eysenck, open-mindedly prepared to consider Gauquelin's case on its merits, as the following 'field notes' attest.

JH: On the face of it his [Gauquelin's] work looks remarkable. He looks at the rising planets at the moment of birth, and, using French and German records, which are precise on the moment of birth, he found astonishing correlations between high achievers in sports and Mars as the rising planet at the birth-time, Nobel Prize winners in science and Saturn as their rising planet.

'We'll get him!'

Now as you know, scientists are very defensive of their territory, and when someone like Uri Geller comes on the scene claiming occult powers, they band together to denounce these frauds, as, well they might in Geller's case. They tried to do the same with Gauquelin, but thus far all their efforts have failed. He took up the statisticians' challenge and submitted his data to the re-analysis they had demanded, but the significant correlations still remained. He did that several times, and all efforts to debunk him have so far failed.

I remember seeing a TV programme concerning an association of scientists dedicated to debunking bogus claims to paranormal powers and knowledge, like those of Geller. One of them said, referring to Gauquelin, 'We haven't got that man yet, but we will!' But so far nobody has, so you can see Eysenck's point: there's something strange going on here.

Unlike Eysenck, however, my scholarly interlocutor ventured an explanation for Gauquelin's 'inexplicable' findings. Suppose, Henry suggested, that human beings naturally conformed to a limited number of personality types:

Then if we could pin this down, we could see why particular personality types were born at particular times and that would maybe account for what Gauquelin sees, and so it's not really an astrological influence, it's a biological clock ticking . . . There don't have to be influences, it's just that what's occurring on earth happens to be synchronous with what's going on in the sky.

That expression of Henry's, 'a biological clock ticking', struck me as eerily resonant with the Enlightenment doctrine of the world as a great machine (cf. Capra 1982), and, sensing we'd reached the end of that particular avenue of thought, cast about for some other approach to this amorphous topic I was committed to researching, and which appeared to run the whole gamut from the esoteric-magical to the tabloid-tawdry. Why was it, I asked, that astrology continued to be so popular with the multitude, whereas its sister discipline alchemy had virtually disappeared with the advent of the modern scientific era. Now I was on Henry's home turf, and his response this time was forthright: the comparison was misleading.

JH: It's very easy for us to look back at both astrology and alchemy and say they are just occult pseudo-sciences and therefore they're the same, but in fact they're not the same. Historically what happened to alchemy was that it was largely absorbed into mainstream chemistry, while its spiritual and mystical side faded away. In the case of astrology it wasn't fragmented like that. None of it was taken over by modern science as it developed.

RW: But wasn't Johannes Kepler an astrologer as well as a scientist?[6]

JH: Yes, Kepler was, but as far as he is remembered today it's for his laws of planetary motion and his rigorous mathematical work. His astrological work is just regarded as a curiosity. I suppose what I mean is, well, let's take the case of the Moon. In mediaeval times many suspected that the Moon affected the tides, and they also thought the Moon affected human destiny in an equally mysterious way. Then Isaac Newton came along and showed how the Moon affected the oceans by means of gravity, but he didn't address himself to the Moon's influence on personality or anything like that. But astrology retained its integrity as far as believers were concerned, while intellectuals from the eighteenth century onwards almost unanimously rejected it, as being completely unfounded. Gravitation wasn't thought of as a force that could affect human destiny or personality, just a physical force that could affect bodies.

Feeling thoroughly rebuffed by this expert, I then tried a different tack, one that harked back to my boyish interest in exploring the universe. I asked Henry if he thought there could be a connection between why astrology is so big in popular consciousness at present and the advent of space travel and space science? Human beings were already exploring these formerly divine objects in the sky: Venus, Mars, Jupiter, etc. As the anthropologist Charles Laughlin (1997) has put it, we are on the verge of becoming a space-faring species, a development that could put us on more of an equal footing with those 'divine' beings out there. Could there be any mileage in that?

> *JH*: My own response to this is straightaway to reject it as a reason for the continuing popularity of astrology. They're completely different approaches to the nature of the heavens, if you like. The mentality behind Ufology and so on is that there are intelligent beings out there who are likely to be technologically more advanced than we are, and wouldn't it be great if we could contact them? Whereas the astrological approach is that the heavens themselves, nothing to do with whether there is life out there or not, have an influence on the Earth: the astrologer wants the heavens to remain different, aloof and mysterious, except as interpreted by the astrologer. But the X Files-type people want to go out there and explore. I see these as very different things.

Well into his stride by now, Henry went on to expound his own 'take' on the effect on astrological beliefs of Copernicus's discovery that the Earth orbited the Sun, rather than the other way about.[7]

> *JH*: You know, it used to be thought that the Copernican theory had knocked astrology on the head by showing that the Earth moved round the Sun rather than vice versa, but rather the reverse happened: new planetary tables were developed which were much more accurate than the old charts based on Ptolemaic astrology, so people thought, 'Aha, now astrology is going to be better because of this greater accuracy'. And of course this was helped by someone like Kepler who was the leading mathematical astronomer of his day and also a committed astrologer. Incidentally, Kepler rejected the signs of the zodiac and things like that and concentrated on the aspects of the planets, opposition, sextile and trine and so on. He even invented new aspects.

I came away from this absorbing and chastening discussion with John Henry better informed, but little the wiser, and aware of a faintly disturbing echo of infant apprehension of a deadening world. It was time, I decided, to experience something of 'live' astrology, by betaking myself to a practising exponent of the craft. A suitable subject suggested itself in Charmaine Chinniah, an enthusiastic astrologer with an academic background in mathematics and computer science.

Unfazed by Copernicus

As she described her background to me, Charmaine began life in Sri Lanka as the offspring of a middle-class indigenous couple. The marriage was not happy, and the couple separated soon after Charmaine's birth in 1963.

> *CC*: My maternal grandmother went to an astrologer when anyone was born, including me. My horoscope was mysteriously 'lost', and I always thought it was because it was

'bad'. In fact, the 'bad' indications were realized when I was eight years old, when my estranged father tried to kidnap me. My mother responded by taking me to Britain. While she studied medicine in London, I went to several schools in different places, eventually entering Edinburgh University. It was there I began in my spare time to study Western astrology and was astonished to find that my [Western] horoscope accurately predicted the 'kidnapping' incident with my father when I was eight years old. That horoscope has given me a sense of my own life, who I am.

I asked Charmaine how, with her scientific training, she saw astrology, especially in the light of post-Copernican astronomy. She had no problem with the Copernican Revolution: 'We don't live on the Sun!' She added that 'as a sort of scientist myself', I can't make a theoretical case for astrology – I just know, from experience, that it works'. This is a statement I was to encounter frequently during my research.

> *CC*: It makes sense if everything is connected. Think of chaos theory and the beating of a butterfly's wings causing a tornado on the other side of the globe.[8] To me, astrology makes sense as a form of divination The so-called supernatural powers which come into play during a divinatory session are not outside the domain of natural law. It's just that because we are unable to understand these laws in a 'rational', left-brain manner, and because consensus reality is so unbalanced at present about this form of consciousness. That means that knowledge systems like astrology and Tarot, which use an intuitive, right-brain consciousness, are denigrated or seen as abnormal.

To put this interesting argument of Charmaine's to the test, I then asked her to devote our second interview to an analysis of my own horoscope. (I was born at Ilford just before 2 p.m. on Thursday 15th September 1927.) What then ensued proved a quite unsettling account of my childhood, a topic on which I was certain Charmaine could have known nothing from ordinary sources. She made me aware of the pervasive influence in my life of the antithetical powers of the planets Saturn and Uranus, the first conveying discipline and restriction, the second anarchic revolt and chaos. Conjoined with a powerful and persistent Jovian influence, this planetary combination presaged a need to communicate unorthodox ideas, in both teaching and writing. That was my first exposure to astrological ways of knowing, and it was followed by a consultation with Jane Ridder-Patrick, a professional astrologer and herbalist, that brought my first intimation of transcendence in an astrological setting.

Ridder-Patrick is the author of *A Handbook of Medical Astrology* (1991), in which she describes astrology as 'one of the finest and most advanced tools for understanding the individual psyche'. Like Charmaine, Ridder-Patrick made no attempt to give me a 'scientific' justification of astrology, beyond asserting that it 'provides an objective map of subjective reality'. Well, does it? Not long into my hour-long session with Jane, I had to admit that the 'map' composed of planetary/

psychic interactions corresponded remarkably well with my inner perceptions. Interestingly, Ridder-Patrick also identified a conjunction of Uranus and Saturn as crucially significant for me. About two-thirds of the way through her absorbing analysis of my horoscope, I had what seemed like a momentary glimpse of that 'dialogue with the divine' aspired to, and supposedly experienced in some cases, by postmodern astrologers (see our Chapters 5, 9, 10 and 11). This is what I wrote immediately after the encounter with Ridder-Patrick:

> She was calmly rational at first, and it seemed to make sense. Then, about two-thirds of the way through the hour-long reading, the atmosphere changed. The relatively mild-mannered Jane became suddenly powerful and authoritative, as though someone or something was speaking urgently through her, something quasi-divine. She became a priestess, possessed of Spirit, able to make all clear. Evidently, she had moved into an altered state of consciousness in which she was 'seeing' things, connecting things together, as though a master plan or pattern had suddenly become apparent. It was weird, and impressive.

There is obvious common ground, explored in Chapter 11, between a divinatory and participatory astrology, and that segment of current anthropology called 'experiential', committed to first-hand investigation of the altered states of consciousness peculiar to divination and ritual healing. The area we are concerned with, where the Lyotardian 'grand narratives' of orthodox Christianity and mainstream science no longer hold sway, is also that of phenomenological philosophy's struggle for liberation from the millennial division and conflict in the European soul between mind and body, spirit and flesh; a place of outrageous pluralism, trickster sprites, demons and dreams, chaos magic, the Yoruba-derived cults of Haitian Vodun, Cuban Santería and Brazilian Candomblé.[9]

The astrology that lives in this tumultuous territory is warm-blooded, egalitarian, anarchistic and erotic, it seems. At this point I particularly want to thank Kathryn Earle, for inviting me to embark on this project, and Patrick Curry for his initially 'wild' idea that we collaborate, an idea that, in its development, revealed a remarkable congruence in the thinking of two academics from differing disciplinary, social and generational backgrounds. I also express my gratitude to Charmaine Chinniah and Jane Ridder-Patrick, for vivid insights into astrology in action. Finally, I thank my lucky stars.

Marginalization

Patrick Curry writes: I came to astrology early, and fell in love with its richness, subtlety and complexity as a symbolic system. It seemed to offer a Key, and being young, I was interested in anything that promised to save time. It also combined spiritual and intellectual properties in a way that perfectly suited my character; so if character really is fate, then I was fated for astrology (or vice versa).

Eventually, however, I tired of a double insecurity: the personal/professional marginalization of being an astrologer, and the lack of certainty that haunted astrological interpretation. I resolved to deal with these together by returning to university. I first studied psychology for a BA, which seemed then to be the mainstream discipline most closely related to astrology. (I was quite wrong, and today would choose anthropology.) But that study threw up meta-questions in turn, so in my MSc. I turned to the philosophy of science. That proved ultimately to be intolerably bloodless, as well as endlessly self-referential, so for my PhD I shifted to the history of science, which at least dealt with real persons and allowed one to bracket some of those frustratingly undecidable epistemological questions. My thesis, on the decline of astrology in early modern England, was really a social history of ideas, strongly influenced by the work of E.P. Thompson.

By then I had, after considerable involvement, given up on the attempt to prove or disprove astrology scientifically. I came to realize that science itself depended on various assumptions that were not only highly questionable but themselves insusceptible to scientific validation. In other words, science was attended by as many mysteries and as much ultimate uncertainty as astrology, which rendered absurd pinning any hopes on clearing up those of the latter by resorting to the former.

Yet the absurdities of astrology were also unattractive, as was its intellectual poverty (albeit this is not entirely its own fault, given its marginalization in the West for the last three centuries). In addition to frequent banality, too many astrologers were happy to ape the scientism of their critics and pretend that astrology was, potentially if not yet actually, the perfect and complete system in which all problems could be treated as technical ones. The arrogance and ignorance of this attitude is such that I might well have abandoned astrology altogether. But around that point, two things happened. One, I realised that astrologers' mainstream critics were, in these respects, just as bad; and they had many times more power to broadcast and enforce their views, which were evidently a party line on the part of a party – let's call it the modernizers – I wanted no part of.

The other event was that I became acquainted with the work of Geoffrey Cornelius, Maggie Hyde and the embryonic Company of Astrologers. Instead of trying to narrow astrology down and shut out mystery which, since it cannot be done, only deadens the former and turns the latter bad, they contextualized astrology as a kind of divination, a dialogue with the unknown, which opens it up and enlivens it. It also both requires and encourages a very attractive humility in one's practice.

To be fair, a living astrology of this kind was also true of the actual practice of several astrologers I knew; but I had never heard or read it articulated before, and being incorrigibly intellectual, that was very exciting. At the same time, however,

I had charted an independent course for too long to sign up uncritically, so I subscribed only to whatever I had personally determined. The result is a complex series of intellectual debts. In a typical example, I discovered and wrote about *metis* as the mode appropriate to divination, only for someone to gently point out that I had attended a seminar (led by John Heaton) on that very subject a few years earlier.

More recently, I had the exhilarating if unnerving experience of reading the essence of all my hard-won insights and conclusions about astrology, as delivered in lectures nearly a century ago by Max Weber. As will be obvious in what I have written, I have learned a great deal from many other writers, but his concepts of enchantment/disenchantment, rationalization and concrete magic now seem to me to offer the best overall way of understanding astrology, among many other things; they also connect the latter with other of my interests and values (ecological, political, cultural and literary),which would otherwise appear incoherent. To toil away in a few corners of the great field Weber uncovered is an honour.[10]

For my part, this book represents the latest development of an involvement with the subject that goes back 35 years, in the course of which I have naturally acquired many personal and intellectual debts. To try to specify them all without unjustly leaving out some would be impossible. But I would particularly like to thank my dear sister Kathy, for introducing me to astrology; subsequent teachers, including Zipporah Dobyns, Liz Greene and the late Richard Idemon; Geoffrey Cornelius and Maggie Hyde, for waking me from my dogmatic neo-Ptolemaic slumber, and for our subsequent discussions; everyone involved in the Sophia Project (not least its founder), for doing so much to enable the scholarly study of real astrology; my colleagues Michael York and Nicholas Campion at the Sophia Centre, BSUC, and our students (from whom I have already started to learn); Bernard Eccles, Chantal Allison, Lindsay Radermacher, Pat Blackett, Graeme Tobyn and Bernadette Brady (together with others already mentioned) for reminding me that a living astrology enlivens; Roy Willis, who, together with Berg Publishers, made my participation in this book possible; Michael Winship, Garey Mills, Clay Ramsay, Joanna Savory, Neil Platt, Angela Voss, Garry Phillipson and Stephen Fitzpatrick, for critical but sympathetic companionship in exploring these issues; Ernesto Laclau, Zygmunt Bauman, Eduardo Viveiros de Castro and Patrick Joyce for their encouragement; and my other friends and family, for being here. Not one of these people will agree with everything I have written, but I am very grateful to all of them for their support.

In what follows, Chapters 4, 5, 6, 7, 8 and 9 are written by Patrick Curry, and chapters 1, 2, 3, 10 and 11 are by Roy Willis. The introduction is a collaborative product. Quotations or citations should be referenced accordingly.

Notes

1. There is now evidence that the zodiacal constellations may be much older. See Liza K. Hall, 'Prehistoric Archaeology', in *Mercury Direct* (December 2002/ January 2003), discussing BBC science editor David Whitehouse's report at http://news.bbc.co.uk/hi/english/sci/tech/neswsid_975000/975360.stm
2. For an empirical refutation, see Durant and Bauer 1997.
3. With thanks to Mary Aylward.
4. Such traditions of minor fraud are, apparently, features of a wide range of industries in Britain (see Mars 1982).
5. The Gauquelins divorced in 1982. Michel Gauquelin's suicide in 1991 seems to have placed a further question mark over the whole controversy, though thus far even the most the strenuous efforts of his scientific enemies have failed to invalidate his data.
6. Johannes Kepler (1571–1630), a German astronomer and astrologer, who showed that each solar planet travels an elliptical orbit with the Sun at one focus.
7. Copernicus (Mikolaj Kopernik, 1473–1543), a Polish monk regarded as the founder of modern astronomy and now chiefly known for his originally heretical theory that the Earth and the other planets revolved around a central Sun.
8. Modern chaos theory stems from the work of the American meteorologist Edward Lorenz, who showed how minuscule perturbations in a complex system could generate large-scale effects.
9. As William Gibson, the novelist inventor of the term and concept of 'cyber-space', has observed, 'The African religious impulse lends itself to a computer world much more than anything in the West. You cut deals with your favourite deity – it's like those religions already are dealing with artificial intelligences' (quoted in Davis 1998: 196).
10. To my [Curry's] mind, the next step beyond where the present book stops is in the direction indicated by the 'actor-network theory' of Bruno Latour.

–1–

Astral Science before History

An earthy proverb of the Fipa people of southwest Tanzania, among whom I [Roy Willis] was privileged to do my first stint of fieldwork as an anthropologist in the early 1960s, observes that 'Who sleeps under the bed can't piss on the one on top'. The most obvious thing about the sky and its luminous inhabitants is that it's always *up* in relation to Earth-dwellers. 'Up', being above or on top, means superiority and 'power over' in every human culture known to anthropology, including our own Western one. So figuring out what's going on up there has, understandably, been a millennial human concern. And until very recently, until the Enlightenment-induced death of God and disenchantment of the world, humans attributed life and super-human consciousness to the awesome celestial domain.

The Animist 'Illusion'

When I began studying anthropology at Oxford under the legendary Edward Evans-Pritchard, one of the first works I was introduced to was the two-volume *Primitive Culture*, published in 1871 by E.B.Tylor, the 'father' of British anthropology. Tylor's best-known contribution to anthropological theory is his concept of 'animism', from the Latin *anima,* meaning 'soul' or 'spirit' or 'mind'. According to Tylor, 'primitive' peoples around the world imagined that every significant object in their environment, both animate and inanimate (as Science thinks of it) embodied a normally invisible spirit or intelligence capable of influencing, and being influenced by, human beings. For Tylor, a free-thinking rationalist of the late Victorian age, the problem of why apparently intelligent people just about everywhere, except the privileged inhabitants of what is now called the 'Western' world, entertained such patently absurd ideas called for a logical explanation. Tylor found it in the universal experience of dreaming. The dreamer seems to enter another world, not unlike the 'real' world of the waking state. There he encounters other beings, some of whom he recognizes as folk who had died. Hence, Tylor argued, there arose all around the world the notion of an 'ethereal' essence which could be called a 'soul', which survived the death of the mortal person. By extension, such insubstantial essences were then attributed to other objects in the environment, both animate and inanimate, and a multitude of spirit beings of varying degrees of importance came to people the imaginations of 'primitive' humans. In 1960 such a world-view seemed to me as self-evidently absurd as it did to the Victorians: a lamentably sloppy way of dealing with and understanding hard reality, having to cope with all these imaginary and unnecessary entities clogging up the works of what was, as Descartes and Newton had shown, no more than a vast machine. No wonder these deluded peoples were so materially ineffective in comparison with the industrially organized populations of Euro-America! And as for attributing soul or mind to the heavenly bodies, as even our own European ancestors had done, well, it might be poetic, but it was patently nonsense in the light of modern astronomy.

'Relegated to the Trashheap'

How then to account for the persisting viability of astrology in today's world? Right from the start, we face the blatant fact that the great majority of the scientific and scholarly establishment in the Western world regards astrology with a contemptuous hostility which at times borders on the pathological, if not the psychotic. The general attitude is summed up in the American philosopher Daniel Dennett's comment that astrology has been 'relegated to the trashheap of history' (1996: 31). Richard Dawkins, an appointed guardian of scientific orthodoxy, laces his latest venture into popularization with particularly venomous attacks on astrology, taken as a specially egregious example of what he sees as the regrettable tendency of the non-scientific majority of the population, motivated by a deplorable 'appetite for wonder', to relapse into pre-Enlightenment irrationality: 'Astrology . . . is an aesthetic affront. Its pre-Copernican dabblings demean and cheapen astronomy, like using Beethoven for commercial jingles' (Dawkins 1998: 118). Astrologers as a body seem inured to this kind of scholarly contumely, customarily countering with the assertion that astrology 'works', nonetheless. The scientific sceptic will naturally greet such statements with a condescending smile and perhaps a reference to Dawkins's pathetic 'appetite for wonder'. For wondrous indeed, for all us denizens of Weber's iron cage of rationality, were we to find that we are all players in a cosmic drama of divine authorship, with just possibly, according to those astrologers I'm here calling 'postmodern', a chance of writing some of the script.

A Crucial Breakthrough

In understanding the whys and wherefores of an alien culture, which the world of astrology is for one such as myself, the anthropologist seeks to apprehend the basic assumptions structuring this world, then to see how real, living people are using these assumptions to create meaning for themselves and others. The first question that then occurs is: Where did it come from, where and how did it begin?

Standard histories of astrology inform us that the craft, if one chooses to call it that, 'originated in Mesopotamia, perhaps in the third millenium BC' (*Encyclopaedia Britannica*, Vol. 2: 640). Yet the hierarchic, literate, centralized kingdoms of Sumer and Babylon did not spring out of nowhere, and neither did their stellar lore and practice. The celestial science of prehistoric humanity was highly developed, though it is only recently that this fact has begun to be recognized in academic circles.

The crucial breakthrough in discovering that human beings of thirty thousand and more years ago were observing and recording the cyclical phases of the moon, using a precise system of notation, was made by Alexander Marshack. In *The Roots of Civilization* (1972) this American polymath and brilliantly gifted amateur archaeologist showed through exhaustive analysis of the material evidence that the incised markings on bone and stone from the Upper Palaeolithic, markings that earlier archaeology had taken to be no more than meaningless 'doodlings' by our savage ancestors, constituted a complex system of lunar notation common to human communities around the globe. Already far developed in 30,000 BCE, in Marshack's view its origins are much earlier (1972: 57). By the later Magdalenian period (*c*.16,000 to *c*.10,000 BCE), best known for the magnificent cave paintings of Altamira and Lascaux, Marshack shows that this system had developed into 'the integrated beginnings of arithmetic, astronomy, writing, abstracted symbolism and notation' (1972: 218).

This was an extraordinary change in our estimation of the cultural stature of prehistoric humanity, suddenly revealed as the authors of a cosmological system in no sense inferior in complexity, grandeur and beauty to the finest intellectual and artistic productions of modern 'Western' civilization. The revolution in archaeological thought seemingly portended by Marshack's landmark discovery appears on the face of it to be similar to the slow change in anthropology initiated seven decades earlier with the researches of Cushing and Boas among the Native Americans of the United States and Canada, Rasmussen's work among the Inuit (Eskimo), followed in the 1930s by the French ethnographer Marcel Griaule's description of the elaborate cosmic philosophy of the Dogon people of the western Sudan (now Mali), and the publication of comparably devoted studies among the aboriginal peoples of Australia and Oceania. Cumulatively, these first-hand studies broke the conceptual link – unquestioned in Victorian anthropology – between perceived economic 'backwardness' (by comparison with 'advanced' industrial complexity) and an associated and presumed intellectual crudity.

In fact the parallel is less than exact, because unlike anthropology, which has, though not without much travail, managed to free itself from the straitjacket of the linear model of social progress which pervaded the discipline in the nineteenth century (and is still potent in popular consciousness), academic archaeology remains dominated by a version of Darwinian evolutionism. In this perspective, our prehistoric forebears, living in small hunting-foraging groups with minimal material infrastructure and unable to read or write, necessarily represented a less developed social and cultural form than their present-day descendants. As Giorgio de Santillana has well observed, referring to the cultural achievements of pre-historic humankind, 'In former times, when the Humanities had not yet been "infected" by the biological scheme of evolution, scholars showed better confidence in the capacities of the creators of high civilization' (de Santillana and von Dechend 1969: 142, n. 9). De Santillana tells us that this high, global civilization, was one in which geography and the science of heaven were 'woven together', in which time was cyclic and Number was 'the secret of things':

> Cosmological Time, the 'dance of stars', as Plato called it . . . was potent enough to control events inflexibly, as it molded them to its sequence in a cosmic manifold in which past and future called to each other, deep calling to deep. (1969: 332–3)

When did this archaic civilization begin? De Santillana thinks the Neolithic, but betrays uncertainty on this matter, suggesting the decision should rest with the archaeologists (1969: 340). Marshack's evidence, of which de Santillana of course knew nothing when he wrote, obliges us to set the origins of this grand pan-human culture of an arithmetically measured, cyclical cosmic time much further back.

'Masculinist' Bias

As William Irwin Thompson puts it,

> The implications of Marshack's observations were enormous, for they meant that as early as fifty thousand years ago primitive humanity had observed a basic periodicity of nature and was building up a model of nature. The human being was no longer simply walking in nature; it was miniaturizing the universe and carrying a model of it in its hand in the form of a lunar calendrical tally stick. (Thompson 1981: 95)

Marshack's work does indeed portend a massive 'paradigm shift' in an archae-ology still substantially dominated, as de Santillana observed, by a borrowed Darwinian conceptual framework. Yet for all his paradigm-busting insights into the prehistoric human mind, it has to be said that Marshack's interpretation contains a singular flaw. It's pervaded by an unconscious 'masculinist' bias that is first signalled in the subtitle of his masterwork: *The Cognitive Beginnings of Man's First Art, Symbol and Notation,* when the evidence he presents tells us un-mistakably that the inspiration and most likely executants of this complex and marvellous Palaeolithic cosmology was and were female. For notwithstanding his magisterial demonstration of the fundamental position of the lunar cycle in pre-historic cosmology, Marshack fails to address the rather obvious question of why the moon, rather than the far more spectacular sun, was such an overwhelming preoccupation for our remote ancestors. Yet the reason would seem to be clear: uniquely among celestial objects, the phenomenal behaviour of the moon appeared to mirror, indeed, be synchronized with, the menstrual cycle of the human female. Citing recent studies showing that modern women living in close proximity to one another tend to have their menstrual periods at the same time, William Irwin Thompson suggests the same would have been true of prehistoric women living together in small hunting and gathering bands (1981: 96). These women would thus have experienced their own bodies, the source of human life itself, as harmonized with the rhythm of the cosmos as manifest in the cyclically changing face of the moon. As Vicki Noble, a modern-day American shaman, has noted, ancient astral science was 'body based and biological', referring of course to the female body (Noble 1991: 85). Knowing themselves as living parts of a universe that was itself alive, Stone Age women were uniquely placed to be the original scientists, mathematicians, artists, theologians and cosmological world-makers. Unsurprising, therefore, that they occupied a special place of honour in their world, simply by virtue of being female. Yet Marshack assumes without question that the nameless author of these notational series, incised with a delicate precision that Marshack says would require the skill of a jeweller equipped with a lens to duplicate, miniaturized to the extent that Marshack was obliged to use a powerful microscope to 'read' them, was necessarily male.

However, as Thompson points out, Marshack's own discoveries contradict the masculinist bias introduced by his own unexamined preconceptions. A particularly blatant example of this bias are the enigmatic objects from the later Palaeolithic Magdalenian period named by the Abbé Breuil, the revered 'father' of modern palaeontology, as *bâtons de commandement*. Thus named because of a fancied resemblance to the short ceremonial staffs carried by the military marshals of France, these objects from 16,000 to 10,000 BCE are typically engraved with lunar-notational symbols and finely executed portraits of animals and plants associated, Marshack suggests, with cyclical seasonal changes. Marshack also assumes that these 'bâtons' belonged to men, but, as Thompson points out, its owner is more likely to have been 'not man the mighty hunter but the midwife' (1981: 100). There is also, Thompson notes, an exciting suggestion in Marshack's reading of the baton symbolism, of a continuity between ancient astrology and the religion of Ice Age humanity:

> The ram's head or Aries is the astrological sign for the beginning of spring. If Marshack is on to something, then astrology does not begin (as often thought) with the Mesopotamians, but it goes back to a lunar astrology in the Upper Paleolithic. (ibid.)

Or indeed earlier, as Marshack also suggests. The most powerful of all images of that lunar astrology, it seems to me, is the wonderful rock-engraving from the Dordogne region of south-west France, known to archaeology as 'the Venus of Laussel'. Dated to *c*.19,000 BCE in the Upper Perigordian period, the image depicts a mature female holding aloft in her right hand a bison horn engraved with thirteen sequential marks, most likely referring to the thirteen lunar months in the annual solar cycle. Her left hand points to her well rounded, and probably pregnant, belly. The image was originally coloured red, a colour universally associated with life and also with the feminine menstrual flow and the blood of child-bearing. The horn resembles the shape of a crescent moon. As a whole the figure is splendidly iconic of the high Stone Age civilization based in the primarily feminine experience of participation in the cosmic rhythm of birth, life, death and rebirth. Combining Marshack's insight that the engraved animals are, like the lunar notation, expressions of time-factoring patterns, with the French palaeontologist Leroi-Gourhan's discovery of the juxtaposition in Stone Age cave art of male animals and female signs – notably the vulva – and vice versa, male signs and female animals, Thompson concludes:

> The animals become the early forms of the zodiacal images for lunar months, and expressions of the basic dualistic nature of existence: male and female, Yin and Yang, life and death . . . the vulva is the magical wound that bleeds and heals itself every month, and because it heals itself in sympathy with the dark of the moon, the vulva is an expression not of physiology but of cosmology. The moon dies and is reborn; woman bleeds but does not die, and when she does not bleed for ten lunar months, she brings forth new life. It is easy to see how Paleolithic man would be in awe of woman, and how woman's mysteries would be at the basis of a religious cosmology. (ibid.: 108–9)

When I learned anthropology in Oxford in the early 1960s, Victorian theories of a 'matriarchal phase' in human prehistory were mentioned as part of a fallacy labelled 'conjectural history', peculiar to the childhood of our discipline, and long since outgrown. According to one of this exploded theory's exponents, the Swiss jurist J.J. Bachofen, ancient archaeological evidence proved that women once ruled human society in the same way that men clearly did in his day.

Curiously, Robert Briffault, a later scholar who contributed more weightily than anyone to the 'matriarchal' thesis, never figured in our reading lists in Oxford, probably because he published in the inter-war period of the twentieth century, when ahistorical functionalism had succeeded linear developmentalism as the dominant paradigm in anthropology. To this day many in anthropology and other branches of scholarship assume that talk of a prehistoric era when human religion was focussed on the cult of an all-powerful Earth-Goddess and females enjoyed social pre-eminence is so much feminist myth-making. They are wrong. The mass of evidence painstakingly marshalled in Briffault's masterwork proves incontrovertibly to anyone who takes the trouble to read it, that such an epoch did indeed exist, and for a period of time probably to be measured in hundreds of thousands of years. What is misleading is the idea, initially propagated by Bachofen and his peers, that prehistoric society was some kind of inverted mirror image of the present set-up, under a female ruling class. Modern first-hand studies of human groups, based on a hunting and foraging economy similar to that of our Stone Age ancestors, show that such an economy presupposes an egalitarian and communitarian ethos that is incompatible with class stratification. Female ascendancy in the prehistoric, 'Goddess' era was ceremonial and symbolic, not hierarchic.

The 'religion' of that immensely long prehistoric epoch did not feature a remote, authoritarian deity analogous to the father-gods of patriarchy. It takes no 'act of submission' or 'leap of faith' to sense the solid, sustaining earth beneath our feet, nor do we have to absorb a complex theology to breathe the ambient, life-giving air: these things happen naturally and instinctively. We are *in* the Goddess, and She is in us.

The archaeological researches of Andrew Mellaart and Marija Gimbutas into the 'matristic', Goddess-focused cultures of the Middle Eastern and European Early Neolithic, offer abundant confirmation of this picture. They also demonstrate clear continuities with Palaeolithic cosmology (see Gimbutas 1982 [1974]). Further, the wide-ranging mythological research of de Santillana and von Dechend and their unveiling of a hitherto neglected astrological/astronomical dimension to ancient myth, also reveals connections between mythical tales first written down in the Neolithic era and likely origins in the Palaeolithic.

If indeed there once existed a global cosmology co-ordinating celestial phenomena with terrestrial experience in a measured and rhythmic process, as these diverse and widely distributed evidences from archaeology and mythology suggest, there must obviously have been an epochal social and cultural transformation at some point in the human story. Is there evidence of such a fundamental change? There is. Countless myths worldwide tell how power and knowledge, originally the preserve of women, were seized or stolen by men. Such stories are part of the indigenous heritage of Americans, Australians, Oceanians, Eurasians and Africans.

Over much of Africa and Australia the world is said to have been made from the vast body of a cosmic serpent: according to Monica Sjöö and Barbara Mor's classic account of the Palaeolithic 'religion of the earth', *The Great Cosmic Mother* (1987), the serpent was the prime symbol of the Mother Goddess. In Middle Eastern myth the origins of kingship are described in terms of the triumph of a divine male solar hero over a cosmic serpent identified with the chaotic powers of the earth. In ancient Egypt the battle between the sun-god Re (or Ra) and Apep, the serpent of chaos, was renewed every night before the god's triumphant rebirth with the dawn. In Mesopotamia the earliest myths tell of a female serpent called Tiamat emerging from the sea and teaching humankind the arts of civilization. Later stories describe how one of the first kings, Marduk, fought a gargantuan battle against Tiamat, now seen as the chaotic enemy of hierarchic order, eventually killing her and splitting her vast body into two halves. One half became the earth, the other the sky, implying that previously these were a unity – seemingly a reference to the organic universe of Palaeolithic cosmology.

Gendered Divinities

Standard histories of astrology, already mentioned, place its origins in the early dynastic civilizations of Mesopotamia and Egypt. This Mesopotamian and Egyptian astrology, though inevitably inheriting many elements from the astro-science of the Palaeolithic, was specifically designed by the male priesthoods to serve the interests of the newly emergent god-kings of the region. Around 2000 BCE these priests were diviners who sought to find in the stars information bearing on the fortunes of the king as embodiment of the state, and it was not until around 500 BCE that the divinatory function of astrology was extended to non-royal individuals. Dynastic Egypt, however, retained something of the Palaeolithic sense of human participation in cosmic process, though metamorphosed into the congress of sacred royalty with the heavens. Thus the Pharoah, the god-king identified with the Sun, was held on death to enjoy sex with the star Sirius, identified in Egyptian cosmology with the great goddess Isis, deity of the Nile. Later, with the demise of the millennial civilization of Egypt and the ascendency of Greek concepts of mathematics and geometry, the idea of a pantheon of stellar divinities ruling the world of humankind became dominant in the eastern Mediterranean and, ultimately, mediaeval and early modern Europe. The most systematic and comprehensive statement of this view of astro-science is contained in the work of the brilliant Egyptian astronomer-cum-astrologer Ptolemy (100–178 CE) who, in the introduction to the third book of his *Tetrabiblos*, lays it down that.

> ... the cause both of universal and of particular events is the motion of the planets, sun, and moon; and the prognostic art is the scientific observation of precisely the change in the subject natures which corresponds to parallel movements of the heavenly bodies through the surrounding heavens. (1940: 221)

Nowadays, of course, it's genes, rather than stars, which are attributed with sovereignty over human destiny. And stellar objects, no matter how visually impressive, are understood not as embodiments of divine intelligence but as mindless components of a mindless cosmic machine.

As Patrick Curry demonstrates in his historical account, European astrology has demonstrated a chameleon-like ability to accommodate itself to the world-view of its environing society, whether this be pagan-polytheist, Christian-monotheist, or scientific-atheist. In the perspective of the *longue durée* that includes the whole immense panorama of human prehistory, however, it seems that running through the changing astrological story since about 3000 BCE is what could be described as the 'masculinization' of what was once a feminine body of knowledge rooted in a participatory model of humanity's active role in the creation and maintenance of cosmic rhythm. The feminine Moon yields to the masculine Sun, part of the wholesale inversion of symbolic values wrought by the patriarchal revolution. Similarly, the female menstrual flow, cosmic mirror of the celestial lunar cycle, changes from being the sacred symbol of life itself to become the prime sign of woman's pollution and ontological inferiority. From the time of the rise of hierarchic, centralized and patriarchal civilization in the Middle East five thousand years ago, the planetary deities became predominantly masculine, only the Moon and Venus (a version of the once-great goddess Inanna/Ishtar) being accorded feminine status. Mars, Jupiter and Saturn were deemed masculine, although Mercury was considered gender-neutral or hermaphroditic.[1] In modern times, the outer planets Neptune, Uranus and Pluto, invisible to the naked human eye and thus unknown to pre-modern humanity, have all been accorded masculine status in astrology, a seemingly blatant case of gender bias.

A Remarkable Convergence

Where stands astrology today, this ancient art and science with an intellectual gen-ealogy far older than most of its exponents appear to imagine? My research for this present book has, most surprisingly, led me into an encounter with a set of ideas, indeed a whole climate of theories and paradigm-challenging insights, strangely congruent with the philosophical radicalism associated with those anthropologists, including myself, who are presently seeking to interpret their first-hand experience of 'spirit' phenomena in Africa and elsewhere (see Chapter 11). As Curry remarks in his introduction to what appears to be a 'key text' in contemporary astrology, Geoffrey Cornelius's *The Moment of Astrology* (1994), we have here a 'meeting of contemporary postmodernism and ancient paganism' (1994: xiv). Cornelius, in a carefully constructed critique of those modern-day astrologers who present their craft as a misunderstood branch of objectivist science, argues for a view of astrology as *divination*, in the strict sense of an entering into dialogue with the divine.

Let us see what this remarkable claim really means. It is breathtaking in its suggestion that we abandon not only the cosmology of modern science, with its model of a mechanical universe devoid of consciousness, but the entire mono-theistic and transcendent tradition of Christianity, Islam and Judaism. Curry further draws our attention to the structural homology between monotheistic religion and the 'single vision' of modern science in its project to produce an all-embracing grand narrative of the universe. In place of these two oppressive accounts of our human situation, postmodern astrology proposes a privileged relationship between astrologer and client, a relationship in which a multiplicity of deities, in the form of the planets, the sun and the moon, show themselves to us, a situation in which our destiny can, in the striking phrase of Cornelius (1994), be 'negotiated'.

The picture of astral science before history now emerging from archaeology and mythology suggests a surprising resonance with postmodern astrological dreamings. The prehistoric association of woman and the moon, William Irwin Thompson says, tells us that

> women were the first observers of the basic periodicity of nature, the periodicity upon which all later scientific observations were made. Woman was the first to note a correspondence between an internal process she was going through and an external process in nature. She is the one who constructs a more holistic epistemology in which subject and object are in sympathetic resonance with one another . . . The world-view that separates the observer from the system he observes, that imagines that the universe can be split into mere subjectivity and real objectivity, is not of her doing. (1981: 97)

This chapter began with a proverb from the Fipa ethnicity, and I'll end it with another, suggestive of the futility of supposing that we finite, mortal humans can ever, contrary to the pretensions of modern science, of Stephen Hawking and Richard Dawkins, grasp the totality of things: *Uwaala-ntaanda, ng'usiku unga ca!* (The night is over before one has finished counting the stars!).

Notes

1. Personal communication from Patrick Curry.

–2–

The Sky as Mirror

As above, so below; as below, so above.

Hermes Trismegistos

Since the dawn of time human beings have spent precious moments of freedom from the exigencies of making a living beneath 'this inverted bowl men call the sky', in Fitzgerald's rendering of the Sufi master, and rehearsing to each other the meaning of what is majestically spread before them. Of all the inhabitants of the heavens, the Sun is by far the most spectacular object in the daytime firmament, so bright that for most of the time we paradoxically can't look at it for more than the briefest moment on pain of going blind, making it effectively invisible. As John Lash has observed, this paradox of invisible solar hyper-visibility has the corollary that the brilliance of our neighbour star the Sun renders all the other members of the astral firmament except the Moon invisible during its diurnal occupancy of the heavens (Lash 1999: 24–5), producing the rhythmic alternation of day and night that conditions our consciousness and that of virtually all other earthly life-forms.

Given the sensory salience of the Sun, it's remarkable that the relatively unobtrusive and shape-changing Moon should have dominated the consciousness of prehistoric humankind, as Marshack and others have demonstrated.[1] Of all the 'storied meanings' (Marshack) engraved on the stone and bone artifacts of the Palaeolithic era, mythic tales about the Moon are probably the oldest. Prehistorian Stan Gooch has traced the global spread of a story which he thinks originated among the Neanderthal peoples and which portrays the Moon as the mother of Earth herself, a mirror in the sky reflecting in its cyclical phases the bodily rhythms of earthly womanhood in its alternation between sterility and fertility, blood of menstruation and blood of childbirth, and the larger cycle of life, death and rebirth in its monthly progress round the girdling heavens. With the formalization of astral science in the literate and hierarchic kingdoms of Mesopotamia, this constellated path was divided into the twelve 'houses' still recognized in present-day astrology, but there is evidence that the number of celestial divisions was originally thirteen, reflecting the thirteen lunar months in a solar year.[2] We have already seen in Chapter 1 that the moon and its cyclical changes were the focus of human cosmological imagining during the long ages of organization in nomadic hunting and foraging groups and through the brilliant early Neolithic period of settled agricultural communities with an egalitarian and pacific social ethos. Astrologer and mythologist John Lash, after noting that the solar zodiac constructed in Babylon in 2200 BCE was preceded by a lunar version, identifies thirteen constellations under the names Ram, Bull, Twins, Crab, Lion, Virgin,[3] Scales, Scorpion, Snaketamer, Archer, Goatfish, Watercarrier, and Fishes. These anciently named and unevenly numbered constellations, occupying varyingly extensive areas of the celestial panorama, relate loosely and imperfectly to the equally divided segments allotted in modern astrology to the twelve zodiacal 'Sun' signs: Aries, Taurus, Gemini, Cancer, Leo, Virgo, Libra, Scorpio, Sagittarius, Capricorn, Aquarius and Pisces. Notably missing from the present-day astrological zodiac is the vast constellation of the Snaketamer, formerly known by the Greek name Ophiuchus and, according to Lash, the prototype of the 'wounded healer', the central figure in all shamanic traditions (1999: 63):[4]

> His enormous stature . . . can be seen as complementary and balancing to the massive elongated figure of the Virgin, the female figure that stretches for 47 degrees. (ibid.)

Lash comments that the exclusion of the storied Snaketamer from the modern zodiac 'says a lot about ourselves as a species', since it represents the suppression in us of the ecstatic Dionysian powers owned by prehistoric humankind (ibid.).

Moon as a Measure of Time

Anthropologist Gary Urton argues on the basis of ethnographic evidence for an ancient lunar zodiac among the Quechua-speaking peoples of the Peruvian Andes in South America. After noting the local association between the phases of the moon and the female menstrual cycle, and the observed tendency for the cycles of women living in small groups to become synchronized, Urton adds:

> . . . it is not generally recognized that the importance of the moon for females also involves the stars. In correlating the menstrual and lunar cycles, it would become a regular practice to observe not only the phases of the moon, but also its movement against the background of the stars. These periodic observations could easily lead to the standardization of a female lunar zodiac. (1981: 79)

Urton also notes the frequent association between the moon and the feminine menstrual cycle in other indigenous South American groups, and a widespread association between the dark lunar spots and menstrual blood (1981: 85). In discussing the stars and constellations with female informants, Urton found they usually tended to rely on the moon as a point of stellar orientation. When locating constellations on a star map, women were 'almost always disoriented by the absence of a moon on the map'. In contrast, this absence didn't worry male informants (ibid.). Evidence of a thirteen-member lunar zodiac in North America has been found on a carved boulder associated with the Mound Builder culture, located in the Ouachita river at Hot Springs, Arkansas (Gooch 1995: 145–6).

Looking at the prehistoric material in South America, Urton points to the institution of the Incan 'Virgins of the Sun', who lived together in the sacred capital of Cuzco in a palace called Acllahuasi, dedicating their lives to the performance of religious rituals in the Coricancha, or Temple of the Sun. The Acllas, Urton thinks, 'could well have served not only as the 'biological standard' for a coordinated lunar zodiac, but also as the record-keepers of nocturnal celestial cycles (1981: 79).[5]

Today the indigenous peoples of the Andes and the Amazon forests still observe and practice an ancient astral science that precisely correlates the apparent movements of the planets and constellations, including the super-constellation known in English as the Milky Way, with fundamental mundane activities, notably the tilling of the soil and the sowing and harvesting of food crops (1981: 3). For the Quechua-speaking peoples, ideological heirs of the elaborate culture of the Incan empire, Urton describes a still viable, complex cosmology in which stellar and planetary cycles are integrated with solar and lunar cycles, all keyed to the economy and ecology of present-day Quechua society. In this cosmology as it was in pre-Conquest times the sun, as in ancient Egypt and Mesopotamia, was identified with the king, while the Incas equated the moon with the female aristocracy (Urton 1981: 197).

In the ancient Near East where what became the great European astrological tradition had its origins, there is evidence of an earlier, lunar-oriented astral system of knowledge. As Gooch observes:

> Islam, Israel, the ancient Greeks, the Celts and all other early cultures in this arena date the commencement of the month from the appearance of the new moon. In Hebrew the word for month, *chodesh*, means 'the newness of the new moon'. The very emblem of Islam today is still the crescent moon . . . Mecca itself was originally the chief shrine of the moon, where popular local tradition relates that Abraham bought Mecca from the old woman of the moon. The black stone of Mecca is still the most sacred object in Islam – but this (as we might judge from its colour) is originally the altar and symbol of the Moon Goddess. (1995: 137)

In Israel, the sixth-century zodiac in the Beth Alpha synagogue has been shown to betray evidence of having been changed from a more ancient thirteen-figure layout to its present twelve-figure format (Gooch 1995: 147). According to Lash, the famous zodiac at Dendera in Lower Egypt shows a putatively ancient thirteen-figure arrangement (1999: 56–60).

Christianity also has its pagan underlay, of course, since the holiest buildings constructed by the Church in medieval Europe were deliberately located atop ancient sacred sites. Only recently has it been discovered that these sites formed a configuration mirroring the celestial firmament and originally dedicated to the worship of stellar deities. Thus the great cathedral of Chartres in northwest France conceals the remains of a solar oracle, and the hallowed edifice of Santiago de Compostela in northern Spain hides a pagan temple devoted to the moon.[6]

More directly relevant to our present purpose, however, is Urton's exposition of the Incan-Quechua conception of the fundamental architecture of the celestial domain, dominated as it is by the immense, over-arching structure of the Milky Way. For the Incan-Quechua people, what modern astronomy knows as our home galaxy seen edge-on is a vast river in the night sky that reflects the terrestrial river called Vilcanota that flows through the sacred Inca city of Cuzco. The very name – *Mayu* – used to designate the Milky Way, literally means 'river' in Quechua. Conversely, Urton was told, the Vilcanota river 'is like a mirror reflecting the Mayu, the River in the sky' (1981: 56). The reciprocal reflectivity between the structures of heaven and earth goes further still, because the four cardinal directions, understood by Quechua-speaking people as dividing the earth into four quarters, are a 'mirror image', as Urton puts it, of the quadripartition of the heavens created by the apparent nightly and seasonal movements of the Milky Way (Urton 1981: 63).

These two mutually reflecting aspects of the cosmos are in fact connected in Quechua cosmology, which sees life-giving water as continuously circulating between earth and sky. On earth, water is said to flow from south-southwest to north-north-east, while in the sky terrestial water enters the Milky Way River in the north and flows southward, returning to earth in the form of rain (1981: 64). This cosmic system of reciprocally mirroring earth and sky resembles what the Orientalist Alain Daniélou has reported for ancient India, where the holy city of Benares is held to be the place where the rivers of three worlds cross each other on the same axis. These rivers are the Milky Way, the Ganga (Ganges), and 'an enormous underground river descending from the Himalayas towards the south' (Daniélou 1984: 131).[7] A similar idea arose in China, where the Milky Way was seen as the celestial counterpart of the Ho or Yellow River that flows through northern China into the Yellow Sea (Krupp 1991: 264).

Cosmic Participation

In their industrious 'field research' among the yet numerous non-Western cultural groups worldwide, anthropologists – these errant children of the Enlightenment – have unearthed precious indications of how human beings (before the triumph of the scientific mythos) entered into dialogue with divinity, knowing themselves as part of the living cosmos whose features they scanned in the starry heavens. Thus Allen Roberts, sensitive ethnographer of the Tabwa people of East-Central Africa, has shown how the collective imagination of these Bantu-speaking agriculturalists sees the Milky Way as reflected in the most prominent feature of the Tabwa homeland, a mountainous ridge called Mwila that runs north-south through the country, and in a supposed 'piling up' of the waters in the middle of Lake Tanganyika, forming a 'back' that defines the western and eastern sides of this huge inland sea. Moreover, for Tabwa the same cosmic feature defines and structures the human body itself, being evident in the vertical dividing line known to medical science as *linea nigra*, the 'dark line' projected down the middle of the abdominal epidermis by an underlying muscular formation. All these celestial, terrestrial and corporeal features are known by a single term, *mulalambo,* in the Tabwa language. In human beings, Roberts says, this line

> is most visible on the abdomen, where an actual line, darker than the surrounding skin, becoms evident at puberty and may be accentuated by body hair. It darkens with each successive pregnancy a woman may have, and can become a veritable track, some millimeters wide, leading over the belly toward the vagina. (1980: 92)

Roberts's carefully documented account makes clear that this cosmically replicated midline comprehensively constituted the symmetry of both female and male bodies from the crown of the head to the genitalia, and was integrated with a symbolic system that associated the left and right sides of the body, as well as the 'vertical' opposition of 'head' and 'loins', with sets of contrasting and complementary values embracing philosophical, religious, social and psychological domains (Maurer and Roberts 1985; Roberts 1986).[8]

In the late nineteenth and early twentieth centuries Tabwa consciousness of a felt corporeal co-presence with the living architecture of earth and sky was fleetingly externalized in an extraordinary efflorescence of plastic art which has only recently been noticed in the Western world. It took the form of wooden sculptures depicting stylized human figures bearing on their bodies elaborate tattoo work typical of the period and most prominently representing the cosmic corporeal midline.[9]

Tabwa awareness of cosmic identity participates in a much wider system of ideas pervading indigenous southern Africa. As the Belgian anthropologist Luc de Heusch has grandly demonstrated in his synoptic study of southern Bantu mythology entitled *Le roi ivre* (*The Drunken King*) (1982 [1972]), the orally-transmitted stories of these peoples dramatize the mythic personae of kings, divine animals and celestial powers to infuse with cosmic significance the organization of society, the succession of the seasons, the phenomena of life and death and rebirth, the dialogue of earth and sky, rain and drought. In this vast cultural region that includes the Tabwa people, the primitive beginnings of human society are symbolically identified with the sun, the advent of kingship and hierarchic authority with the moon, an interesting inversion of the Eurasian and South American celestial symbology. As in Ancient Europe, the cyclical rhythm of the seasons, epitomized in the regularly changing face of the moon, provides the living background to mythical drama. For these peoples of the southern African savannah and Congo forests, the modulated moon represents the principle of measurement and control essential to civilized human society, in contrast to the uncontrolled violent energy of the sun, symbolizing pre-civilized anarchy and lack of manners. The mythic mind weaves a semantic network out of the Morning and Evening Stars, birds of dawning, the speaking animals of paradise, the ever-changing, dying and reborn moon, the ambiguous solar serpent Nkongolo whose name means Rainbow, the nocturnal and lunar aardvark or scaly anteater whose subterranean tunnels go on for ever and who is also the culture hero who created human society and the cosmos, vainglorious men who foolishly try to build a tower to the sky,[10] the tragic queen Lueji whose unceasing menstrual flow condemns her to permanent sterility, the mysteries of life and death and the rhythmic flow of the seasonal cycle, all connected together in a vast, unending semantic web of cosmic powers spanning time and space. De Heusch quotes a Lunda creation myth that gives some sense of this semantic interconnectedness:

> The primordial serpent, Tianza Ngombe (or Chinaweshi) the mother of all things, divided up the world with the lightning, Nzashi, her husband. The latter set himself up in the sky with the sun, the moon, Venus, and the stars; his urine became the beneficial rain. Tianza Ngombe, on her side, had the earth and the rivers. When the thunder rumbles in the sky, Tianza Ngombe responds in the waters and the rivers become swollen. Tianza Ngombe bore a son, Konde, and a daughter, Naweshi. These two united incestuously and had three children, among them Lueshi (Lueji). At the confluence of two rivers Lueshi met Chibinda Ilunga, the tireless hunter with the long hair who was a master of his art and became chief. (De Heusch 1982: 183)

Western social science has managed to decode, dissect and demarcate the total and totalizing experience that is mythic consciousness, and the industrious clerics of enlightenment have labelled the separate parts history, social evolution, religion, kinship system, and so on. A disenchanted world, indeed.

The Luba-speaking peoples, whose year consists of thirteen lunar months, the number engraved on the lunar-crescent horn in the upraised hand of the goddess of Laussel, express their sense of the moon's moral ascendency over the sun in this story:

> The sun and the moon each claimed to be greater than the other. They brought their dispute to God, who decided in favour of the moon, because it gave life to men: on one of its thirteen annual journeys, the moon brought back the rain, so causing the plants to

grow. Incensed at this verdict, the sun threw mud in the moon's face. Since that time the moon has produced less light than the sun. (1982: 51)

From the eastern margin of the huge mythic domain surveyed by de Heusch, anthropologist Allen Roberts contributes a special understanding of these Bantu peoples' complex sense of cosmic inter-connection, grounded in four years of field research with the Tabwa. Here he learned the story of Mungaleza, the tyrant king whose repeated bids to achieve immortality by building a tower to join the mirrored realms of earth and sky ended in catastrophic failure and the scattering of human groups which had originally been one. As both Roberts and de Heusch make clear, this assertion of separation and discontinuity, most grandly exemplified in the separation of heaven and earth, also gives rise to the cyclical alternation of the wet and dry seasons, rain and drought, life and death and life's return. In Roberts's vivid words:

According to Tabwa thinking, the year is divided into two six-month seasons, one wet, the other dry. Nkuba, the chimera causing the lightning, and Nfwimina, the solar serpent producing the rainbow, are locked in a never-ending, head-over-heels spin, the one dominant for its season, to be replaced by its other at the appropriate moment. Each defeats its other, but assures its return. (1980: 10)

'The most incomprehensible thing about the universe is that it exists' – Albert Einstein

It took the greatest mind in twentieth-century science to pose the grandest of all problems, the meaning of multiform creation itself, the problem of Being that, as Heidegger has argued, engrossed the pre-Socratic thinkers of Greece. Yet long before their fragmentarily surviving cogitations, it seems, the anonymous tale-singers of humankind's remote prehistory pondered the strange mutuality of life and death, order and chaos, unity and multiplicity. As mythic consciousness unfolded in dialogue with itself, it established the necessary connection of separation and otherness with felt communion. Among the diverse powers of heaven and earth, humankind's complex relationship with the ever-changing moon has a primal and archetypal quality well evoked by Allen Roberts for the Tabwa-speaking fisherfolk of southern Lake Tanganyika. In this region of Africa, as in ancient Mesopotamia, and commonly in Amazonia and many parts of aboriginal Australia, the moon is regarded as a masculine entity. For Tabwa, the male moon is a celestial being allied with the earthly divinity of the subterranean aardvark, avatar of Mtumbi the culture hero and creator of human society, with the mystery of the female menstrual cycle, and exemplar of the ambiguous powers of chiefship. For, says Roberts, a chief has two 'faces' like the moon, 'one shining, with which he guides and nurtures his people, the other dark as he turns aside, allowing sorcerers to slaughter these same' (1980: 13).

The dark of the moon, the two or three days when it sheds no nocturnal light, is also the time when Mtumbi the Aardvark 'is out and about, reveling in the primordial obscurity', but equally it's the time when dangerous beasts such as snake and lion are most to be feared (1980: 166). While nocturnal game and, it is said, fish abound, the hidden moon is said to make them peculiarly hard to catch. Supposedly, it does the same thing when directly overhead at dusk, leading people to describe the moon, too, as a two-faced 'sorcerer'. A Tabwa woman called Mumba gave Roberts a revealing description of her terrifying encounter with an earth spirit called Ngulubia, an immense serpent which 'sparkles like the stars' and whose behaviour falls under lunar influence. During the period of nocturnal moonlight this powerful spirit remains peacefully at its 'male' home up a mountain, but during the dark of the moon it descends to its 'female' site by the lake, when it is liable to cause trouble for unwary humans:

> Mumba herself tried to cross the path it had made at such a time in its descent from the mountain, and the spirit seized her feet; she was unable to move, and there was sparkling light all about her. It then released her, but she stood there for a long moment, bedazzled and stricken with fear. At the *mwandamo*, the appearance of the new moon, it reascends the mountain. (1980: 168)

It is not in sub-equatorial Africa, however, but in the vast rainforests of Amazonian South America that the pattern of the cosmic dialogue that is mythic consciousness has revealed itself most elaborately in the work of de Heusch's mentor, the great mythologist Claude Lévi-Strauss. Lévi-Strauss's crucial contribution to mythology was his adaptation of the form of human dialogical discourse newly developed in structural linguistics as a model for decoding the global species-dialogue of myth. In the Lévi-Straussian reading of myth we see the human mind engaged in a constructive debate with itself on the nature of dialogical thought, a debate that takes as its illustrative subject matter the entire range of sensible phenomena. It is this mind that, as Merleau-Ponty has it, discovers consciousness, intelligence, spirit in every thing, making a subject of every object.

Ordering of Chaos

Adrift in a talking universe of numberless voices, *Homo sapiens* creates an always provisional, open-ended order from the boundless chaos of perceived phenomena, always by imagining and exchanging stories, articulated accounts of his or her situation in the world. And the very paradigm of that cosmic dialogue that ever seeks to embrace all things in a singular net of meaning, is the mirrored reciprocity of that grandest and most inclusive of all dialogical actors, the conversation of heaven and earth. The mythography of Lévi-Strauss shows the sky-earth couplet to be one of a theoretically infinite set of binary oppositions, contrasted and reciprocally complementary conceptual pairs. The 'binary' couplet is not just the simplest form of linguistic structure, as Lévi-Strauss once remarked, it is also the most basic model of the dialogical process through which humankind turns the chaos of phenomenal experience into a meaningful universe. Viewed through the lens of an anthropology which is both comparative and participatory, both objective and subjective, we notice at once that the division of earth and heaven which is also a relation of mutual implication is in all cultural entities joined in narrative with that singular human characteristic that transcends all local particularity, that of being subject to the limitation of death. So countless myths associate the inexorable fact of human mortality and finitude with the most generally apparent feature of cosmic architecture, the gulf between earth and sky. In Africa, missionary-anthropologist Matthew Schoffeleers tells how the creation myth of the Mang'anja people of Malawi begins with the descent of God, together with the first human beings and all the animals, on to an originally lifeless earth. Thereafter all these beings lived together in a timeless harmony until one day man accidentally discovered fire, causing a devastating conflagration that ended with all the animals except dog and goat becoming enemies of humankind, the withdrawal of God to the over-arching sky and the advent of death. From that moment time began in the dual sense of the perpetual succession of the seasons of drought and rain and the subjection of all living things to the cycle of birth, maturation and death (Schoffeleers 1992: 33–4).

The mythic imagination aligns the sky-earth and life-death oppositions with a rich assortment of conceptual contrasts that in the extensive culture region of the central African savannah includes the idea that the seasonal occurrence of the great bushfires toward the end of the six-month period of drought itself precipitates the first rains. According to Allen Roberts, the Tabwa see the fires as 'building' the rain-bearing clouds, while the rains in their turn clean or purify the moon, causing it to rise:

> the great message of Tabwa thought (and of Luba as well) is to look to the fugue of the seasons, to the counterpoint of these forces, to their harmonic relationship which none-theless preserves the individuality of each within the greater universe in which they are bound and define. (1980: 318)

In northeast Africa the Dinka people of the southern Sudan suppose that originally earth and sky were connected by a rope, people lived contentedly in company with God, and there was no death. This state of primal unity was ended when Abuk, the first woman, decided to plant more than the one grain of millet allowed by God, and in doing so struck God with her long-handled hoe. Offended, God withdrew to his present great distance from earth, and sent a small blue bird called *atoc* to sever the rope joining heaven and earth. From that time humans knew hunger, disease and death, but also experienced a new freedom to live their own lives (Lienhardt 1961: 36).

'At the beginning of time, night did not exist' – Amazonian myth

In his monumental study of South American myth, Lévi-Strauss rehearses the 'symphony' (his term) through and in which the mythic imagination of the Amazon rainforest peoples expresses their sense that the cosmic interdependence of heaven and earth is of a piece with the temporal rhythms of human and natural life. In the Amazon, he tells us, many myths deal with the relationship between sky and earth, 'whether the theme is cultivated plants resulting from the marriage of a star with a mortal, or cooking fire which disunites the sun and the earth, once too close to each other, by coming between them, or man's shortened life-span, which is always in all cases the result of disunion' [between earth and heaven] (1978: 181).

Lévi-Strauss succeeds by dint of exhaustive analysis in establishing his case that 'primitive' or mythopaeic thought exhibits a uniformly patterned matrix consisting of a combination of binary contrasts and analogical relations. It's worth noting that the binary couplet, the fundamental structural unit in Lévi-Strauss's scheme, is also the very paradigm of dialogical communication between Self and a reciprocal, mirroring Other. Examination of the numerous examples Lévi-Strauss analyses shows that the essential characteristic of all myth is its interrelating within a single narrative of actors rarely if ever found together in the texts considered in the four volumes of the *Mythologiques*, a bringing to order of the chaos of perceived cosmic 'voices'. This ordering process is a creative or 'worldmaking' human activity, but it is always and inevitably incomplete and provisional, being itself a part of an endless dialogical exchange between narrators. This exchange has the form of a semantic chain in which each narrated myth itself emerges as a reponse and in opposition to, another myth, while generating a similar oppositional response in its turn. We could say, then, that beneath the concrete manifestations of mythopaeic thought in the form of individual narratives, structured in terms of analogous and opposed clusters of binary pairs, and the endless unfolding of mythic 'conversation', lies the same conceptual paradigm of 'self' in dialogue with 'other'. This relation is always asymmetrical, otherwise there would be no impulsion to response: equality and absolute alienation alike preclude dialogue, the first state by making it superfluous, and the second by rendering it impossible.

Summarizing his results, Lévi-Strauss concludes:

> It cannot be said purely and simply of the world that it is: it exists in the form of an initial asymmetry, which shows itself in a variety of ways according to the angle from which

– 34 –

it is being apprehended: between the high and the low, the sky and the earth, land and water, the near and the far, left and right, male and female, etc. (1981: 603)

Many myths in Lévi-Strauss's grand collection appear to be implicitly concerned with the conditions of fruitful human dialogue, which requires distance, difference, and asymmetry between the parties in dialogue, together with the fact of necessary relationship. 'So it is not surprising', Lévi-Strauss comments, 'that myths dealing with the impossible arbitration between the near and the far, should frequently take as their theme the shortness of human life, which was instituted by the demiurges at the same time as the reasonable distance between the sun and the moon, the inevitable discrepancy between upstream and downstream canoe-journeys, and the degree of mobility permitted to women' (1978: 171). So cosmic relations such as that between earth and sky, sun and moon, are seen as analogous to geographical distances such as the optimum length of a canoe journey, and with temporal sequences such as the proper alternation of night and day.

Lévi-Strauss quotes a myth from the Arawak people of Guiana that illustrates both the combination of cosmic and human relations typical of myth and the mythic concern with the proper preconditions of dialogue. According to this story, the sun and moon were formerly human beings who kept light shut up in a basket. The sun wanted to marry a Native American woman, but he was too high up to come down, and so the girl had to climb into the sky. No sooner had she got there than she opened the basket, light poured out and from then on day and night shared time between them (1978: 174).

In North America indigenous imagining of the relationship of earth and heaven has constructed stories about a war between the earth and sky people, these hostilities featuring mythical animals known to anthropology as 'culture heroes', who founded human society. These stories describe the temporary connection of sky and earth through the medium of a ladder constructed by the terrestrial animal-people, who use it to invade the sky and capture cooking fire. Grizzly Bear, the last animal to attempt to climb the ladder, broke it with his great weight. The other animals found nothing to eat in the sky and, starving, some floated back down to earth, but most of them died in the sky, or were changed into stars (Lévi-Strauss 1981: 463–7).

Notes

1. See above, pp. 17–20. Briffault (1927, ii, 583 ff.) maintains that the moon was 'originally' seen as male by prehistoric humankind, but his argument appears to be grounded in evolutionist presuppositions. The important point is that,

whether perceived as male or female, the moon is everywhere and in all eras associated with women and their menstrual cycle. On this association see also the scholarly work of Shuttle and Redgrove (1978).

2. Cf. the thirteen marks on the lunar-crescent horn held aloft by the Palaeolithic goddess figure at Laussel (p. 20 in this volume). See also evidence from the Americas and the ancient Near East, below.

3. The original meaning of the term that has come down to us in the Latin form *Virgo*, denoted a free and independent woman. The connotation of chastity was a concept introduced with the advent of patriarchal society in the Middle East about seven thousand years ago, along with the idea of male proprietorship in females (cf. Sjöö and Mor 1987: 158–9).

4. As Lash notes, the Snaketamer figures prominently in the famous painting of the zodiacal images by the sixteenth-century German artist Albrecht Dürer.

5. Cf. discussion in Chapter 1 of prehistoric evidence for female control of a lunar-based system of cosmological notation. In Africa, the cosmic significance of the moon and its rhythmic cycle of apparent 'birth', 'growth', 'death' and 'rebirth' has been well described by Allen Roberts (1980). Here too, as universally it seems, the people explicitly correlate the lunar and menstrual cycles (Maurer and Roberts 1985: 39; on the prehistoric evidence see Briffault 1927, ii, 583: 'The moon is the regulator and, according to primitive ideas, the cause of the periodical functions of women. Menstruation is caused by the moon; it is a lunar function, and is commonly spoken of as 'the moon'').

6. See Wallace-Murphy and Hopkins 1999: 127 ff. Other holy Christian buildings, in a huge arc extending from Compostela to the mysterious Roslyn Chapel near Edinburgh in Scotland, had each a specific planetary association. It is note-worthy, in view of the argument developed in the present book, that the 'lunar' site of Compostela appears to have been accorded pre-eminence by medieval pilgrims.

7. The Quechua peoples also have a concept of an invisible underworld where 'everything happens just opposite to the way it happens on this earth; our sun-rise is their sunset, our day is their night, and our earth is their sky'. It is to this underworld that the dead go (Urton 1981: 38).

8. This complex body-based symbolism, general throughout the southern Lake Tanganyika region, associated 'head' and 'right' with masculinity, intellect and political authority, with the cardinal direction east, with light and life, while 'loins' and 'left' were associated with femininity, emotionality, sexuality, dark-ness, sorcery and death.

9. An impressive exhibition featuring a selection of these Tabwa sculptures was organized in 1985 by Allen Roberts and museologist Evan Maurer under the significant title of 'The Rising of a New Moon' and presented in the United States and Belgium (see Maurer and Roberts 1985).

10. This is of course the widespread motif that appears in the Christian Bible as the story of the Tower of Babel. Another biblical motif commonly found in Black Africa is the Mosaic tale of the leader who parts the waters of a lake or river and allows his followers to escape to the farther shore.

–3–

Actors on the Celestial Stage

... the constellations, for which the Salish not only have descriptive terms, but which they deal with in special myths explaining the origin and configuration of each: frozen in characteristic poses, terrestrial people are transported to the sky where they hold their positions, as in a *tableau vivant*. (Lévi-Strauss, 1981)

It is time to consider in more detail the interrelations between the mythic stories told through countless ages by human beings as, the daily chores over, they relaxed around the camp fire and contemplated the grand pageant arrayed before them in the night sky, a pageant of illustrations from the book of ancestral memory. Because each and every myth in some measure evokes, through a network of analogies and inversions, the entire range of human experience, we could say that the symbol-strewn heavens are the very mind of the species made visible, speaking to us with ageless authority. On this unique, earth-spanning stage, the minded past of humankind, told in the cosmic, multi-layered language of myth, presents itself in the living present to those with eyes to see, or at least all those who have not been blinded by the uni-dimensional narrative of 'science'.

So we find there the wondrous animals whose strange, non-human intelligence irresistibly suggests, as it did to our Palaeolithic ancestors and the ancient civilizations of Australia, Africa, Asia and the Americas, the sense of divinity in its all-powerful otherness; we find the gods and goddesses themselves, and the heroic archetypal figures of our own unconscious.

Now, if the essence of mythic thought is its cosmic reach, then the gigantic Emu visible in the Milky Way as it appears in the clear night sky of central Australia, its powerful beak pointing south toward the Musca constellation, is not just the image of this great bird of the desert spaces, it's also the altered-state experience of dancing the Emu spirit; it's the miracle of creation in what English-speaking Aborigines call 'the Dreaming' and the continuing wonder of the living earth imprinted with ancestral memory; it's the awesome mysteries of initiation into adulthood, sexuality, life and death.[1] For these desert people, too, the constellation astronomy and what white culture calls the Southern Cross is the claw of an enormous celestial Eagle-hawk, likewise the emblem of sacred myth and ritual. In this mythic world the powers of heaven are living beings, the sun is a woman with a fiery exterior who daily traverses the sky before returning at dusk to her special haunts on earth, and the moon was once an earth-dwelling man (Basedow 1925: 267, 332–49).

It is said that long ago in the Dreamtime, seven virgin sisters called Kung-karangkalpa came from the north beyond Atila, fleeing from the unwanted attentions of a man called Nyiru. At midday they rested briefly at Kungkalililpa, where they gathered some bush fruit to satisfy their hunger. At sundown they reached Waliny. Weary and anxious, the sisters made a wide *yu* of brush as an overnight shelter. Next day they discovered that as well as water and plenty of firewood, there were abundant food-bearing trees and bushes. So they built a *wiltja,* a more extensive and durable shelter, secluded by a stand of *ili* bushes.

> But the man Nyiru followed them. Finding their *yu,* he made a small shelter for himself overlooking the sisters' first camp, thinking he could spy on them from his vantage point. When the women did not return to their *yu,* Nyiru searched about, tracked them to their *wiltja* hidden beyond the grove of *ili* bushes and heard the women's voices. Making a sudden attack, he terrified them, but the women escaped by breaking a small opening in the back of the *wiltja* and continued their flight, leaving clear tracks in the sand as they ran towards Alkanyunta. (Wallace and Wallace 1977: 64–5)

These are the words of Phyl and Noel Wallace who, in *Killing Me Softly* (1977), eloquently mourn the destruction of the spiritual universe of aboriginal Australia by the agents of disenchantment. The myth ends with Nyiru and the seven sisters climbing into the sky, where the drama of pursuit and flight continues for ever. Today the Dreamtime shelters made by Nyiru and the women are granite caves in certain hills in South Australia, while the cave that is Nyiru's shelter is decorated with sacred symbols:

> It is well known to be *watiku* (belonging to man) and no Desert woman or child would approach it. Through the ages its immediate environs have been used – and still are – as a *Nyi: nka* camp for segregated boys in training for manhood . . . Animals, birds, chains of waterholes, tracks, mythical serpents that guard all waterholes and soaks, sacred symbols and totemic designs abound. In a rich medley of ochre, charcoal and ash, the secret and the sacred stand together (1977: 66–7)

The very earth is shaped by this story that binds together so many elements of Aboriginal culture. 'The tracks the Dreamtime women left in the red sand as they fled from Waliny are preserved forever in the now rock surface leading away from the little escape cave', while four tall monoliths are the man Nyiru, searching for his human prey (ibid.: 67). At night also the epic story is mirrored in the brilliant desert sky, the immortal sisters are the constellation of the Pleiades, while their eternal pursuer Nyiru's pounding foot is seen in the belt and sword of the constellation known to the West as Orion.[2]

Actors in a Cosmic Drama

In his monumental *Golden Bough*, J.G. Frazer remarked on the important role played by the Pleiades in the calendars of tribal peoples worldwide, adding that 'for reasons which at first sight are not obvious savages appear to have paid more attention to this constellation than to any other group of stars in the sky' (1925, vii, 307). More recently Gooch, after quoting Frazer on the Pleiades, further notes the global occurrence of tribal myths linking the constellation of Orion with the Pleiades, suggesting that 'Warrunna', one of the Australian names of the hunter elsewhere called 'Nyiru', is the same word as 'Orion' and that both are versions of a Neanderthal term (1995: 27). Whatever the truth of this assertion by Gooch, there is certainly a striking resemblance between the Australian myth of Nyiru/Warrunna and the seven sisters and the Greek myth of the Pleiades:

> To the ancient Greeks, the Pleiades were originally the daughters of Atlas, the giant con-demned by Zeus to support the sky's vault upon his shoulders. Their mother was Pleione.
> While travelling through Boeotia, northwest of Athens, the Pleiades and their mother had the misfortune to cross the path of Orion the hunter. Infatuated with the women, he started to chase them. It was a long race: some say five years, some say seven. Zeus term-inated this marathon by transforming Pleione and her attractive daughters into doves. Later they flew to the sky to become the stars we now see clustered together west of Orion and still outrunning him. (Krupp 1991: 250)

Lévi-Strauss also draws attention to a structural similarity between mythic relations between Orion and the Pleiades found in the ancient Mediterranean and widespread ideas among the forest peoples of Amazonia, again suggesting – as with the parallel stories from Greece and Australia – a common origin in remote prehistory. In Greco-Latin tradition Orion was associated with destructive storms and torrential rain, while the Pleiades are linked in myth and custom with fertility and growth. While not dismissing the 'common origin' theory, Lévi-Strauss advances a no less plausible explanation of this remarkable similarity in mythic formulations in Old and New Worlds, one grounded in the nature of dialogic thought engaged in cosmic construction. Citing a Greek myth where humans send an archetypal Raven in search of water and Raven, failing in his mission, is condemned to be forever thirsty in summer (hence his characteristically 'hoarse' voice), Lévi-Strauss shows that this ancient European tale is paralleled by a similar story involv-ing the same bird in the Americas.

> The Greeks and Romans associated Orion with the 'bad' season for empirical reasons. It is enough to postulate, first that in their hemisphere the Bororo [a people of the Amazon forest] make a similar deduction in associating the constellation of the Raven with the rainy season, and secondly, that Orion and the Raven dominate the southern sky during

different periods, with the result that if two myths are systematically opposed but use the same lexicon, one myth being concerned with the origin of celestial water, the other with terrestrial water – then, it follows that if one myth relates to the Raven constellation, the other will relate to Orion, on condition only that such an opposition is explicit in indigenous thought . . .

And indeed, as Lévi-Strauss proceeds to demonstrate in the pages that follow, the Raven constellation fulfils the same function in the mythic universe of the southern hemisphere, including both South America and Polynesia, that the Orion constellation serves in the northern hemisphere (Lévi-Strauss 1964: 235).

These apparently opposed interpretations of some remarkable commonalities in mythic themes around the world are resolvable if we recognize that mythic 'dialogue' is both a developmental process, a 'history', and a timeless, time-binding totalization. Every myth is a response to another, a moment in the unending dialogical chain, but also an ever-renewed creative process of cosmic reach, an erotic movement reaching toward, while never finally attaining, total communion of self and other.

Origin Stories

Numerous Amazonian narratives are concerned with the origin of the stars, and this story from the Bororo people is typical of myth in its interweaving of the 'binary' contrasts of sky and earth, domestic and wild, old and young, male and female, language and silence (non-communication):

> The women of the village went out to harvest maize, but with but a poor result. Then they took with them a little boy who managed to find a whole heap of maize cobs. The women ground the maize on the spot and made cakes for their menfolk who were out hunting. But the little boy stole much of the flour and took it to his grandmother, asking her to make cakes for himself and his young comrades.
>
> The grandmother did so, and the boys enjoyed a grand feast. To conceal their theft, they cut out the grandmother's tongue, then the tongue of the domestic parrot. After that they sent all the other domestic parrots back into the wild.[3] Then, fearful of their parents' anger, they fled up to the sky, using an immensely long vine set there by the humming-bird.
>
> Shortly afterwards, the women returned to the village, looking for the boys. In vain they questioned the grandmother and the parrot, deprived as they were of the faculty of speech. Then one of them noticed the long vine and the line of boys climbing up it. The women tried to call them back, but they merely climbed faster. In desperation, the women climbed up behind them, but the thief, who brought up the rear, cut the vine as soon as he arrived in the sky. The women fell to earth, and changed into wild animals when they landed. In punishment for their wickedness the boys were changed into stars

and spend every night looking on the sad state of their mothers. It is their eyes we see shining up there.

Another myth quoted by Lévi-Strauss, from the Matako people of the Amazon, illustrates the characteristic nature of mythopaeic thought in the way it plays on the same set of cosmic contrasts apparent in the Bororo story, although here the overt theme addressed by the Matako tale is the origin of women:

> Formerly, men were animals with the gift of speech. They lacked women, and lived on fish, which they caught in abundance. One day they noticed that someone had stolen part of their food store, and left a parakeet to keep guard on the rest. From his perch in a tree, this bird saw some women descend from the sky on a long rope. They ate as much as they could from the store of fish, then went to sleep under the tree. Instead of raising the alarm as he had been instructed, the parakeet contented himself with throwing twigs down on the women. In response, the women threw grain at the bird, hitting his tongue, which remains black to this day.
>
> The iguana heard the noise of this battle and alerted his comrades. But, believing him deaf, they refused to listen. As for the parakeet, he remained silent.
>
> The next day, the lizard mounted guard, but the women caught him, and tore out his tongue. The men discussed the situation and entrusted the job of guarding the village to a sparrowhawk, who was invisible to the women as his plumage was the same colour as the treetrunk where he perched. The sparrowhawk duly raised the alarm, and despite being pelted with missiles by the women, he succeeded in cutting the rope by which they had descended from the sky, preventing their return. From then on men had women with them. (Lévi-Strauss 1964: 122–3)

In east-central Africa the Tabwa people recognize the 'hunter' motif, already encountered in Europe and Australia, in the three visible stars constituting what in European myth is the 'belt' of the great hunter called Orion. According to Allen Roberts, this asterism is the only significant stellar cluster recognized by Tabwa. Of these three stars, Delta, the westernmost and lowest of them, is seen as a cane rat, Epsilon, the middle star, is a dog chasing it, and the third and easternmost star, Zeta, is the hunter following behind. The asterism as a whole is called Kabwa, 'Dog' (1980: 69).[4] For Tabwa, as Roberts explains, the symbolism of these three animated stars evokes other constituents of the Tabwa cosmos, including the Milky Way, seen as congruent with the geography of Tabwa country and the medial *linea negra* of the human body, and the underground journey of the culture hero Mtumbi the Aardvark down its 'endless' subterranean passage:

> As the wet season progresses, from November when the asterism is first visible, to May when it no longer is, the three stars move across the sky (when viewed at the same hour nightly), as though the cane rat were being chased from east to west, which is associated with the place of the dead . . . it is in the east [associated with birth and renewal] that

Mtumbi, the possessing spirit, resides, and whence it is called to possess those chosen. Just as the way to and within the cavern of Kibawa [terminus of the geographic median line, the Mwila ridge] where the spirits of the dead reside, can be analogized with the tunnel of the aardvark, so does the celestial hunter pursue the cane rat along the Milky Way toward the west, toward death. Furthermore, just as cane-rat hunting implies the wet season within the dry because of the nature of the animal and its habitat, so does the asterism Kabwa, visible in the rainy season, imply the dry within the wet, because of the usual timing of the activity itself. Finally, hunting and masculinity are closely associated, with Mtumbi as a mediator. In Orion's Belt, the number three (for the stars) joins that paradigm with celestial brilliance; it will be encountered in many other contexts as a subtle reference to its masculine set. (ibid.: 71)

This sampling of Roberts's brilliant exposition of Tabwa mythopaeic thought is apt to our exploratory purpose here. His method comes straight from Lévi-Strauss's application of the theory of structural linguistics, the first scientific discipline to uncover the laws of human discourse at the basis of all particular languages, to ethnographic data. A similar patterned commingling of cosmic elements is to be found in the pre-scientific foundations of all human cultures, including our own, 'Western' one.

Inveterate Dualism

The sub-science of mythology has come a long way since Max Müller's nineteenth-century project of reducing all mythical stories to expressions of primeval sun-worship. The grandeur of humankind's mythic heritage later became a preoccupation of such famous twentieth-century names as Carl Jung, Mircea Eliade and Joseph Campbell, all of them concerned to demonstrate the universality of mythic themes, an idea most abstractly formulated in Jung's famous concept of 'collective uncon-scious', a hypostasized entity that unfortunately reflects the inveterate mind/matter dualism millennially inherent in 'Western' civilization. In contrast, our approach here sees the global body of mythical tradition as a 'history before history', a trad-ition that yet lives, generally unbeknownst to us, in our very bodies.

Another notable twentieth-century contribution to the work of mental arch-aeology in the field of myth is Giorgio de Santillana and Hertha von Dechend's 1969 volume *Hamlet's Mill: an Essay on Myth and the Frame of Time*. Despite being written in a style that is often an irritating mix of obscurity and whimsicality, this immensely learned volume is a major, if still largely unacknowledged, contribution to mythological studies. Drawing on a wealth of sources ranging from the Edda and Kalevala collections of ancient Europe, the mythic traditions of Greece, the Near East and the Orient, the codices of the Mayan and Aztec civilizations and the Incan traditions, and a host of ethnographic materials worldwide, the authors build a powerful case for the existence of a global human culture in prehistoric times. Writing as they did before the remarkable work of Marshack, Gimbutas, Sjöö and Mor, among others, the authors can hardly be blamed for seriously under-estimating the temporal depth of that universal civilization which would now seem to have originated in the Palaeolithic world of 50,000 years ago, and possibly earlier.

The authors' single most sensational conclusion, one that has been virtually ignored by the scientific and scholarly establishment, along with the rest of their work, is that the bearers of Megalithic civilization were aware of the cyclic celestial phenomenon which modern astronomy calls 'the precession of the equinoxes'. This regular 'wobble' of the earth on its axis – the effect, science tells us, of the differential gravitional attractions of the sun and the moon on the planet's mass – has a cycle of close on 26,000 years, and its discovery is conventionally attributed to the brilliant Greek astronomer Hipparchus (190–120 BCE). It's hardly surprising that the 'experts', convinced *a priori* of the scientific ignorance of our putatively 'savage' prehistoric ancestors, have paid no attention to de Santillana and von Dechend's heretical assertion, despite the impressive weight of evidence advanced in its favour.

Be that as it may, the central argument of *Hamlet's Mill* is that the language of mythology is a coded means of transmitting, artfully disguised as mundane adventure stories, complex information about changes in the heavens during prehistoric times. In the authors' formulation:

> The main merit of this language has turned out to be its built-in ambiguity. Myth can be used as a vehicle for handing down solid knowledge independently of the degree of insight of the people who do the actual telling of stories, fables, etc. In ancient times, moreover, it allowed the members of the archaic 'brain trust' to 'talk shop' unaffected by the presence of laymen: the danger of giving something away was practically nil. (1969: 312)

In other words, the celestial information de Santillana and von Dechend have discovered in myths purporting to describe the doings of earth-bound actors conveys the 'real' meaning of these ancient tales, one known only to the intellectual elite, or priesthood, of prehistoric human society. There are two principal objections to this one-dimensional 'reading' of mythical language. The first is that all we know of hunter-gathering peoples from first-hand modern studies and ancient story suggests that our prehistoric ancestors lived in nomadic, socially unstratified and normatively egalitarian groups until the later stages of the Neolithic and the so-called Bronze Age. In these social circumstances, it would be surprising to find a closed elite possessing 'secret' knowledge, as posited by the authors of *Hamlet's Mill*. The second objection to their theory is provided by the monumental work of Lévi-Strauss and his exhaustive demonstration of the complex transformations of mythical narrative across cultures and continents, together with the work of his disciples and emulators in Africa and Asia. To suppose that this kaleidoscopic material conveys a stable, precise mapping of celestial events that could be seen as congruent with the ordered, mechanical universe of Newtonian astronomy seems less than plausible.

Yet there is a wealth of information in de Santillana and von Dechend that is very much grist to our mill, if not to Hamlet's. Let us take for example, their treatment of the Epic of Gilgamesh, the action-packed quest for immortality of the Mesopotamian culture hero.[5] Here is what de Santillana and von Dechend have to say about this first written text in the meta-narrative of Western civilization:

> . . . all the adventures of Gilgamesh, even if ever so earthily described, have no conceivable counterpart on earth. They are astronomically conceived from A to Z – even as the fury of Era does not apply to some meteorological 'Lord Storm' but to events which are imagined to take place among constellations. The authors of Sumer and Babylon describe their hair-raising catastrophes of the Flood without a thought of earthly events. Their imagination and calculations as well as their thought belong wholly among the stars. (1969: 323–4)

Elsewhere the authors note affinities between the warror-hunter Gilgamesh and the biblical Old Testament figures of Samson and Nimrod, with Marduk, the dragon-slaying king of the Babylonian origin myth, with the Greek Orion and much further afield, from the Chinese war lord Tsan, master of the autumn hunt, to Cambodia, where the Orion constellation is seen as a trap for tigers, to Polynesia, where he is a net for catching birds, and in South America, where his analogue is said to be Hunrákan, great god of hurricanes (1969: 166). To this inventory could be added the ancient Indian concept of Orion (called Skanda or Karttikeya in Sanskrit), who headed a great celestial army and let his arrows fly against the White Mountain, or Milky Way (Krupp 1991: 215). The list could certainly be prolonged, though to little purpose, since our point here is that, *pace* de Santillana and von Dechend, we do not need to choose between terrestrial and celestial dimensions of mythical semantics: our theory of myth as cosmic dialogue requires instead that we admit both on equal terms.

Accordingly, let us consider the myth of Gilgamesh, the hero-king of Uruk in Sumer, whose epic story was first recorded in the fifth century BCE. Although de Santillana and von Dechend loftily dismiss the terrestial implications of Gilgamesh and his deeds, it has become evident in recent years that the Sumerian epic is of epochal importance for the emergence of human consciousness out of its embeddedness in Nature through the Palaeolithic and early Neolithic periods, into what became Nature-dominating 'Western' civilization. Gilgamesh, this sexually aggressive male who takes on and defeats the great goddess Inanna/Ishtar herself, epitomizes a historically novel individualism. The symbolism is blatant in Gilgamesh's killing of the forest guardian spirit Huwawa, and his subsequent destruction of the cedar forest itself; in his sacrilegious defiance of the great goddess of love called

Inanna by the Sumerians and Ishtar by the Semitic Akkadians of Babylon; and in the slaying by Gilgamesh's beloved friend Enkidu of the Bull of Heaven, sent by the goddess to punish Gilgamesh for his errant behaviour. According to William Irwin Thompson, the Gilgamesh myth is 'the very foundation of Western literature, for what we are witnessing here is to set the pattern for all Greek and Hebrew literature to come' (1981: 198).

> Contained in the conflict between Ishtar and Gilgamesh is the conflict between the institutions of the temple and militaristic monarchy, between the civilized remnants of the old neolithic religion and the new masculine order of civilization. (ibid.)[6]

Small wonder that such a socially and historically portentous myth should also be written in the stars, for the 'Bull of Heaven' sent to earth by the goddess to punish the blasphemous upstart Gilgamesh, is, of course, the constellation Taurus, just as Gilgamesh is Orion. As Gooch observes, '[i]n the sky, Taurus is immediately adjacent to the north of Orion, and a glance at the star map at once suggests that these two are confronting each other' (1995: 33).

The signal achievement of *Hamlet's Mill* is its discovery of the hidden astrological dimension in mythic narrative; its error is concluding that the astrological element is the underlying or even the sole source of meaning in a cosmic discourse embracing all areas of life and extending through all time and space.

Notes

1. In other Aboriginal contexts the Milky Way is an an epiphany of the bisexual and cosmic Rainbow Serpent (Buchler and Maddock 1978).
2. Personal communication from Robert Layton. Professor Layton added: 'The belt stars are his [Nyiru's] toes'.
3. In Bororo culture adult males customarily kept parrots as pets, supposing them to incarnate the spirits of dead kinsmen.
4. I encountered this story among the Fipa of southwest Tanzania in 1964. The cane rat is a sought-after game animal for these peoples.
5. Gilgamesh was a king of Uruk in Babylonia (now in Iraq), who lived *c*.2700 BCE. He became the focus of a cycle of myths, originally narrated in the Sumerian language. Our knowledge of the epic comes from a version inscribed on clay tablets in the Semitic Akkadian language and discovered in the ruins of the library of the Assyrian king Ashurbanipal by British archaeologists early in the nineteenth century.

6. Cf. Sjöö and Mor: 'This new individuating, mocking, arrogantly alienated ego of Gilgamesh, established in defiance of the Old Religion of the Goddess and the earth, becomes in Western religious and secular history the ego of man, 'mocker of the past, builder of tomorrow', etc.' (1987: 246).

–4–

The Astrological Story

A Brief History of Astrology

Western astrology as we know it today appeared as first Mesopotamian, then Greek, astral divination with some Eygptian influences. The planets and prominent stars, identified as divinities in ways that have remained extraordinarily stable over time, were omens conveying the will of the gods, largely in response to royal concerns. The origins of many key elements of the astrological tradition – the planetary identities, zodiacal signs, risings and settings, etc. – developed between its origins around 2000 BCE and the fifth century BCE, when natal astrology first appeared. The same period saw an effort to systematize divination through what we would now view as astronomical and empirical observations.

This astrology was then affected by Greek geometric and kinetic models, which added the aspects, or angles of separation between planets and points, and emphasized the importance of the *horoscopos* or Ascendant, the degree of the sign rising on the eastern horizon. (The first known horoscopic nativity dates from 4 BCE.) Astrology also interacted significantly with Empedoclean elements, Aristotelian cosmology, Hippocratic humours and (slightly later) Galenic temperaments. The general movement – especially as influenced by Ptolemy (*c*.100–170 CE) in his *Tetrabiblos* – was in the direction of a more universal and systematic application to any individual or event. At the same time, however, the ancient astrological interrogation of the stars *qua* divine will in relation to human desires met with and mutually strengthened Greek practices of *katarche* and Roman *aurispicium* and *augurium*, giving rise to horary astrology – the practice of seeking (and sometimes finding) the answer to a question in a map of the heavens for the moment it is asked, or received. Persistently insusceptible to a 'rational' explication, it has commonly been disowned even by most astrologers (see Curry 1989; Cornelius 2003 [1994]).

Astrology played an increasingly important role in Roman life, although largely in populist and overtly political contexts. One response was a capable critique by Cicero, but a more fruitful course followed in the wake of Alexander the Great's conquests, whereby Greek astrology spread to Persia and throughout Eastern Asia as far as India, where it interacted with local cosmo-religious knowledge to produce

Indian astrology. In this way, astrology also eventually contributed to, as well as benefited from, all the learning of Arabic civilization. It was then reintroduced into medieval Europe by retranslations into Latin, predominantly Aristotelian, in the thirteenth and fourteenth centuries.

Astrology was never favoured by the Christian Church. It survived the condemnations of St Augustine and other early Church Fathers, who saw it as pagan, and more precisely polytheistic, and an offence to both human free will and divine omnipotence. Augustine did not deny that astrologers could speak truthfully, maintaining only that when they did so it was with the help of, and in the service of, demons. Despite the hostility of the authorities, however, astrology in medieval Europe remained entrenched, in one form or another, at both popular and elite levels. In the late thirteenth century, St Thomas Aquinas finally formulated a compromise which secured for it a long-lived and relatively secure, if limited, niche. His synthesis of Christian theology and Aristotelian natural philosophy permitted 'natural astrology' to influence physical and collective phenomena but not (directly) human souls; the individual judgements, and in particular predictions, of 'judicial astrology' were therefore illicit. Since Aquinas admitted that most people were in turn influenced by their bodies, however, there was a kind of tacit legitimation of astrology, and the possibility of its truthfulness, in practice. (Judicial astrology was so called because it involves making interpretive judgements.)

In the late fifteenth century, a series of influential translations by Ficino made available more rediscovered Greek texts, including much of Plato, Plotinus and Iamblichus and the *Corpus Hermeticum*. These placed a renewed magical and/or mystical astrology at the heart of the Renaissance revival of neo-Platonism and hermeticism. Typically, it managed to evade Pico della Mirandola's powerful critique by finding shelter elsewhere in the very set of ideas that had so inspired him (for example, occult sympathy and antipathy).

The Protestant Reformation in the fifteenth and sixteenth centuries, however, soon presented a serious new challenge. Reigniting Augustine's earlier attack, Luther and Calvin objected violently to astrology's idolatry – in other words, the illicit worship of the stars as intermediary deities – which they stigmatized as 'superstition'. In response, the Catholic Counter-Reformation also undertook to reform the beliefs and practices of popular culture (see Burke 1978).

The seventeenth century was pivotal in the history of astrology, but (notwithstanding Keith Thomas's influential *Religion and the Decline of Magic*, 1973 [1971]) the question it raises is not why so many otherwise intelligent people believed in astrology, at a time when this was not extraordinary, but why did many people stop believing in it? (Lloyd 1979; Curry 1991). There was a strong social and political dimension to its fall from favour. In the English Revolution the pamphlets and almanacs of astrologers on both sides (especially those of William Lilly [1602–81] for Parliament) played a major and highly visible role. In the late seventeenth and eighteenth centuries the new patrician and commercial alliance sought to put sectarian strife and upheaval behind them, and astrology became firmly identified as vulgar plebeian superstition – now understood in class more than religious terms – to be contrasted with the new spirit of rationalism and realism. This perception was now most often articulated by a new set of opponents: the metropolitan *literati*. It was epitomized in 1707 when Jonathan Swift issued a mock almanac predicting the death of the prominent astrologer, John Partridge, followed by another putatively confirming its fulfilment. Partridge became a laughing-stock in coffee-house circles although, significantly, his almanacs continued to sell. Benjamin Franklin later employed the same tactic in the American colonies (see Curry 1989).

At the same time, increasing political centralization in France made astrologers' unlicensed prophecies unwelcome there too. And after a short period of ambivalence, most prominent European natural philosophers also started to close ranks against astrology, alternately ignoring or criticizing it as part of the old Aristotelian order, and/or magical (whether plebeian or Platonic). To a considerable extent, Isaac Newton's success set the seal on this development. He borrowed the old astrological idea of attraction at a distance, but substituted a single universal and quantifiable force for an astrological *sine qua non*: the planets as a qualitative plurality. So natural astrology – including the moon's effects on tides, and the cosmological functions of comets (see Schaffer 1987) – was gradually absorbed, and renamed, by natural philosophy; but judicial astrology, as a symbolic rather than mathematical system addressing merely 'secondary' qualities and 'subjective' concerns, became out of place as never before in an ever more disenchanted (and commodified) world.

It was in this context that the charge against astrology of 'superstition' began to acquire its present meaning as a cognate of stupidity or ignorance. To begin with, scientific hostility to astrology largely coincided with that of the guardians of religious orthodoxy; but as natural philosophy turned into modern science, its opposition became increasingly secular.

The early modern period has too often been described, by those wilfully mistaking contemporary rhetoric for reality, as marking the death of astrology. There was indeed a serious decline, as astrology was pushed into largely (but not entirely) rural strongholds, where *Moore's Almanac* was so central, and a relatively simple and magical set of beliefs. But early in the nineteenth century, as the middle classes grew in power and began to break away from patrician hegemony, a new urban astrology appeared which is still with us. More individualistic than before, it succeeded in adapting to consumer capitalist society. And in the early twentieth century, through the work of Alan Leo (1860–1917) and his commercially canny Theosophy, astrology secured a firm footing in both the popular press and the thriving middle-class market for psychology-cum-spirituality. At present it still seems to meet a demand for re-enchantment which no amount of technical, technological or purely theoretical progress can obviate (see Kontos 1994, Curry 1999b).

What is 'It'?

What is evident from even this brief history? Most basically, that notwithstanding clear constraints and setbacks, astrology has managed to survive, adapt to, and sometimes even take advantage of, every challenge thrown its way. But – to ask a naive but heuristically valuable question – what is 'it'?

As noted above, there have been, and remain, three main enemies: in chronological if overlapping order, the Christian Church, scientists, and metropolitan literary professionals. Each group has answered that question in terms of a different form of superstition: that astrology is, respectively, a pagan religious practice (and therefore illicit), an unscientific kind of knowledge (and therefore delusory), and a vulgar or parochial belief-system (and therefore ignorant). The answers they have supplied are thus all negative: astrology is a not-religion/not-science/not-truth. In response, most astrologers have countered by insisting that astrology is indeed conformable to Christian tenets, or is susceptible to scientific 'proof', or is a kind of exalted universal truth; in other words, to assert that it is a religion/science/truth, albeit still largely unrecognized as such. This, of course, simply concedes the grounds of the argument to their opponents, and thus materially assists their triumph.

But by no means all of astrology's critics have been fools, as some astrologers assume. So let us examine the possibility that in important respects, they are right about astrology – if not necessarily in the valuation placed on what they perceive – and that astrologers, in their attempted defence, not only often misunderstand their own art but unwittingly endorse the values of their critics. Granted that astrology *isn't* a religion, science or even 'true' – in the ways its critics would recognize – then what is it?

J.S. Morrison (1981: 91) points out that 'The *mantis* [diviner] is listed in the *Odyssey* among the common craftsmen (*demioergi*) who were always welcome at a prince's table. The others are: the carpenter, the singer, the doctor and the herald'. That changed long ago, but the astrologer was still welcome, as such, at some princes' tables until at least the eighteenth century. In the intervening centuries between then and now, however, he or she has become a figure of fun, or if taken seriously, only to be consulted privately. (Even coming from California, where acceptance of astrology is fairly mainstream, Ronald Reagan tried to keep his personal astrologer a secret.)

The mainstream public view thus came to be just as it was spelled out in the statute of English law that was long used to persecute astrologers as any 'Person pretending or professing to tell Fortunes, or using any subtle Craft, Means or Device . . . to deceive and impose on any of His Majesty's subjects . . .' (see Curry 1992: 13). In other words, it was held to be something that could not be done *at all*, let alone well or badly. And although astrologers are no longer imprisoned, and have staged a comeback among some parts of the middle classes and in the horoscope columns of the tabloids and magazines, the same broad attitude obtains.

Ann Geneva (1985: 9), introducing the great English astrologer William Lilly, describes the problem well:

> Astrology in seventeenth-century England was not a science. It was not a religion. It was not magic. Nor was it astronomy, mathematics, puritanism, neo-Platonism, psychology, meteorology, alchemy or witchcraft. It used some of these as tools; it held tenets in common with others; and some people were adept at several of these skills. But in the final analysis it was only itself: a unique divinatory and prognostic art embodying centuries of accreted methodology and tradition.

Thanks to the work of a few such authors, it has now become possible to throw off the inherited mentality of anachronism that has so long patronized and diminished its subject matter, and its human subjects. But is there some way of extending this understanding to take in not only astrology in its origins and heyday, but now?

Divination and the Stars

On Fate

One way to begin to answer to this question is to look at astrology's origins in, and as, divination, and the worldview implicit in such a practice. There is already an excellent discussion of this subject by Geoffrey Cornelius (2003) which will unavoidably overlap with ours, but another promising starting-point is offered by Alby Stone in an extended essay on *wyrd*, the Old English term for 'fate'. Stone points out that in the understanding of North European paganism, the idea of fate was very far removed from its subsequent common versions – whether later (post-Homeric) Greek, Christian or secular, and later scientific – as an inexorably predetermined and objective truth. Rather it combined the concepts implied by the three *nornir* or Fates: worth (the value a life has by the time it ends), death (as the price of life which must eventually be paid by all), and that which, at any given time, will come to be. But the latter can change. As Stone (1989: 22–3) notes, with profound implications for astrology, 'The shaping of destiny did not stop at birth . . . fate was perceived as a steady, ongoing process, only fully completed at the end of a lifetime.' To anticipate a connection to be developed below, this under-standing of fate closely resembles that of Max Weber, who argued that 'every single important action and finally life as a whole . . . signifies a chain of ultimate decisions through which the soul, as in Plato, *chooses* its own fate – that is, the meaning of its doing and being' (quoted in Scaff 1989: 92).

Why? Sometimes fate is identified just as the will of the gods, but in other cases, as H.E. Davidson (1981: 133) writes, 'it is the gods themselves, as well as men, who wait upon [the seeress], and seek to know what is hidden from them by a greater power still, that of Fate'. But ontologically speaking, in either case the powers concerned can always (so to speak) change their minds.

There is another reason too, this time epistemological. The very act of cognizing and recognizing one's fate changes it, the paradigmatic instance of this being the act of divining: a 'foretelling' the reception of which cannot but affect what it fore-tells. (This is true even if, as with Oedipus, the efforts to evade it are instrumental in its realization.) Thus every prediction is necessarily also an intervention. While this truth precludes any fantasies of perfect and complete foreknowledge, it entails something much more valuable: namely, in Cornelius's (2003: 144) resonant phrase, that 'destiny is negotiable' (first cited in his 1984: 18). As Stone (1989: 25, 34, 35) writes,

> How is it possible to foresee the future if fate is a continuing process of becoming, with all factors in constant – if limited – flux? . . . The art of divination . . . [depends] on harnessing the very forces of creation, by a form of imitation that places the operant in the role otherwise occupied by the cosmogonic processes . . . The essential equation [is] between finding out what is going to happen, and actively making things happen . . . Magic, as a creative activity, and divination, the foretelling of future occurences, are one and the same thing: to foretell the future is to assume the mantle of the Fates, and thus to create the future. In this way, the constant process of creation is maintained, and although the future has already been written, its shape is constantly being redrawn.

Now in terms of historical origins, the divinatory discourse Stone describes was still relatively common cultural currency in North European paganism, in the tenth century in England and as late as the twelfth century in Scandanavia and Iceland. The reason was twofold: the relative marginality of this area to the Mediterranean-centred power, knowledge and culture that dominated Europe for so long, plus the fact that the transition away from the indigenous discourses here took place relatively peacefully and gradually. In the new view, 'fate' had become a causal, naturalistic and (in principle) completely determined system, transmitted in one direction only – no dialogue here – from God, or the Unmoved Mover, through the perfect motions of the heavenly bodies, to the corrupt and changeable sublunary Earth. This view, adumbrated initially and most powerfully by Plato and especially Aristotle, spread in the wake of Alexander's conquests and later the Graeco-Roman dispensation until it was adopted and institutionalized, suitably adapted, by Christianity. But the question can still be posed, and we shall: did the old divinatory discourse survive, and is it therefore in any meaningful sense still present?

The older chthonic emphasis ('of the Earth') survived longer on the European fringes, but even there it became remarkable by virtue of its rarity and contrast with the new dispensation. Thus, as Davidson (1981: 126) records, one early Icelandic diviner of renown, Thorstein, 'is not said to have worshipped the gods, but he made offerings to a waterfall near his farm, throwing gifts of food into it'. Another, Lodmund the Old, venerated the sea in the same way. These survivals, remembered because they stood out, now remained common only among surviving indigenous peoples for whom hunting and gathering was still central. Davidson (1981: 127) comments, 'Such a search for guidance, linked with waterfalls, mountains and the sea, resembles methods of consultation used by the Lapps in the relatively recent past, when they desired to know whether or not to proceed on a journey or hunting expedition, according to whether they had the goodwill of the local spirits of the land'.

Given how early (and in many cases drastically) indigenous pagan discourse of the kind described by Stone was displaced at the heart of Europe, its traces are naturally much harder to find; but they certainly exist. They are more easily perceptible now thanks to the work of E.R. Dodds (1951) and G.E.R. Lloyd (1979) in overcoming the anachronistic rationalist superstition that the Greeks 'must have been', and therefore were, supremely rational. Divination and oracles were obviously long at the heart of Greek cultural, social and political life.

More specifically, J.S. Morrison (1981: 91) stresses that in ancient Greece, '. . . the *mantis* is not merely a forecaster of future events, his sphere of knowledge embraces the past and present as well; he tells the truth as opposed to the appearance of things'. Similarly, as he notes (1981: 110), in Aeschylus' *Choephorai*, 'the dream does not foretell the future. It does what Calchas did in the *Iliad*, it reveals the truth about a situation'. Another highly significant point arises from studies of the records of responses at the Delphic Oracle after 750 BCE, which show that about three-quarters of all consultations concerned matters of *res divinae*, or religious law: in other words, not 'What is going to happen?' but 'Is this course of action in accord with divine will?' (Fontenrose 1978).[1]

This understanding is also true in the classical Roman context. As J. Warde Fowler (1911: 298) noted, 'The augural art never provided an answer to the question, "what is going to happen?" but only to that much more religious one, "are the deities willing that we should do this or that?"' A sympathetic understanding of the importance of this point, incidentally, was still possible in the early sixteenth century, as Machiavelli's (1970: 148–50) superb analysis of augury in the Roman Republic shows; he points out that 'knowing how to accommodate nicely [one's] plans to the auspices' must nonetheless respect the authority of the latter; simply defying them was invariably and, he maintains, rightly punished.

Note that the answer can only ever amount to advice; so the asker (whether diviner or client) is left perfectly free, in principle, to proceed or not. By the same token, there is no need to protect the appellant's free will – nor, for that matter, the omnipotence of God; there is nothing here to imperil them. Another corollary is that divination essentially concerns not the future but the present, because it really asks: what course of action should I undertake now? Given this understanding, it is easy to see that even where prediction is apparently of the essence, what it amounts to in practice is the question: what should my attitude be, here and now, to a future and therefore (by definition) hypothetical event? Thus the paradigmatic divinatory question is not 'What will happen?' but '*What should I do?*' This bears careful unpacking, for each element is vital:

- 'What' – cognitive knowledge, or rather wisdom, is sought;
- 'should' – this introduces a moral or ethical dimension, whether this is interpreted metaphysically (a deontological good), socially (the greater good) or narrowly (my individual good);

- 'I' – the query concerns the questioner uniquely, and requires his or her particip-ation (both of which points still hold true of a 'we'); and
- 'do' – an action, specific and concrete, is also involved.

It is our contention that this kind of question is still the appropriate one for astro-logy; and that what it entails – a fluid, ongoing, intimate, contingent and messy process of negotiation (within limits) with the divine – still constitutes astrology's essential condition, as well as that of other forms of divination. This claim, particularly its contemporary aspect, cannot, in the nature of the subject matter, be strictly proven; but evidence for it can certainly be adduced. Beyond that, our goal is more to help open up a relatively new perspective, and see what follows if it is taken up.

First, however, two brief semantic clarifications: (1) by 'essential' we mean that insofar as divination is actually engaged in, then the process we have just described is inherent in and entailed by it; and (2) that process includes equally a world-view, an attitude and a set of concrete practices which, although analytically disting-uishable, actually all operate together and which, for convenience, we shall call 'discourse'. (The latter term does therefore *not* just refer, as it is often understood, to linguistic phenomena.)

Astrology as Divination

In Mesopotamia, the principal original home of astrology, a deterministic and 'objective' view of fate did not yet obtain. Not only were chthonic omens potent-ially as significant as heavenly ones, but the latter were apparently not held to cause earthly events; nor were the events they signified necessarily unavoidable. Destiny, through magical intercession, was still negotiable (see Baigent 1994: 41, 87–8; Barton 1994).

Against this, however, it must be noted that in relation to its pre-Neolithic antecedents, Mesopotamian astral divination was already decadent (so to speak) compared to the earlier, more fluid, vivid and messy mythicity (still surviving in aboriginal societies) as already described by Willis. This process of simplification and rationalization can be specified in at least two ways. First, as elsewhere around the same time, there was still an effectively unlimited number of local chthonic and animistic deities, who were therefore ultimately unrepresentable as a whole or externally, and certainly unmasterable; and insofar as these were gendered, they were almost certainly predominantly feminine. But these were being increasingly supplanted by a pantheon of predominantly male Indo-European sky-gods; so already, with a limited number of deities, there was a hint of the promise of mastery. This marked a significant break from the earlier emphasis, evident from North European material but also true of early Greece, on 'closeness to earth', which hitherto was 'always regarded as a source of prophecy . . .' The 'shaman-like figure of Apollo', for example, replaced the earth-goddess who had earlier occupied the prophetic seat at Delphi (Morrison 1981: 96, 99). And crucially, this *coup* also broke with the effectively endless multiplicity of animistic spirits associated with sacred places in and of the Earth (see Kane 1994).

There also arose a deliberate Mesopotamian programme to compile a systematic and codified body of putatively objective omen-knowledge; so the discourse of omen divination was already moving toward doctrine, compared with the fluidity and openness of an oral tradition. And relatedly, there seems to have been an attempt to use this knowledge to predict the future as such: 'If Nergal [Mars] approaches the Scorpio, there will be a breach in the palace of the prince', and so on. So on the one hand – and this is a tension that characterizes nearly all actual astrological discourses – there was a clear movement away from the pure ideal type of astral divination; but on the other, compared to later developments, this astrology was still definitely, if only relatively, divinatory.

In Greece at the time of the arrival of Mesopotamian astrology, there was already a divinatory discourse which must have constituted the context for its reception and understanding. (For a more detailed discussion, see Appendix.) This was *katarche*, a term linking concepts analytically distinct but a unity in practice: a human initiative and the ritual seeking of an omen by 'impetrating' the gods, in order to discover their will in relation to that desire. The ritual is thus a 'performative' one: it does not refer *to* the desire but *enacts* it, linking the human and divine dimensions; and the moment of asking is itself the moment both of initiating the action and of involving the gods.[2] The same discourse existed in the Roman almost precise equivalents of *aurispicium* (to begin something, attend to an omen at or for a beginning) and *augurium* (to begin, divine, or consecrate). Cornelius (1984: 20) comments that

> Since an omen is only an omen if it is recognised as such, it is clear that its significance is dependent on the participation of those for whom it is present. Its validity does not depend in any way on some general or theoretical law governing the production of omens. Its power comes precisely from its unique appearance 'for us, here, now'. For this reason, the significance derived from omens and embodied in ancient divination may be called participatory significance . . . It stands in contrast to the modern non-divinatory attitude which assigns an apparently non-participatory theoretical significance to events.

So *katarchic* astrology connoted not only 'beginning' but to *make* a beginning; and the presence of a human desire, expressed in an initiative, entailed not a detached reading of the will of the gods as expressed through the stars but participation in a dialogue with them.

This was exactly what was displaced by Ptolemy's *Tetrabiblos*, written in the second century CE. It seems likely that he was responding, at least partly, to Cicero's attack on divination (argued convincingly in Long 1982), in which case it is significant that Ptolemy felt obliged to defend astrology. But Cicero (1923: 233) had already defined divination as 'the foreseeing and foretelling of events considered as happening by chance', which precludes just the participation and pluralism we have been discussing. And Ptolemy's defence, accepting Cicero's rationalized and naturalized definition, accepted Cicero's definition, and then attempted to demonstrate astrology's plausibility and probity in those terms. In order to do so, he created an essentially abstract theoretical structure – mainly Aristotelian, with some Stoic elements – that set the basic pattern for astrology for millennia. (Neo-Platonic and Hermetic astrology, almost contemporaneous in origin, long provided a 'spiritual' counterpoint – but largely within the terms set by Ptolemy.)

One of the effects of Ptolemy's approach – entirely consistent with its central naturalistic metaphor of birth as a 'seed' moment, in which the future development of the relevant entity is perceptible – was to depose horary astrology, the direct heir of *katarche*, and enthrone natal astrology. (In horary practice, the answer to a question for guidance is sought, according to a fairly strict set of rules, in a map of the heavens at the time the question was asked.) Indeed, Ptolemy ignores horary altogether. He does discuss inceptions (maps for the beginning of an enterprise) and elections (attempts to choose a propitious time for beginning an enterprise), but precisely because these can be covered, by analogy, by his Aristotelian root-metaphor of birth; horary cannot. This move was what Bouché-Leclerq nicely termed a 'metaphysical *coup d'état* by natal astrologers, who pretended to integrate in a unique moment the totality of causes predetermining the destiny' (quoted in Cornelius 2003: 177).

Then and Now

We have already mentioned the movement away from what Max Weber (1991: 282) called 'concrete magic', uniting what we now distinguish, and indeed polarize, as 'spiritual' and 'material'. That process was greatly strengthened by the rationalist and realist spirit of Greek philosophy, both Platonic and Aristotelian, especially as incorporated into Christianity. And the split between subject/spirit and object/matter – that dualism which actually comprises 'two vying "monisms"' – had momentous consequences for astrology and all such discourses (Everndon 1992: 95, citing Jonas 1982: 16; cf. Latour 1991). That human beings are divided into spirit and body only, with no intermediate and ambiguous 'soul', has been official Christian orthodoxy since a Church Council of 869. Descartes's version then became a cornerstone of modern science (see Burtt 1924).

As that split deepened and hardened, astrology became metaphysically homeless. Divinatory astrology, as a symbolic art which is necessarily both subjective (participatory, contextual) *and* objective (requiring a world of persons and stars)

– and therefore neither alone – almost disappeared from view. Perforce, astrologers from the late seventeenth century onward aligned themselves with either the 'scientific' or the 'spiritual' side. The former itself divided into neo-Aristotelians and Baconian-style empiricists, while the latter became increasingly caught up in supernaturalist magic and occultism – each, of course, reacting against and encouraging the other. But both options left unquestioned the assumptive split itself; and neither left any room for concrete magic (see Curry 1989). In their *practices*, however, and probably among those of the unrecorded urban heirs of village cunning men and women, it survived. And since the 1990s, crystallized by and around the recovery of the astrology of Lilly, it has once again become possible to recognize and begin to theorize astrology in such terms (see Hyde 1992; Cornelius 2003).[3]

From the earliest astrology to the present, then, two characteristics can be perceived whose coexistence seems paradoxical, but both of which should be kept firmly in mind. On the one hand, in practice, astrology is still essentially divinatory, with an intimate relationship with the divine, the attendant humility, and a propensity to subvert (or simply ignore) all the painstakingly constructed and defended categories of subject/self/culture *vs* object/world/nature. On the other hand, and at the same time, it has been consistently subjected to increasing formalization, systematization and naturalization in the modern sense (which therefore ultimately includes secularization), with a view to ever greater mastery. It is likely that these two aspects of astrology have always coexisted, and will as long as there is such a thing.

At the other end of the chronological scale, namely astrology in present-day practice, it may reasonably be asked: how can interpreting a map of the heavens for the moment of someone's birth, almost always in 'secular' psychological terms, possibly be construed as divination? Hyde (1992) and Cornelius (2003) have devoted extended discussions to this question, and there is no need to rehearse their arguments here. I would just add that close analysis of the lineaments of astrology – the precision of the planetary positions for a certain time and place, the moment of birth taken as the seed of the life or blueprint of the mind, and so on – shows these things do not signify the objectivity that many astrologers take them to be, as indeed scientific researchers have been keen to show. Of course, the latter then go on to say this shows that they are meaningless or worse, fraudulent: something that only follows from a scientism which should be rejected.

These characteristics of a contemporary astrological consultation are indeed highly meaningful, but in other terms: they comprise a *ritual*, including not only precision, essential for any ritual, but the whole tradition of disciplined and skilful metaphoric interpretation which constitutes the astrological tradition at its best. (That is, the symbolic 'language' of astrology is a special case of metaphor, just as astrology involves a special kind of ritual.) This emphasis on metaphoricity does not itself make astrology unsound; scientific practice too would be impossible without metaphor.[4] Nor does recognizing the need for objective accuracy to be a ritual requirement incriminate it, unless you happen to think that inquiry of any kind can proceed without ritualized rules.

Indeed, there is a good case for arguing that just as science now essentially functions in society as a religion (see Feyerabend 1978, 1987), 'the scientific method' is its corresponding central ritual, in which the white-coated priests interpret the pythian gibberish of experimental data . . . That role would not be surprising, since science, whatever else it may be, is a human activity; and ritual, as Roy Rappaport (1999) has delineated in depth and detail, is central to the 'something else' – which he calls 'the holy' – that is itself integral to being human (including, need we add, researchers). This situation is reflected, for example, in all human beings' commitments to values which motivate, guide and inform that are effectively ultimate or intrinsically valuable, and therefore cannot be further grounded or justified without question-begging.

Even the most 'objective' and 'secular' astrological consultation thus turns out to be a ritual in which the unknown (an idea which P.L. Travers once suggested virtually exhausts the meaning of the 'unconscious') is invited to speak to the inquiry at hand. And since the parties involved admit, perforce, the power of the unknown, and that of its principal perceptible aspects, it might be more honest to simply call them by their old names: those of fate, and divinities. 'No psychology since has ever gone beyond this; all we have done is invent, for those powers that act upon us, longer, more numerous, more awkward names, which are less effective' (Calasso 1993: 94). Liz Greene (1984: 33) too questions modern psychological secularization of the planets, 'which for so many centuries were perceived and experienced as gods. We still do not really know what they are.'

It might be objected: surely a horoscope is a symbolic map of someone's psyche or (in the same spirit of calling a spade by its name) a soul, in some 'objective' sense? Doesn't that map 'belong' to that person, or vice versa? But this overlooks the fact that every interpretation of a horoscope necessarily proceeds in response to questions, whether explicitly or implicitly. (Again, the same is true in science, where no pure empiricism or induction is possible.) And it too easily reifies that soul-map by assuming that it is already set at or by birth, as distinct from something that provides a symbolic guide to the ongoing negotiation between what one wants and what is advisable (itself partly a function of what is possible) that constitutes a life, whose 'fate' is only determinable when it is finished. Even more fundamentally, what is the moment of birth but an essentially 'random' occurrence, in terms of objective time – every bit as much as a spread of cards, or a throw of coins?[5]

Finally, objectivism underplays astrology's strongest hand – arguably its very point – namely what occurs on those occasions when the astrologer voices an interpretation that falls into place for the other party with a truthfulness that is undeniable by the parties present, accompanied by a powerful recognition that 'they [are] in the presence of a mystery and that they themselves [are] a part of it' (Brown 1969: 131). Although necessary, no astrological technique, be it ever so refined or powerful, is sufficient – that is, can be relied upon to produce such an experience automatically. As John Heaton (1990: 18) aptly remarked, 'astrology predicts but you can't predict when it is going to predict'. And no scientific analysis, no matter how theoretically sophisticated or empirically sound, can explain that experience away without doing it violence. What is there important about this situation, then, that is not divinatory?

Notes

1. With thanks to Geoffrey Cornelius for this reference.
2. With thanks to Geoffrey Cornelius for spelling this out (in a personal communication).
3. Work by the astrologers Derek Appleby and Olivia Barclay was also an important part of the horary revival.
4. See the discussion of 'Science and Astrology, True or False?' below.
5. As pointed out by Geoffrey Cornelius (Cornelius 1982).

-6-

Varieties of Astrological Experience

At this point, let us take a closer look at the different astrological schools or sub-traditions. Of course astrology has an immensely varied and complex past, and generalizations by definition may not apply to any particular individual case. So, for example, an astrologer could subscribe to the tenets of any of the following philosophies and yet actually practice a craft horoscopy which embodies a symbolic attitude, and thus invites divination. But it would be fatuous to deny any connection whatsoever between philosophies and practices. Particular discourses encourage some kinds of practice and discourage others; that is a great deal of their very point. So a scientific practitioner of horary astrology, for example, will not only be considerably rarer than most other kinds, but must perforce act secretly, or dishonestly, in relation to his or her own conscious beliefs – and to that extent, be hindered by them. And it is our business here to try to perceive and think about these things as clearly and sensitively as possible. For that, flexible, non-dogmatic categories, in an ongoing mutual relationship with social and historical evidence, are the most promising way to proceed.[1]

All the schools or streams of astrology that follow have contemporary forms, albeit some more implicit or covert than others. (To pick just one example, the Aristotelian/Ptolemaic metaphor of a determining 'seed moment' remains powerful among astrologers today, but it is rarely recognized as such.) In addition to this taxonomy, however, there is also what we may call 'popular astrology'. That is the astrological discourse (both theory and practice) of those who consult, with varying degrees of avidity and confidence, the sun-sign colums and articles in tabloid newspapers, women's magazines, websites and call-lines.

It is not our intention to address this subject in the detail it deserves here, but a few remarks at least are in order. First, popular astrology is vastly more widespread, per capita, than the kind of those who actually consult an astrologer, let alone those who practice it seriously for themselves and others. But it is also correspondingly much shallower: more evanescent, ineffectual, and unconnected with the rest of one's life. However, it does not follow from the last point that it is therefore wholly inauthentic. Popular astrology draws on elements of, and is therefore related to, aspects of virtually all the other more serious and specialized kinds. Keeping pace with urbanization, it has largely replaced the rural kind so widespread until the beginning of the twentieth century. Although its content is thus different, popular astrology now is no less validly and inextricably a part of contemporary life than its rustic forebear was formerly. (For a good discussion, see Eccles 1996.)

Popular astrology can also, in its own way and within those limits, also involve the divination that we have identified at the heart of astrology proper. The moment when a reader on an Underground train is struck by the truth of an observation in his or her sun-sign column for the day is a divinatory moment: an experience, however fleeting, of concrete magic and enchantment. The widespread desire for such moments can therefore be seen – potentially, at least, and in part – as expressing a desire, however inchoate, for re-enchantment; and its satisfaction should be seen as meeting it: not apparently (as the universal church of science would have it) but actually.

Such an understanding certainly survives sociological analysis. A recent study, defining 'serious believers' as 'those who reported that they read horoscopes often or fairly often and that they took them seriously or fairly seriously', concluded that they tend to be 'female rather than male; single rather than living with partners; younger rather than older; religiously motivated rather than indifferent; and inclined to attribute scientific status to astrology' (Durant and Bauer 1997: 59, 68). And what conclusions can be drawn about the 'truth-value' of astrology from this portrait? None (either way), of course.

That does not at all reduce the possibility of a defensible critique of popular astrology as being harmful, overall, in its *effects*. But it is interesting that Bauer and Durant's results contradict Adorno's (1994) heavyhanded attempt to pin on astrological believers an 'authoritarian personality' – as if all astrological believers were, *ipso facto*, fascists. They do support his insight into its 'semi-erudite' social nature; but such a provenance is easily explicable as charcterizing those who have acquired sufficient intellectual tools (as well as possessing sufficient wit and inclination) to enquire, but not so much as to have become effectively part of the dominant ideology which, by and large, is responsible for supplying of such tools, and remains overwhelmingly hostile to astrology: a somewhat crude point, perhaps, but certainly not therefore without some truth.

(Openly) Divinatory Astrology

To summarize the discussion so far, astrology originated in the formative matrix of experience in which what we now distinguish as mythic, scientific, spiritual, physical, divine, animal and indeed human itself were inseparable. This situation then became locally more defined as astral omen-reading in Mesopotamia and katarchic astrology in Greece. As such, it involved treating the heavenly bodies as divine omens in which the will of the gods, who are identified with the planets, can be discerned in relation to the question (concerning a human desire) that is asked.

Such omens are signs, not causes. Nor is it assumed that the future is fixed, inasmuch as the will of the gods, or Fate(s), can change, and the diviner, and the divination, are not predicting a fixed future but necessarily intervening in and re-creating the future as an onging process. Animistic and then polytheistic, metaphorical/symbolic and at once both practical and spiritual, this is the original form of astrology, and the latter still bears its mark – as long maintained, albeit with hostile intent, by the Church. Its most eminent exemplar is probably William Lilly, the last astrologer whose practice was able, in essence, to unite unselfconsciously divinatory magic, religious piety and premodern *scientia* (see Curry 1985, 1989, 2003; Cornelius 1985; Geneva 1985). Without denying its earlier roots, modernist disenchantment – including but not limited to the scientific revolution – really started to get a grip in Lilly's lifetime, and with it divination went into a steep decline. As a result, it was very largely (although not entirely) eclipsed by the following successors for centuries, surviving only in popular astrological practice until very recent times, when divinatory astrology has made a modest comeback.

Horary astrology is clearly the direct heir of katarchic astrology and, as such, the most unambiguously divinatory kind of contemporary astrology. But we are not suggesting that all other kinds of astrology (nativities, elections, inceptions, mundane, etc.) can be reduced to species of horary; rather – and it is a significant difference – that *all* these could best be understood as divinatory, each in its own way. Thanks to the long absence, even suppression, of such an awareness, however, these are early days for this issue, and a lot of hard thinking about it still waits to be done.

Neo-Platonic and Hermetic Astrology

This 'school' originated with the second-century CE Alexandrian *Corpus Hermeticum* and the classical neo-Platonic philosophers, but it was revived in the fifteenth century Florentine Renaissance, largely by Marsilio Ficino (1433–1499) (see Voss 2000). Actually there was a significant difference between the more intellectual neo-Platonists, such as Plotinus and Porphyry, and the emphasis of Iamblichus (240–325) on ritual and *theurgy* (literally 'god-work') (see Shaw 1995). The former reserved astrology for philosophy, in the sense of 'pure' wisdom. But in the approach of the latter, especially, astrology was still participatory as well as symbolic, and retained a strong sense that destiny is negotiable – i.e. in this case, that the otherwise 'fated' outcomes of planets can be transformed, or at least modified, by the skilful use of philosophical or magical knowledge (there being no essential difference here). But although the world and the psyche are still mutually implicated in cosmic lawfulness, the practice of astrology is less of an ongoing process in a world which is itself living (i.e. equally 'material' and 'spiritual'), and more the discovery and development of one's individual soul – a kind of spiritual psychology.

Not surprisingly, that is how Ficino's work has been developed by modern astrologers (taking their lead from Moore 1982).

A corollary is that successful astral divination depends not only on technical knowledge, however complete, but also the soul-knowledge of the practitioner. Here too, neo-Platonic astrology occupies an ambiguous position between earlier (and surviving) participatory astral divination and the later (albeit also partly contemporaneous) objectivist discourse of Aristotelian/Ptolemaic astrology.

The same characteristic is perceptible in other ways. For example, astrological polytheism is subsumed into a synthesis of Platonic philosophy and Christian theism. The result is a divine hierarchy which includes the fixed stars and planets as distinct spiritual powers but under, and ultimately subject to, the one God, whose will they ultimately signify. So there is a movement toward unity while retaining a limited but real pluralism. This kind of astrology also remains undeniably spiritual, but in a more self-consciously distinct sense – as defined, most influentially, by Plato, against the material, the feminine, and the Earth – than that of the divinatory approach.

Similarly, participation through theurgic ritual remains central but in a more rationalized way, in the sense of a systematic use of magical appeal and/or manipulation. Such magic proceeds by the law of correspondences uniting macrocosm and microcosm, encapsulated in the dictum, 'What is below is like that which is above, and what is above is like that which is below, to accomplish the miracles of one thing.'[2] Thus each planet corresponds to a part or organ of the human body, animal, plant, metal and so on, in a complex system of sympathetic and antipathetic resonance which doesn't depend on purely physical considerations, such as size, proximity, etc. Finally, the question of whether astral configurations are signs or causes is more ambiguous here.

Is neo-Platonic astrology divinatory? In keeping with the 'two tendencies' already noted, the answer is yes and no. On the latter point, Roberto Calasso, in his marvellous book *The Marriage of Cadmus and Harmony* (1993), puts his finger on a key point. Homer's refusal to distinguish between gods and '*daimones*', he writes, 'precludes any idea of a ladder of being, on which, through a series of purificatory acts, one might ascend toward the divine, or alternatively the divine might descend in an orderly fashion toward man. This idea, which forms the point of departure for every form of Platonism, is already implicit in Hesiod's division of beings into four categories: men, heroes, *daimones*, gods'. And he quotes Plutarch:

> those who refuse to admit the existence of a class of *daimones* alienate the things of men
> from the things of gods, making it impossible for them to mix, and eliminating, as Plato
> said, 'the interpretive and ministering power of nature', or alternatively they force us to
> make a general hotchpotch, introducing gods into our human passions and goings-on and
> dragging them down to our level whenever it suits us, the way the women of Thessaly
> are supposed to be able to pull down the moon.

Calasso adds that 'When the Christian Fathers railed against Homeric debasement, they were really doing no more than dusting off Plato's sense of scandal, and likewise those of his followers, here so lucidly summed up by Plutarch' (1993: 275–6).[3]

Here, in the philosopher Plato's hostility to the poet Homer, we see a major taproot of the millennia-long rationalist and rationalizing attempt to order, and thereby disenchant, the world. It is, of course, the same programme that has made it so hard to understand astrology (among many other things about ourselves and the world), because 'pulling down the Moon' – which could stand as a poetic summary of everything we have already said about divination and fate in a living world – is precisely what astrologers do, when the magic works. And it hardly needs adding that the rationalist assault has been, from the very beginning, highly gendered.[4]

We have emphasized the critical case here because of a tendency (as we see it) to engage in somewhat wishful thinking about neo-Platonism as a radical alternative to modernist nihilism. It *is* an alternative, and a good one, but not – in the proper sense of the word, a return to the root – radical. It will always be vulnerable to William James's (1977 [1908]: 140–1) rhetorical question: 'Why should we envelop our many with the "one" that brings such poison in its train?' But what about the 'yes' side?

Here it is important to recognize that although neo-Platonism offers a 'complete' and therefore ultimately disenchanting system, it remains a spiritual one. In consequence, although at one remove from a Homerically unmediated enchantment, it retains an appreciation of *ultimate* mystery that places a limit on disenchantment, and acts as a prophylactic against complete rationalist and humanist hubris.

One way to understand why is this: without (for a moment) accepting its ultimate truth, the division of everything into spirit and matter means that by definition, the latter, whatever its form or arrangement, is simply uniform quantitative stuff.[5] In that case, the relationship, pattern or order between two such entities – and note that there must be more than one for these to exist – is necessarily nonmaterial and as such, at least in this context, spiritual. Now suppose a deeper or underlying pattern to phenomena is perceivable; and another, still deeper, metapattern . . . There is no reason to suppose this could not carry on indefinitely, but the human mind cannot; at some point, it must concede its limits. In this way, even within a systemic and lawlike *Weltanschauung*, as long as it is a spiritual one the humility that attends a symbolic and divinatory attitude remains possible.

Aristotelian and Ptolemaic Astrology

Especially as formulated in Ptolemy's highly influential *Tetrabiblos* (second century CE), this 'school' is related to the previous one and retains both the Platonic quest for universal truth and certain knowledge, and its rational systematicity, e.g.

a hierarchy proceeding from cosmic perfection through to chthonic mutability. In a move with far-reaching consequences, however, that system is recast as a causal and material system; the planets are no longer considered semi-autonomous spiritual entities, but merely transmitting the will of God, who now affects without being affected. But He is also now confined to the ultimate sphere.

This development places correspondingly more emphasis on astrology as a kind of natural philosophy: not only systematic but fully rational and natural. Here the planets are treated not as signs but as universal and unidirectional causes – the dominant metaphor for which is 'influence' (see North 1986) – and only our imperfect knowledge of them and their effects prevents us being able to comprehend and predict all phenomena in this imperfect sublunary world. Each individual is imprinted with a specific set of attributes determined at, and therefore assessible by, the moment of birth – the 'seed moment', in Ptolemy's metaphor – and what happens subsequently is a function of that given and the subsequent 'ambient' on Earth – itself ultimately astrologically determined. Here indeed we have the cosmos as 'the Machine of Destiny' (Cornelius 2003: 169–72), with astrologers, at least potentially, its technician-priests. (Actually, there was another version, harder and tighter because less mediated, in Stoic determinism, which Ptolemy also incorporated into his model in order to undercut Aristotle's inconveniently sharp distinction between the super- and sub-lunary worlds.)

A careful examination of Ptolemy's rhetoric shows a series of promises that certain knowledge derived from universals can indeed be applied to even minute particulars, alternating with qualifications admitting the problems in doing so in practice. (This is a rhetorical strategy that will be duplicated by advocates of modern systematicity.) For example, after presenting the case for the powerful influence of the planets, Ptolemy is careful to admit other non-astrologiccal determinations: the country of birth, its customs, rearing of children, etc. In the next breath, however, he suggests that these too are ultimately functions of the surrounding cosmic conditions or 'ambient', which is itself astrologically determined.

A later version devised by St Thomas Aquinas (1225–74) in the mid-thirteenth century provided the basic framework for astrology for the next four centuries. A synthesis of Aristotelian/Ptolemaic astrology and Christian theology, Thomism introduced considerations of angelology at every level of the system, as well as qualifying the unmoved Mover as the Christian God; but having thus 'guaranteed' its spirituality, Aquinas cemented its Aristotelian rationalism firmly into place, remarking that 'Reason in the man is rather like God in the world'. (*Opuscula* 11, *De Regno*). He drew a sharp distinction between natural and judicial astrology, and confined astrological influence – and therefore legitimate astrological knowledge – to the material world, both human and natural (the weather, crops, epidemics, etc.), arguing that 'nothing stops any man from resisting his passions by his free will' (quoted in Tester 1987: 181), and even citing the astrological maxim that 'The wise man rules his stars'. The specific individual prognostications of judicial astrology therefore offended both human free will and God's omnicompetence. However, he admitted that without the inclination and ability to resist, such influences were commonly transmitted via the body to the soul; hence astrologers do often make true predictions.

In practice, astrologers frequently transgressed the terms of this compromise to make the kind of specific judgements they were always asked for – and were pilloried for doing so, when caught at it, by the Church. Note, however, that Aquinas' concern is predicated on the assumption that judicial astrology necessarily involves prediction of a predetermined fate and not, as has been suggested, insight into or advice concerning the present; in the latter case, the so-called problem of free will does not arise.

On the one hand, the Thomist arrangement gave astrology a new lease on life without which it might conceivably have diminished into just another popular mantic practice. On the other hand, that extension was bought at the price of strict limits (if only intermittently enforced) on what was permitted; and even that was constrained by a determinism and quasi-materialism which is a far cry from divination. In the Neo-Platonic Renaissance, as already described, there was a qualified return to the latter. But not long afterward, and more influentially in the longer run, the Protestant Reformation (and to some extent Catholic Counter-Reformation) largely stigmatized astrology *en tout* as a survival of pagan astral idolatry; and any successes, while still not denied as such, were attributed, after St Augustine, to the intervention of demons.

Scientific Astrology

In the modern sense of 'scientific', this programme began in the late seventeenth century with efforts by some practitioners to reform astrology in keeping with the new natural philosophy, particularly Bacon's empirical and experimental programme. But these failed, and natural philosophers gradually incorporated a few parts of what had hitherto been considered natural astrology, such as lunar tides, but rejected the rest, i.e. judicial astrology. The subsequent impact of science was broadly as follows. First, the divinatory approach was anathematized as vulgar superstition – a term originally conveying Christian (especially Protestant) disapproval but now that of scientific reason – and became confined to the horary practices of astrologers to the common people. Second, neo-Platonic astrology largely succumbed as well, before reappearing (to a limited extent) as part of the nineteenth-century occult and magical revival, but still beyond the scientific pale. Finally, formally Ptolemaic astrology gradually almost disappeared, as the

Aristotelian natural philosophy upon which it depended became incredible, having been supplanted by a system even more thoroughly material-causal, thus largely redefining 'rational' in terms of what we now call 'scientific'.

In the late twentieth century, scientific astrology reappeared, thanks almost entirely to the research of Michel Gauquelin, but after nearly fifty years his findings remain controversial. His results centre on very weak – but statistically very significant – correlations for professional eminence with, to varying degrees, the Moon, Venus, Mars, Jupiter and Saturn in the diurnal circle (see Gauquelin 1988, 1983). None of the other planets remain, nor signs, houses as such, nor aspects. In other words, symbolism – which is appropriate for the planets with such 'effects' (e.g. Mars with athletes, etc.) – survives, but only just. Subsequent work by Dean et al. has produced no significant positive results whatsoever; on the other hand, attempts to explain away Gauquelin's results as artefactual have also been unconvincing, and none more so than Dean's most recent effort (see Dean 2000; also Ertel 2001–2003). The 'Gauquelin effect' remains stubbornly provocative for astrologers and scientists alike: the 'effects' too weak to be useful but too significant to be entirely ignorable.

Broadly speaking, in trying to 'test' astrology by elimating the astrologer, the scientific 'school' simply replaces it with a different kind of human experience: that of astrology as considered by a scientific researcher. In the course of such an operation, the price of success is that the patient has died: there is nothing openly symbolic or metaphorical – and therefore properly astrological – left. Thus the logical terminus of scientific astrology is none at all – which is precisely the goal of this set of researchers, despite their protestations of disinterestedness. In Weber's terminology, their object is pure disenchantment: the opposite end of the spectrum from participation in a living and meaningful, but unbounded and unmasterable, cosmos, with the mediating span being its increasingly rational and natural (in the modern senses) prediction.

Psychological Astrology

This 'school' grew out of the Theosophical astrology of Alan Leo at the beginning of the twentieth century; it was most influentially developed by Dane Rhudhyar, Liz Greene and Stephen Arroyo, among others (and more recently Hillman 1997). It is psychological not in the sense of the academic social science but rather in the popular apprehension of that term which, significantly, is closer to the original meaning of *psyche* as soul: an individuality partaking of, and mediating between, spirit and matter. The rise of psychological astrology was part of the ascendency of the 'possessive individualism' of modern capitalism (MacPherson 1962). In its most basic populist version – the ubiquitous sun-sign columns of tabloid newspapers and magazines, which date from the 1930s – even the self is arguably a kind of possession, whose nature is marked by one of the twelve solar signs.

This was a new development. Although even simpler than the older astrology of nonliterate rural people, it no longer depends on phenomena observed in daily life (lunar phases, eclipses, etc.) but on a mass-produced literary artefact, however often crude, which is a daily feature of modern urban life. And however paradoxically, the way mass consumption has been accompanied by an atomized individualism is also reflected in astrology; the Sun, formerly one planet among others, has become elevated to unprecedented importance as a symbol of the self. Even among the small number of people who take the further step of consulting an astrologer, the sun-sign remains a common starting-point, on the part of both client and astrologer, that receives far more attention than it would have received 150 years ago, compared (say) to that of the Ascendant or the Moon.

Despite its extreme youth compared with all but the scientific school, psychological astrology should be mentioned for two reasons. One is that it is now the dominant kind of astrology among contemporary practitioners. The second is that in many ways, it is a development and renewal of neo-Platonic/Hermetic astrology, with its emphasis on self-knowledge and self-transformation, but unevenly and inconsistently secularized. The tensions and contradictions of this school are thus very close to those, already mentioned, of the neo-Platonic astrologers. (We should add, however, that psychological astrologers have borrowed from Ptolemy the metaphor of an originary 'seed moment' of birth.)

That characteristic can partly be attributed to the figure who exercised the strongest, albeit largely indirect, influence on its formation: C.G. Jung. Caught between the conflicting demands of a thirst for mainstream recognition requiring sober scientific probity, on the one hand, and his wild subject matter requiring very diffferent virtues (essentially metic – a term we shall come to) on the other, Jung never succeeded in resolving his ambivalence, both personal and theoretical, as to whether his subject matter was spiritual or psychological, objective or subjective, some combination of all four, or neither/both; hence, for example, the unconscious as 'psychoid'. Perhaps, as Liz Greene (1984: 278) argues, the term is indeed apposite, because archetypes have 'a unity which encompasses, and transcends the opposition of, psychic and physical, inner and outer, personal and collective, individual and world'. In any case, Jung's ambiguity bought a significant breathing-space for spirituality among modern Western people at a time when scientific secularism was the dominant ideology.

There is a parallel here, both strategic and substantive, with the way both Ptolemy's and Aquinas's earlier ambiguous accommodation purchased a new lease of life for astrology in a fundamentally Aristotelian cosmos. To some extent, both share the price, namely acceptance of the basic (and fundamentally anti-divinatory) premise that the perceptible cosmos runs entirely on 'natural', material and even mechanistic principles with no direct spiritual input or dimension (and in the case of the fully scientific cosmos, none whatsoever). The result is an astrology, like a world, divided into those bits which can be naturalistically appropriated and a 'supernatural' remainder – at best inexplicable, but from a scientific-theoretical point of view, impossible, and therefore fraudulent.

Archetypal/humanistic/transpersonal astrologers often try to claim scientific support in woolly ways that are easily disposed of by their critics, in which case they fall back on an inexplicable supernaturalism, often of 'New Age' provenance. But they tend to shrink from recognizing and reclaiming what at their best, they actually *practise*: 'concrete magic'. Ultimately, they fail to contest the modernist carve-up, merely claiming the so-called subjective or spiritual half of the equation as their own; and even that is first domesticated into secularist safety. The birth-chart is thus seen as a map of the psyche, now understood to be not so much the soul as the Self; the planets are no longer divinities but psychological functions (cognition, volition, affection, etc.), and the symbolic elements aligned, somewhat awkwardly, with Jung's four-fold psychological typology (intuition, feeling, thinking, sensation). But the so-called outer world is largely either ignored or reduced to a reflection of the so-called inner, and the latter's unconscious contents are 'projected' onto the former (see Hyde 1992: 85–6). Thus astrologer Howard Sasportas (1985: 20): 'the philosophical premise upon which psychological astrology is based is that a person's reality springs outward from his or her inner landscape of thoughts, feelings, expectations and beliefs'. And compared to a world without binding regulations about which aspect of it is prior, or real, or permissable, this is certainly a kind of impoverishment; half of enchantment, so to speak, is the world!

In this arrangement, not only is the Cartesian split accepted but there is still a unidirectional determinism at work, albeit a subjective/spiritual one. The need for participation is still recognized (unlike in scientific astrology), but only in a constrained way that does not really amount to negotiation: one's fate is only 'transformed' by recognizing and accepting the pre-existent unconscious forces revealed by the birthchart. The primacy of the latter is another feature shared with psychological astrology's materialist and objectivist Ptolemaic twin. In other words, the only way to get what you want is to accept what fate offers, and convince yourself that that is what you really want too.[6] And since fate is what most psychological astrologers claim to be able to find in the birthchart, then by implication, fate is ultimately determined with, if not by, the stars.[7]

However fluffy, then, this is still a Machine of Destiny. Consequently, psychological astrologers are forever having to 'save' the client's 'free will' (and their own fallibility) with recourse to the tired old Ptolemaic-Aquinian formula, dressed up in Aquarian garb, that the wise man (now 'person') rules his stars. The latter version stems almost entirely from Alan Leo, who replaced 'inevitable destiny' with 'character reading', and 'influence' with 'tendency'. His motto was 'Character is destiny' (see Curry 1992). But this doesn't solve the problem, because its starting-point is still skewed; Leo's move was simply a refinement, with character as an intervening variable between the stars as fates and one's personal destiny that they have fixed. If, however, the stars cannot state immutable facts, let alone predict future facts – because there are none – but only ever advise courses of action in relation to a constantly shifting future, the entire dilemma, even in its soft 'humanistic' version, is unnecessary.

Another way to understand modern psychological astrology is suggested by one of the touchstones of divination, namely pluralism. Applying this test, we once again find ambiguity. On the one hand, polytheistic pluralism survives to the extent that the Sun is not allowed to swell into undue dominance. On the other, that is exactly the impetus given to psychological astrology by Jung and his heirs in their emphasis on the archetype of the Self (easily translated as the Sun) and what follows: a tacit valuing of monotheism over polytheism and integration/unity over diffusion/multiplicity. And the former values are, of course, those that disenchant.

In a fascinating new development *within* psychological astrology, James Hillman (1997; also 1981) has recently suggested applying the pluralism he has been developing within archetypal psychology since the 1980s. This involves a significant break with the monistic emphases of Jung as just noted, and a move toward a genuine (and uncomfortably agonistic) pluralism of the kind embraced by Weber, James and Berlin among others. In such an astrology, each planetary deity would receive its due without any attempt – virtually a reflex, among astrologers no less than anyone else – to arrive at an overarching meta-principle which would magically accommodate all differences and reconcile all conflicts; and the inevitable conflicts would just have to be borne with! (That was just what Weber, after Machiavelli, saw as developing character, and criticized Christianity for discouraging.) This hare Hillman has started, with its obvious affinity with the existential divinatory situation, thus has real potential for re-enchantment within, and probably beyond, psychological astrology.

Notes

1. That was precisely what Weber intended with 'ideal types'; see Scaff (1989): 50–9. It was also the kind of history memorably practised by E.P. Thompson.
2. From the *Tabula Smaragdina*, or Emerald Tablet of Hermes Trismegistus; see Shumaker 1972.

3. Note here the way the role of nature is reduced to that of being a handmaiden of the divine, rather than coterminous with it.

4. As another, later instance in the same tradition, note the Prometheanism of one of the most important Renaissance neo-Platonists, Pico della Mirandola, who established magic as unambiguously transcendental (ever ascending into the spiritual) but also involving ever more mastery of the material world. Pico's magical philosophy – masculinist, will-oriented, anthropocentric and freedom-worshipping – was accordingly contemptuous of the dark, the feminine, the ensouled let alone embodied, the Earth, and all limits. This set of values was a major formative influence on modern science, especially via Francis Bacon, who appropriated the idea of the magus wholesale for his new, heroic and definitely male natural philosopher.

5. Which was why Gregory Bateson always felt obliged to insist that 'energy' is such a bad metaphor for qualities.

6. This is the common definition of freedom that Isaiah Berlin always rightly contested: 'The fundamental sense of freedom is freedom from chains, from imprisonment, from enslavement by others. The rest is extension of this sense, or else metaphor' (1969: lvi).

7. This is not, however, the position of one of the most influential psychological astrologers, Liz Greene.

Disenchantment – and Re-enchantment

The Disenchantment of the World

It does not take any great perceptiveness to see that even allowing for all its unevenness and complexity, there is an overall tendency or direction at work in the history of astrology. There need be nothing teleological, predetermined or absolute about it for this to be the case. Nor is it contradicted by such partial retrogressions as the Neo-Platonic/Hermetic and later the modern depth-psychological schools, arising partly as a kind of of Romantic resistance to the more rationalist and materialistic approaches (Aristotelian/Ptolemaic, and later scientific); and all the more so when one considers the compromises the former has accepted.

This process is precisely the one famously identified, on a much larger stage, by Max Weber: 'The fate of our times is characterised by rationalisation and intellectualisation and, above all, by the "disenchantment of the world"' (quoted in Scaff 1989: 224).[1] Weber's work has been very influential, having been taken up and developed by members of the Frankfurt School, within the anthropology of religion, and elsewhere (for example Horkheimer and Adorno 1994; Bauman 1992, etc.; Grauchet 1997; and see Lambek 2002). Michel Foucault arguably not only addressed many of the same issues but arrived at highly compatible (albeit provisional) answers. Its contemporary manifestations have also recently been anatomized by James C. Scott (1998), who follows the logic of 'high modernism' in architecture, politics and ecology. Despite these subsequent developments, however, Weber's original thesis (or at least the aspect of it we shall take up here) retains its cogency today – perhaps more than ever – so we shall briefly summarize it before turning to its specific relevance for astrology.

Weber (1991: 139) characterized this rationalization as purposive or instrumental, and solely concerned with means as distinct from ends. Its central tenet is the belief that 'there are no mysterious incalculable forces that come into play, but rather that one can, in principle, master all things by calculation. This means that the world is disenchanted. One need no longer have recourse to magical means to master or implore the spirits, as did the savage, for whom such mysterious powers existed. Technical means and calculations perform the service.' Note that what is important is the *belief*, especially when collective and institutionalized.[2]

For our purposes here, 'disenchanted' can be used interchangeably with 'desacr-alized' or 'demythologised'. That is because the overlap is large and more important than the differences, although, of course, each meaning is also distinct, and leads off in, as well as arrives by, particular perspectives. The first, it seems to us, emph-asizes a phenomenological dimension of how the world is experienced; the second stresses the spiritual or religious element; and the third the social and anthropo-logical.

Central to Weber's insight is the subsumption of everything, at least in principle, within a unity to which nothing is external. (As usual, the implausibility of such an idea is, *in itself*, neither here nor there; as William Empson [1935: 22] once observed, 'once the philosophy is made a public creed it is sure to be misunder-stood in some such way'.) Being putatively able to compare all things, including values and abstract ideas, to *one* overall master principle, is an indispensable condition; it is what makes them masterable by calculation. Hence the real contrary of monism is not dualism, but plurality (see Viveiros de Castro 1998). The dualisms of mind/body, culture/nature, subjective/objective and so on – with the adherents of one side or the other forever trying to reduce and absorb their opposites – are just what monist rationalization has bred, and to subscribe to one side or the other is simply to sign up to the programme.

Whether such monism is religious ('God') or secular ('truth' or 'reality') is therefore *ultimately* a secondary consideration. Only ultimately because, as we have already mentioned, the disenchanting potential of one God explaining everything in principle is significantly limited by our own inability ever to fully understand the mystery of God. And conversely, as also already discussed, even polytheism involved a reduction of the unbounded plethora of early (and to some extent surviving) animistic divinities. But overall, Weber rightly perceived the major impetus of disenchantment in monotheism. The imperative in Judaism to worship only Yahweh did not entail that He was the only God, however. The key step was taken with Christian universalism, which combined Jewish henotheism with the Hellenic philosophical commitment to abstract universal truth; only now was it asserted, and enforced, that there *are* no other Gods. (This was and remains even truer of Islamic monotheism, which is even undiluted by any equivalent to the doctrine of the Trinity or, for that matter, rendering unto Caesar that which is Caesar's.)

Consequently, modern science's break with religion was not, in this context, radical, and it did not initiate the process of disenchantment: 'Scientific progress is a fraction, the most important fraction, of the process of intellectualisation which we have been undergoing for thousands of years . . .' (Weber 1991: 138). On the other hand, it is now indeed the 'most important fraction', and there is no denying its extraordinary impact in the last two centuries. Together with the immense power of corporate capitalism and the modern nation state, with which it now forms an inseparable whole, each reinforcing and protecting the others, techno-science is integral to the 'progress' of modernity – sometimes not unreasonably compared, for both its impetus and lack of control, to a speeding juggernaut – which post-modern suspicions have done little to restrain.[3]

Such monism is admirably summed up by Barbara Herrnstein Smith (1988: 179) as 'the effort to identify the presumptively universally compelling Truth and Way and to compel it universally . . .'. It invariably entails authoritarianism and impoverishment – the former because nothing, let alone a single view of every-thing, is self-evident, so its universalism must always be more or less coercively enforced; and the latter because although it cannot ultimately succeed (except, that is, with the extinction of conscious life), the *attempt* to do so grievously reduces the richness and variety of available life-experience. Weber pointed out that as a matter of lived and experienced (i.e. phenomenological) fact, we find ourselves participating in various different life-spheres, each one of which involves its own values and ideals, which cannot be subsumed, without such violence, under a single meta-sphere. Ultimately they are, both theoretically and practically, irrecon-cilable; yet in living one's life, one cannot avoid choosing. Hence, whether or not they are secularized as principles, 'different gods struggle with one another, now and for all times to come' (Weber 1991: 148).

This ancient insight – undoubtedly at home among the pre-Socratics – was influentially propounded by Machiavelli, and subsequently Nietzsche; in our times, in addition to Weber, it has been articulated in various ways by John Stuart Mill, William James, Isaiah Berlin, Paul Feyerabend and Michel Foucault. Theodor Adorno and Max Horkheimer developed Weber's version in a way germane to our understanding of modern science, which will be taken up later in this chapter. But a more recent addition to our understanding comes from James C. Scott in *Seeing Like a State* (1998). Scott's analysis of modernist logic reveals the procedure at its heart: converting lived experience into knowledge that can be processed and used requires creating standard units of measurement, in the course of which each particular person, place, activity or situation reappears purely as an instance of a class; then one can arrive at synoptic facts. And 'research' on astrology is, as we shall see, merely one instance of a much greater programme of converting personal experience into instrumentally usable facts: from openly metaphorical to proposit-ionally representational; from wild to domesticated; from living to dead.

Scott (1998: 82) also points out that 'modern statecraft is largely a process of internal colonisation, often glossed, as it is in imperialist rhetoric, as a "civilising mission". The builders of the modern nation-state do not merely describe, observe, and map; they strive to shape a people and landscape that will fit their techniques of observation.' This point offers a very important insight into the relations between the modern mainstream and astrology, as representatives of the former continue trying to brand practitioners of the latter as – simply by virtue of being astrologers – intellectually deficient and, when they resist, morally degenerate. Here too, astrology takes its place alongside other discourses branded as backward. In all its aspects, from the technical to the ideological, religiously sanctioned imperialism was first tried, tested and perfected at home, and its first victims were local. European astrology was 'reformed' – what of it that could not be stamped out altogether – before, as well as alongside, the assault on foreign heathenism.

This process is still taking place. Astrologers in the 'West' are no longer liable to be fined and imprisoned, although the last prominent cases were only in 1914 in the USA and 1917 in England.[4] But the victims of modernist monism, past and present, are of course vastly more numerous. The contemporary world is marked by a double and rival colonialization: economic neo-liberalism on the one hand and Islam and Christianity on the other. One is theistic and the other secularist, but both are monist and, far from coincidentally, actively intolerant in a way that contrasts strikingly with indigenous religious pluralism (see Soyinka 2002, Naipaul 1998). And both ideologies are disenchanting.

Thus Weber's analysis provides an indispensable context for any adequate overall understanding of astrology. Once again, we find the paradox of steady domestication coexisting with a surviving wildness at heart. For example, as Scarborough (1994: 50) remarks of the cosmological dimension of astrology, 'despite the fact that much of earlier Greek cosmogony viewed the world as an organism, if one accepts Thomas Aquinas's definition of a machine as "*partes extra partes*", then the world of the *Timaeus* is already a kind of rudimentary mechanism millennia in advance of Newton's modern picture of mechanism as the world's mute obedience to mathematical law.'

Nonetheless, it remains equally true that astrology is still a unique part of 'the resilience and durability' (Scott 1998: 281) of human cultural diversity which is essential to any resistance and promising alternative to the terminus of what Lewis Mumford called 'the megamachine'. Not coincidentally, again, astrology also preserves pluralism internally, in one of its *sine qua non*: qualitatively different planetary principles which are irreducible (without the destruction of astrology as such). In other words, astrology is inherently pluralist; and as such, it is problematic for the whole ethos – rationalizing, because monist, and vice versa – that Weber identified. (As a tiny but significant sign, it was quite appropriate that the poet Louis MacNeice [1964], whose ultimate apprehension of the world was as 'incorrigibly plural', should be attracted to astrology.)

Among the other consequences of disenchantment directly relevant to our subject is that 'The unity of the primitive image of the world, in which everything was concrete magic, has tended to split into rational cognition and mastery of nature, on the one hand, and into "mystic" experiences, on the other. The inexpressible contents of such experiences remain the only possible "beyond", added to the mechanism of a world robbed of gods' (Weber 1991: 282). Or as Gregory

Bateson (1979: 210) put it, 'A miracle is a materialists's idea of how to escape from his materialism.' Like other such discourses, astrology has now been largely consigned to a category, the 'supernatural', which is in great part the creation of science itself, following on from monotheistic religion, and has no necessary connections at all with the phenomena themselves. Yet this view has so far succeeded as to be accepted by probably the majority of astrologers et al. themselves, thus adding considerably to the general confusion and mystification. So it is now very difficult to speak of astrology as spiritual, or magical, without being *heard* (on both sides of the debate) as decrying the material, or rational. But that is not what we (after Weber) mean by 'concrete magic'; nor, by implication, what we mean by 'astrology'.

Science as Disenchantment

Weber's epistemic and axiological (value) pluralism has powerful implications for modern science, which, as he noted, 'presupposes that what is yielded by scientific work is important in the sense that it is worth being known ... [But] this presupposition cannot be proved by scientific means. It can only be *interpreted* with reference to its ultimate meaning, which we must reject or accept according to our ultimate position towards life' (1991: 143). This point was a cornerstone of the work of the late Paul K. Feyerabend, who remarked (and how much needless suffering would be prevented, were it to be taken seriously enough by enough people?) that 'The objection that [a] scenario is "real", and that we must adapt to it no matter what, has no weight, for it is not the only one: there are many ways of thinking and living' (1995:164).

The same issue has also been excellently addressed by Mary Midgley in a series of books which illuminate a distinction that is very important in this context. *Science* is the disciplined pursuit of a certain kind of knowledge about certain objects of knowledge. Like all human pursuits, it is appropriate in some ways and contexts and inappropriate in and for others, but there is nothing inherently problematic about it; quite the contrary. Nor does it, in itself, rule out enchantment; in fact, we believe that on the part of many of the greatest scientists, their work began and ended with wonder. Unfortunately, they are less typical than ever before of what science (which we should really rename 'techno-science') has now mostly become: a bloated, market-driven and state-protected enterprise contemptuous of ideas as such, let alone wonder (see Forman 1997).

In this context, it may also be relevant that very few of astrology's scientific critics are themselves practising scientists, as distinct from public spokespersons for 'Science'. And *scientism* is what obtains when science is viewed and presented as, in effect, a crypto-religion, with 'the' scientific method exalted as its central ritual. It is also a religion which cannot admit to its own ultimate contingency and (which is to say the same thing) mystery. As Midgley (1992: 108) points out in her analysis of science as salvation, 'Science cannot stand alone. We cannot believe its propositions without first believing in a great many other startling things, such as the existence of the external world, the reliability of our senses, memory and informants, and the validity of logic. If we do believe in these things, we already have a world far wider than that of science' (cf. Habermas 1971: 4). And then there is the provisionality of all scientific findings, which not only always raise more questions but are always subject in principle to revision.

Nothing daunted, however, acolytes of scientism such as Dawkins, Peter Atkins, Stephen Hawking and Lewis Wolpert continue to present answers to the question, 'How?' as answers to the very different question (as Weber pointed out), 'Why?' The arrogance of this totalizing self-deification, which presumes not only to know everything important that *is* the case, but what is and isn't *possible*, is matched only by its equivalent in political cabinet-rooms, company boardrooms and departments of economics – and, unfortunately, by that of the religious fundamentalists whom such 'secular' imperialism has helped to create. Strict monists all, they hate enchantment quite as much as each other.

What Laclau and Mouffe (2001 [1985]: 191–2) argue in a political context thus has much wider applicability: 'This point is decisive: there is no radical and plural democracy without renouncing the discourse of the universal, and its implicit assumption of a privileged point of access to "the truth", which can only be reached by a limited number of subjects.' It follows that it is not reason or rationality per se that is pathologically disenchanting, nor science; it is rational*ism*, and scient*ism*. Scientism doesn't consist of scientific explanations of phenonema, but of the assertion that such explanations, actually or potentially, exhaust all phenomena, and are therefore the only valid kind. So, artistic performance just *is* sexual display, full stop; and so on. But theoretical explanations should add to and enrich our understanding, not occupy it.

Of course, there is a problem with the distinction, which is that to a considerable extent scientism was incorporated into modern science from its very beginnings. This can easily be seen in the breathtaking sweep and assurance of the programmatic statements by its founding fathers: Galileo's intellectual brutalism, sweeping aside everything qualitative and sensual for abstract quantification alone; Descartes, in his obsession with certain knowledge, splitting everything into 'objective' matter (soon to become a cognate of 'real') and 'subjective' mind or spirit (for which the French word, *l'esprit*, is identical); and Bacon's misogynistic fantasies of torturing nature to obtain her secrets and thus extend human dominion. These were less perceptions of the world as it is than vows to compel its perception as such, and if it were not for the scientists who have subsequently shown real humanity and humility (the proper criteria here), it would be easy to think that scientism has infected the whole enterprise.

The template for science which has then tended to scientism was provided by physics, but in recent decades biology too has fallen into line. On the ontological assumption that 'animate things, being innately inanimate [*sic*], are innately simple too', the machine has replaced the organism as working root-metaphor, simplicity has driven out complexity, and natural history driven into extinction by the laboratory-based analysis of the inanimate (Peter Atkins quoted in Midgley 1992: 85; see Jonas 1982, Everndon 1992). Even ecology, of all things, has been thus deformed. This is not mere personal mendacity; it is systematic. As Scott (1998: 290) puts it, 'To the extent that science is obliged to deal simultaneously with the complex interactions of many variables, it begins to lose the very characteristics that distinguish it as modern science.' Advocates of scientism merely take this to an extreme, so that if, in the words of Edward Teller, 'There is no case where ignorance should be preferred to knowledge', and those are the only two choices, then everything that isn't such 'knowledge' automatically becomes 'ignorance'.[5] Consequently, scientists who admit an irreducible dimension of value, judgement, art or wisdom to their deliberations become marginalized by the majority of their peers: the fate of David Bohm, Gregory Bateson and Francisco Varela, now Lynn Margulis and Maewan Ho, and even Steven Rose and the late Stephen Jay Gould. (James Lovelock is proving more resistant.)

In the social sciences the situation is more complex, but basically psychology has been the worst afflicted by 'physics envy', with a correspondingly strong tendency toward favouring the trivial and banal, which is most amenable to quantification. This naturally favours reducing or eliminating experience and behaviour – usually through a mechanistic metaphor such as 'artificial intelligence', 'hardware/ software', etc. – to what can be quantified. Anthropology, in contrast, has managed to preserve and develop (although not without internal as well as external resistance) much of its traditions of participant observation, respect for the integrity of personal experience, and for qualitiative analysis. Anthropologists have been prominent among the intellectual opposition to evolutionary psychology, with its unholy alliance of capitalist and scientistic apologetics (nature-is-capitalist-and-capitalism-is-natural). Sociology seems to exist midway between these two; strong 'residues of unresolved positivism' (Barfield 1977) continue to influence many Anglo-American departments, and evolutionary psychology began as sociobiology. (It is sobering to note that Weber's own work was domesticated into the systemic banality of functionalism, explaining everything and nothing, by Talcott Parsons. In order to do so, of course, the Machiavellian/Nietzschean wildness at its heart had to be sacrificed – in other words, just what makes it special.[6])

Another point to notice is the ever-closer connection between business and science, via corporate-sponsored research, as well as the state and science via the legal and financial protection offered to huge projects such as the nuclear industry, industrialized agriculture, the pharamaceutical business, advanced weapons research and so on. The programme Weber described so well nearly a century ago is now not so much postmodern as hypermodern. As doubts about its legitimacy have grown, so too has its exercise of naked power. But only that part of it concerned with disenchantment is it our job to bring to light here.

The System

Astrology, like every other phenomenon, does not exist unaffected by, and (to a much lesser extent) without affecting, the world at large. Consequently it is not surprising that in both its 'internal' and 'external' relations, its history shows the disenchanting rationalism identified by Weber, that stands in the clearest possible contrast to its divinatory dimension. The attempt – with powerful effects, although 'success' is another matter – has been to replace contingency with certainty by identifying and enforcing a single universal system of knowledge and value, whereby personal experience becomes increasingly rationalized, managed, naturalized and eventually commodified, i.e. ever less personal. Since the goal is to replace personal, plural, concrete, local and contextual knowledges and values, including ultimately the participation and intepretation of human beings (notorious for their imperfections) at all, this attempt identifies itself as 'objective' and the enemy as 'subjective'.

Now all organisms require strategies in order to live; and strategies (if they are to be any use at all) must incorporate, whether conscious or not, systemic knowledge. So we would like to make it clear that systems (plural) are not, so to speak, the problem. Nor is reason; as Kontos (1994: 235) writes, 'The issue is not rationality per se, but a deranged, totalized rationalization which yields disenchantment. The mere presence of rationality does not result in disenchantment.' Indeed, as Lyotard (1988: 2) pointed out, 'there is no reason, only reasons . . . it is never a question of *one* massive and unique reason – that is nothing but an ideology'. The central problem is rather the idea, incorporated into the ideology and then reproduced institutionally, of a System. Because the perfect or complete system exists only as a fantasy, it requires (as pointed out in Barbara Herrnstein Smith 1988) enforcing.

One reason is that such a system is doomed to failure as long as human beings are still required to 'operate' it; their interpretations, conclusions and decisions, being unavoidably perspectival, will necessarily differ, thus introducing 'imperfection' that yet another perspective, however putatively comprehensive, can do nothing to resolve. Proselytizers for the complete system, even in principle – whether scientific, economic, political, religious . . . or astrological – are thus fundamentally dishonest. To be more precise, it cannot interpret itself (nothing is 'self-evident'), so it necessarily falls short of pure objectivity in requiring both production (and reproduction, hence institutionalization) and continuing interpretation – and therefore an ongoing priesthood of licensed interpreters. And since in practice, it just *is* its interpretations, and these will differ (potentially in as many ways as there are differently situated perspectives brought to bear on it), there will be discrepencies and inconsistencies both within any 'one' system and between any of its subsystems, which will then have to be eliminated rhetorically, and if necessary forcefully.

The fact that so many so-called victims of delusion/superstition/false conscious-ness stubbornly refuse to recognize the Truth is then taken to mean that they need 're-education'. And that raises the question of the ethics of this programme's ultimate values, because it follows that the 'success' of the perfect system would require the elimination of human beings as such. It is thus a project, ultimately, of collective suicide. As Foucault (1977: 163) realized, 'Where religions once demanded the sacrifice of bodies, knowledge now calls for experimentation on ourselves, calls us to the sacrifice of the subject of knowledge.'

In this connection, recall Karl Marx's trenchant observation (in *The Eighteenth Brumaire of Louis Bonaparte*) that 'Men make their own history, but they do not make it just as they please; they do not make it under circumstances chosen by themselves' – an insight he went on to betray in postulating the fixed laws of historical materialism, affecting but essentially unaffected by history, which then, as Lenin saw, had to be contingently realized by force (with consequences we all now know). There are exact precedents and continuing parallels in eschatological monotheistic discourse, of course, but also in modern science, where 'the attempt to enforce a universal truth (a universal way of finding truth) has led to disasters in the social domain' – to say nothing of the ecological – 'and to empty formalisms combined with never-to-be-fulfilled promises in the natural sciences' (Feyerabend 1987: 61).

In short, the system-mongers misunderstand (whether deliberately or not) both what they advocate *and* its supposed opposite. There is no 'objectivity' that could even exist for us, let alone mean anything, without subjective selfhood – and there is no 'subjectivity' that could exist without a world to sustain it and be aware of. As Merleau-Ponty wrote, 'All my knowledge of the world, even my scientific knowledge, is gained from my own particular point of view, or from some experience of the world without which the symbols of science would be meaningless" (quoted in Abram 1996: 36). Experience is unavoidably embodied, embedded, perspectival and, given the existence of more than one subject, plural. The only available alternatives are different kinds of personal experience; its transcendence or replace-ment by a single universal 'view from nowhere', even tendentially, is simply not an option. Lakoff and Johnson, seeking to reorient philosophy on the basis of cognitive psychology, have come to the same conclusion: 'In sum, embodied truth requires us to give up the illusion that there exists a unique correct description of any situation' (1999: 109).

This argument coheres with that of Midgley and others, already mentioned, for the inalienability of metaphor. Milton Scarborough builds on the work of Michael Polanyi to make a parallel case vis-à-vis myth, and attempts to evaluate its truth-value. (The construal of astrology as myth has, by way of their intimate relationship, great potential.) Thus Scarborough (1994: 109–10) points out that 'theories and criteria of truth are already and necessarily myth-dependent and are, therefore, both ill-suited and inappropriate as criteria for appraising myth. Rather than theories or criteria judging myth, myths help generate and lend credibility to theories and criteria.' Consequently,

> The ultimate assessment of myth must be of a kind suited to the nature of myth as giving expression to apprehensions of the life-world and as functioning to provide an orientation for living in that world. Within those strictures myth is neither true nor false *in a theoretical sense* but viable or not viable for the tasks (both theoretical and otherwise) which confront us. This viability is not determined in intellectual terms but in the very process of living, by whether or not one is energized, whether or not problems are being solved, whether or not life is integrated at a variety of levels, whether or not it is endowed with a significance that pulls one toward the future in hope (Scarborough 1994: 109–10).

Enchantment

The terminus of a 'successfully' scientific and therefore thoroughly disenchanted society was laid bare by Horkheimer and Adorno (1994: 20), following on from Weber, as scientific faith – which, being illicit, is unconscious – becomes 'an instrument of rational administration by the wholly enlightened, as they steer society towards barbarism.' (It is amusing to observe how uncomfortable their book *The Dialectic of Enlightenment*, first published in 1947 (and in English in 1972), still makes so many intellectuals today, the majority of whom are themselves in thrall to the faith of modernist progress whose effects they often criticize.) As Horkheimer and Adorno write (1994: 20, 5, 8, 7), the programme of disenchantment, demythologization and (as its adherents love to proclaim) demystification requires 'the extirpation of animism', and indeed the 'destruction of gods and qualities alike'. Since 'its ideal is the system from which all and everything follows . . . It makes the dissimilar comparable by reducing it to abstract quantities.' And in a fitting irony, the practitioners of scientism, in their all-embracing and scientifically unsupportable quest to disenchant the world, become the ultimate black magicians *de nos jours* (see Curry 1999).

What, then, was – and perhaps still is – enchantment? Alkis Kontos (1994: 225, 226, 232) points out that 'It was the spiritual dimension of the world, its enchanted, magical quality that rendered it infinite, not amenable to complete calculability;

spirit could not be quantified; it permitted and invited mythologization'. Following Weber, he specifies that 'The characteristics of the anthropologically-historically specific idea of an enchanted world are: mystery and a plurality of spirits.' As he adds, however, these are 'not identical to the spiritual concerns and dogmas of formal religion and theology'. Indeed, as has been said, the latter have been profoundly disenchanting.

But we should be careful of our terminology here. J.R.R. Tolkien (1988 [1964]: 49–50), who was an excellent scholar as well as a very successful writer, drew an important distinction between magic and enchantment: 'Enchantment produces a Secondary World into which both designer and spectator can enter, to the satisfaction of their senses while they are inside; but in its purity it is artistic in desire and purpose. Magic produces, or pretends to produce, an alteration in the Primary World . . . it is not an art but a technique; its desire is power in this world, domination of things and wills.' That is, magic (*magia*), whether as *goetia* (the invocation of spirits to do one's bidding) or *theurgia* (ritual realization of the divine for self-purification or transformation), while indeed spiritual, is purposive; and the instrumentalism it thus shares with science is confirmed by the close historical continuities (see Webster 1982; Henry 2002 [1997]). Essential to enchantment, by contrast, is 'the realization, independent of the conceiving mind, of imagined wonder' (Tolkien 1988 [1964]:18). While not absolute in practice, there is a very significant difference between magic and enchantment; so concentrating on the latter, and therefore wonder, can help to clarify its nature.

As Ronald Hepburn (1984: 140) points out, 'existential wonder' is generated from a 'sense of absolute contingency' – the very opposite of a sense of absolutely determined and therefore necessary, nomothetic, and unavoidable fate – and 'its object is the sheer existence of a world . . . All reasons fall away: wondering is not a prelude to fuller knowledge, though the generalized interrogative attitude may persist.' Furthermore, there is 'a close affinity between the attitude of wonder itself – non-exploitative, non-utilitarian – and attitudes that seek to affirm and respect other-being.' Thus, from 'a wondering recognition of forms of value proper to other beings, and a refusal to see them simply in terms of one's own utility-purposes, there is only a short step to humility. Humility, like wonder, involves openness to new forms of value: both are opposed to the attitude of "We've seen it all!"' (Hepburn 1984: 145, 146) – or as Horkheimer and Adorno (1994: 7) put it, a 'system from which all and everything follows', and not only follows, but can be used. Hence the contempt of what Tolkien (1988: 15) called 'the laborious, scientific, magician' for enchantment; it is useless. But as Chuang Tsu remarked long ago, 'everybody knows how to use what is useful, but no one knows how to use what is useless' (Raphals 1992: 95–6).

The word 'enchantment' literally means, of course, to be inside a song. And what use is it to be inside a song? None at all. But does that mean it has no value?

Only in a value-system that is dominated by an instrumentalist utilitarianism of the kind exemplified by the modernist (economic-political-scientific) complex. And the 'inside' here provides another important clue: that complex wants to reduce everything, including experience, to its 'outside'. In this way it becomes amenable to manipulation, exploitation and commodification. As I have suggested elsewhere, even enchantment can be so processed, and as such is integral to the multi-billion pound entertainment and advertising industries. But it becomes something very different in the process, namely *glamour*; because enchantment is, as we have seen, a kind of experience which is distinctively non-exploitative and non-utilitarian.[61] It is an experience of the world as *intrinsically* meaningful, significant, and whole in a way that is fundamentally mysterious (the opposite of what Weber calls "calculable") and that includes oneself, not observing it from the outside but participating *in* it.

Insofar as astrology partakes of enchantment, then, it properly belongs not with modern science at all, but with the traditional subject matter of the humanities – religious experience, aesthetic experience (art, music, dance, etc.), poetry and prose, and humour – and those of the social sciences that have been most influenced by the humanities, such as some kinds of anthropology and history. Certain kinds of these experiences, at least, are principally evocations of and responses to wonder. It is significant, in this respect, that in antiquity – in Greece, and almost certainly universally in human societies – 'the seer, the poet and the philosopher [were] originally identical, a shaman-like figure . . .' (Morrison 1981: 95)

Science too, of course, started this way. But where *scientia* and its cognates, for most of human history, have simply meant the knowledge resulting from disciplined inquiry, the scientific revolution eventually turned that meaning into something very different. For the most part it now refers implicitly, and often explicitly, no longer to simply one kind of inquiry and knowledge among others, but to the only 'real' or 'true' kind. Part of the price for the latter position is the sacrifice of original wonder; they cannot coexist. Richard Dawkins (1998) patronizingly chides Keats, Wordsworth and Blake, who recoiled from 'single vision, and Newton's sleep'; but on the subject of science, it is he who is the fantasist.[7]

Astrology's contemporary survival, and even in some respects flourishing, outrages Dawkins even more. He fails to see that it does so, in large part, not despite modern science but *because* of it, or rather, its effects. Popular astrology today arose chiefly in response to a widespread public desire for re-enchantment: an attempt, however often inchoate and crude, to re-enchant the world: to (re)place the person in a world where mystery again, or still, has a place; where fate or destiny is a reality; where there are subtle connections even between the highest and the lowest; a world, in short, which is still alive. Of course, sun-sign astrology is also strongly commercially driven, and certainly constitutes a domestication of full divinatory wildness. But the latter, as a potential experience, survives in it (no mean feat, given some of the prose).

Astrological Delusions

Oddly enough, Dawkins's blind spot is shared by many astrologers, who proclaim and 'believe in' astrology (no mere art, this) precisely as an all-encompassing, potentially all-powerful system of knowledge for which they apparently crave recognition. For example:

> We are *all* moving toward knowledge of God which is *the* perfection of life and the goal of the wise . . . The entire system aimed at enabling the astrologer to be wise in *every* area of thought, on every subject at all times. Astrology from this perspective is a unified cosmological system in which science and mystical religion [are] joined. (Zoller 1982: 28)[8]

Or in another, slightly less ambitious version,

> The question often raised by a non-astrologer is the practical proposition: how can this patterning of some trivial life situation have its reflection in the heavens? The answer is found in the general concordance of events in an orderly universe or integral energy system. (Marc Edmund Jones quoted in Greene 1984: 285)

Frankly, this last statement, together with all its sub-atomic, fractal, holographic and chaotic successors (surely it is only a matter of time, so to speak, before someone attempts to corral superstring theory for this purpose?) amounts to so much whistling in the dark.[9] For some years, quantum physics has appeared to reinstate a spiritual dimension at the heart of the physical. But that would be rejected by the overwhelming majority of physicists themselves as an unwarranted metaphoric extrapolation from extremely narrow experimental and theoretical contexts to lived experience. We are perfectly free to do so, of course, but we cannot thereby claim scientific sanction. The only honest answer to the non-astrologer's question is: *we don't know*.[10] That such a reply is intolerable to those who want an Answer simply cannot be helped.

In both cases, however, whether traditionalist or modernist – and ultimately, for that matter, whether materialist or spiritualist – the universalist ambition is quite clear, and its successful realization would be ruinous for astrology itself. As Weber stressed, adherence to all-encompassing systems of *whatever* kind is disenchanting, and the more so the more widespread and general that adherence becomes. It follows, given the nature of currently dominant discourses, that astrology thus draws a significant part of its ability to enchant *from* its marginalization; and its virtue, in relation to them, is precisely in its ability to resist disenchantment and help develop alternative ways of life. Given in addition the highly unequal resources involved, then, if these astrologers' dreams were to be realized and astrology achieved serious mainstream success, it would be at the price of its soul.

The same point applies, *a fortiori*, to scientific research on astrology. As a straightforward function of the enormous difference between the power (institutional, rhetorical, etc.) between the two discourses, if anything now considered astrological was held to have been scientifically verified, it would very quickly stop being astrological, becoming part of science instead. The general message would be: 'Well, well, in your simple way, you've actually discovered something quite interesting, but we'll take over now . . .' So the resistance of astrologers to such research decried by scientists is actually, to this extent, evidence of their perceptiveness. 'What is called "anti-science" feeling is not usually an objection to the actual discovery of facts about the world . . . Instead, it is a protest against this imperialism – a revulsion against the way of thinking which deliberately extends the impersonal, reductive, atomistic methods that are appropriate to physical sciences into social and psychological enquiries where they work badly' (Midgley 2001: 1).

Incredibly, however, even after the débâcle of the last twenty years of astrological 'research', it is still possible to find astrologers confident that, astrology obviously being true, science will confirm its truth;[11] or saying things like, 'Astrology has been flooded with wave after wave of plausible, astrologically sensible, but untested ideas. It is time for us to enter into a culling period to discern which ideas are more reliable than others' (McDonough 2002). Another astrologer recently stated that

> Because astrology has such a long recorded history, it is very reassuring that we can confidently tell any sceptic or client that every statement we make has the backing of empirical research, whether its findings were published BC or in 2002. We know that this is so, and we can well afford to be quite dogmatic about it: our astrological house is built on rock with extremely solid walls, as well as foundations. (Parker 2002)

Such a claim is, of course, pure fantasy; but no less so would be to believe (as many astrologers apparently do) that it *ever could* be true. Such 'testing' or 'research' is never itself unproblematic; astrology – albeit in good company in this respect – is, and always has been, particularly unsuitable to such a process; and astrology does not in any case need such dubious 'validation', especially as its 'success' would spell the end of its chief value. For these reasons, as Cornelius has argued, questions of technique must – if the integrity of astrology is to be respected – be answered *ritually*, not technically.[12]

In this context, those with a critical attitude toward science in practice often rightly also find it necessary to upbraid astrologers. Feyerabend's wonderful attack in *The Humanist* of September/October 1975 on the 'Statement of 186 Leading Scientists' condemning astrology was accompanied by the caveat that it 'should not be interpreted as an attempt to defend astrology as it is practised now by the great majority of astrologists.' Modern astrology 'inherited many interesting and profound ideas, but it distorted them, and replaced them by caricatures more adapted to the limited understanding of its practitioners.' 'It is interesting', he concludes of both astrologers and scientists, 'to see how closely both parties approach each other in ignorance, conceit and the wish for easy power over minds' (Feyerabend 1978: 96).

This is painting with a broad brush, but for the sake of fairness, let us note its truth regarding the starry party. The astrologers of today to whom Feyerabend is referring are the same 'petty ogres', using a fatalistic and superstitious astrology to bolster their own power and profits while exploiting the people, whom Ficino attacked five hundred years ago in the name of a truly divinatory astrology, one both spiritual and practical, and nonfated because participatory.[13]

It is obviously possible to have an inflated idea of astrology and of oneself as an astral master of the key to the universe; to abuse it for personal power and self-aggrandizement, in a pettily tyrannical way; and to have a neurotic dependency on it: for example, being unable to undertake any major action (which then creeps down to minor ones) without first checking the planetary positions in increasingly obsessional detail, which then (not coincidentally) become accordingly confusing and ambiguous as they are asked to do what they cannot do, namely take a decision for you. This sort of behaviour we are entitled to call 'superstitious'. It is not a new problem. J.S. Morrison (1981: 108) quotes Theophrastus on the man whose corn-bag has been penetrated by a hungry mouse: 'he goes to the *exegetes* and inquires what he must do: and if the *exegetes* gives him the answer "give the bag to the cobbler to mend" he doesn't pay attention to this advice but goes away and makes expiatory sacrifice'. Since virtually every other human enterprise has the same potential, however, such abuse is hardly a unique indictment of astrology.

It is not universally appreciated among astrologers, however, that there is a morality of divination beyond the obvious (but no less important) obligation, in the words of Lilly (1985 [1647]: B) to 'the Student in Astrology', to 'afflict not the miserable with terror of a harsh judgement'. It consists of first trying, as far as possible, to answer one's question unaided. The reason is the all-too-human, but unfulfillable, desire for absolute security and certainty, and consequent temptation to a lazy recourse to divination. Unchecked, this eventually leads to a neurotic attachment which necessarily results in an abuse of the art (even, or especially, when it is understood as one with a divine dimension) (see Smith et al. 1990).

It would also be appropriate to point out here that while an experience of astrology from the 'inside' is invaluable to its analysis from the 'outside', the former is no guarantee of the excellence of the latter. The enterprises of practising astrology and understanding (and *a fortiori* explaining) it overlap, but they are two, not one. The same is true, of course, of doctors, bicycle mechanics, birdwatchers . . . and scientists.

Notes

1. Whenever possible I have used Scaff's translations. The phrase 'disenchant-ment of the world' was originally Schiller's.
2. A better metaphor for this than the internet search engine – including the ways it both succeeds and fails in living up to the promises made for it – would be hard to imagine.
3. Cf. Weber (quoted in Scaff 1989: 14): 'One has the impression of sitting on a speeding train, while doubting that the next switch will be correctly set.'
4. Evangeline Adams and Alan Leo respectively; on the former see Christino 2002, on the latter Curry 1992.
5. From an interview with Christopher Hitchens, 'Dr Strangelove, I presume?', *New Statesman and Society*, 30 September 1994, 44–5: 45.
6. For a brilliant analysis, true to the spirit as well as letter of Weber, see Scaff 1989.
7. For an elegant and detailed rebuttal of Dawkins, see Midgley 2001.
8. Here, my emphases are to stress its monist universalism. It would be possible to adduce many other examples of such ill-advised hubris, including for example Elwell 1987. Such was also essentially the promise made by the Addey/Harvey harmonics programme.
9. Here, for once, we agree with the 'researchers' (Phillipson 2000: 159–60).
10. Or as Olgierd Lewandowski once put it to Patrick Curry, 'Ce n'est pas un sécret, c'est un mystère!'
11. For example Edward Snow in *The Mountain Astrologer/Mercury Direct*, December 2002–January 2003 (with thanks to Garry Phillipson for the refer-ence).
12. In a Company of Astrologers seminar on 8 July 2001.
13. Ficino 1981, letter 37, p. 77 (A disputation against the pronouncements of the astrologers by Marsilio Ficino of Florence); with thanks to Angela Voss for this reference.

–8–

Science and Astrology

Astrology as Scientific Heresy

In a radio broadcast in 1996, the only issue of agreement between Professor Richard Dawkins and an Anglican bishop was the iniquity of astrology. This cosy unanimity between otherwise often bitter enemies perfectly illustrates the continuity between monotheistic religion and modern science. As Horkheimer and Adorno noted, endorsing Weber's insight, 'Reason and religion deprecate and condemn the principle of magic enchantment' (1994: 18). It also lends support to the view of contemporary astrology as enchantment that still survives, and/or a kind of popular re-enchantment.

On the religious side, hostility to astrology is not peculiar to the Church of England. There is a long history of papal bulls condemning belief in astrology, most recently in the Catechism of the Catholic Church of 1993 (paragraph 2116), which rejects 'all forms of divination', including 'consulting horoscopes'. By the nineteenth century, however, science had become astrology's chief opponent, almost replacing Christianity and informing the attacks of critical journalists. Since science has had such an impact on contemporary astrology, then, let us turn to the 'scientific' case against astrology.

In 1975, 186 'leading scientists' who signed a statement organized by the American Humanist Society condemning 'the increased acceptance of astrology'. But it seems that when some of the eighteen Nobel Prize Winners included were asked for an interview they declined, explaining that they had never studied astrology – 'which did not prevent them', as Feyerabend (1978: 91) pointed out, 'from cursing it in public'. Even the authors of the statement show a poor grasp of the subject, which he compared unfavourably with that of the Catholic Church's condemnation of witchcraft, *Malleus Malleficarum* (1484). But the strength of their conviction, at least, cannot be doubted.

Dawkins, in his capacity as holder of the Charles Simonyi Chair of Public Understanding of Science at Oxford University, is probably the most visible public proponent of science today. He has also written at some length about astrology, most notably in the *Independent on Sunday* (31 December 1995), most of which also found its way into his *Unweaving the Rainbow: Science, Delusion and the*

Appetite for Wonder (1998). It repays a close look.[1] In aggressively militant metaphors, Dawkins advocates 'fighting . . . these glitzy con-artists'. The late Princess of Wales is nailed as 'an enthusiast for astrology' – a revealing choice of word, since its meaning of 'unbalanced irrationalist' began precisely with the reaction by the founders of the Royal Society in the late seventeenth century against astrology, among other things, as partaking of 'the wildest and most Enthusiasticke Fanaticisme'.[2] The continuity of this vehemence, together with the slenderness of direct acquaintance that accompanies it, evinces a more or less unconscious mentality on the subject, with collective metaphysical and institutional origins that are now at least three centuries old.

This is worth exploring further. With the long tradition, notably Platonic and Aristotelian, of viewing them as perfect and superior to our sublunary muddle, the heavens offered far too important a resource to modern science to be passed up. Not only did they promise perfect and therefore superior knowledge, but if the cosmos could be shown to be mastered then the authority of science would be beyond 'reasonable' dispute. In order to succeed, therefore, modern science had to turn people's remaining experience of the planets and stars from animate and intelligent agents with a divine dimension into fully 'natural' – that is, now, lifeless and mechanical – objects, which scientists alone were qualified to understand.

In other words, science had first to destroy astrology – which it largely succeeded in doing, within elite and mainstream opinion, albeit unevenly and incompletely. So for most scientists today (and this is where the mentality comes into play) contemporary astrology is a reminder, irritating at best and threatening at worst, of the failure of their collective mission of universal enlightenment, i.e. disenchantment. In other words – and this is entirely consistent with the emotional content of their reaction (it would tempting to say 'irrational', if the abuse of that term wasn't one of their own favourite weapons) – *astrology is scientific heresy*. It should be stamped out, and those 'pagans' who still practise it excoriated. But 'Asking for more science and less of something else is itself a social and political move. This move can be quite legitimate but it must not be mistaken for part of a pure, mysteriously objective science which stands outside society' (Midgley 2001: 49).

With this in mind, Dawkins's rhetoric becomes more comprehensible. For example, he asserts that 'a constellation is of no more significance than a patch of curiously shaped damp on the bathroom ceiling.' First, notice his choice of metaphors: a patch of *damp* on a *bathroom* ceiling. This is about as far removed from a disinterested or 'objective' analysis as possible. Second, characteristically, he is stating, without any qualification, what is and is not significant for everyone and all times and places; and the item concerned is one that has had immensely rich significance (religious, cultural, aesthetic) for most human societies for aeons. No awareness here that 'there are many ways of thinking and living'; science alone has the final word. Such universalism is one of the clearest signs of scientism, and the dangerous arrogance that accompanies it needs to be identified as such. The irony of Dawkins's religiosity, as his rhetoric repeatedly betrays value-commitments that cannot themselves possibly be justified scientifically, is impossible to miss (except, notoriously, for him).

He continues that constellations 'constitute a (meaningless) pattern when seen from a certain (not particularly special) place in the galaxy (here)'. Here the deliberate programme of disenchantment is plain. And what is its object? A certain place – clearly any place where anyone happens to be – and therefore, by definition, here. As meaningless is what the person is experiencing in that place – in this case, a constellation – because *here*, no matter where that is, is nothing special. It is no accident that such a perception stands in the strongest possible contrast with the aboriginal mythopoeic human condition (and, we are saying, that of astrology):

> Wisdom about nature, that wisdom heard and told in animated pattern, that pattern rendered in such a way as to preserve a place whole and sacred, safe from human meddling: these are the concepts with which to begin an exploration of myth. Of these, the notion of the sanctity of place is vital. It anchors the other concepts . . . Once the power of the place is lost to memory, myth is uprooted; knowledge of the earth's processes becomes a different kind of knowledge, manipulated and applied by man. (Kane 1994: 50)

That kind of knowledge is just the goal of Dawkins and his colleagues, such as the physicist Steven Weinberg, another scientific triumphalist, who describes human life as a 'farcical' accident in a 'hostile' universe which is 'pointless' (see Midgley 1992: 33). It bears repeating that these are not perceptions of a given reality so much as interventions intended to help bring about, to *create*, such a world, 'and to compel it universally'. Theirs is a programme meant to cleanse the world of personal meaning and start again at epistemological (and axiological) year zero. No astrologer has ever publicly entertained such a disturbed and disturbing fantasy. As Midgley (1992: 33) remarks, 'This cosmos is, after all, the one that has produced us and has given us everything we have. In what sense, then, is it hostile? Why this drama?'

The rest of Dawkins's proclamation need not detain us long. He simply assumes (albeit in numerous company) that astrology is either a *bona fide* science or – there being no other alternatives – the practice of solely fools and knaves. With a blind spot resembling a black hole, he describes it as 'the debauching of science for profit as a crime', without mentioning the billions of pounds of profit resulting from industries exploiting science for the arms industry, industrial agriculture, mining, timber, pharmaceuticals, etc. (Astrologers: in your dreams!) And he concludes by labelling astrology as 'an enemy of truth', whose practitioners, like the IRA terrorists denounced by Margaret Thatcher, should be deprived of 'the oxygen of publicity', and 'jailed for fraud'. Like Fichte – one of the enemies of liberty anatomized by Isaiah Berlin (1998: 222) – he appears to hold that 'no-one has rights . . . against reason'. (It should not need adding that 'reason' always amounts in practice to someone's particular version of it.)

Of course, if Dawkins were alone all this would hardly matter. But articles of the same scope and tone, or worse, feature regularly in the British broadsheet press, at least, presumably informing as well as reflecting educated intellectual opinion. To pick one almost at random, Thomas Sutcliffe, writing in the *Independent* (9 January 2002), condemns astrology as an 'infection', 'a kind of scabies of the intellect', and 'an epidemic'. If astrology were not the kind of tacit heresy we have suggested, it would be difficult to understand this hysterical language of the witch-hunt and show trial, directed against such an apparently insignificant target.[3]

There is also an organization, an offshoot of the so-called humanists of the 1975 statement, devoted entirely to debunking the 'irrational': CSICOP (the Committee for the Scientific Investigation of Claims of the Paranormal, aptly pronounced 'psicop') (see Pinch and Collins 1984; Hansen 1992; Clark 1993). Their foray into direct involvement with research on astrology in the early 1980s turned into an embarrassing débâcle (see Rawlins 1981; Curry 1982), since when they have contented themselves with publishing others' work and op-ed pieces. But a closely related group has been involved in such research for twenty-five years, and Garry Phillipson (2000) has recently produced a very useful summary and discussion, based on extensive interviews, which we shall draw heavily upon below.[4]

True or False?

Most of these researchers' discussion of astrology, in the course of interviews with Phillipson, centres on three issues: is astrology true? Is it objective or subjective knowledge? And does it work? Both these questions and the answers supplied in response repay close examination.

Their stated starting-point, both originally and in this analysis, was to ask themselves: 'Was astrology true?' (Phillipson 2000: 124) This question is itself peculiar, as can be seen if we imagine equivalent alternatives: 'Is science true?' 'Is art true?' or 'Is religion true?' It is very difficult to imagine how one could possibly arrive at an adequate response to such a sweeping and (as it is stated virtually without qualification) impossible demand. So we shall have to figure out for ourselves what exactly is meant by 'true' here.

That is made a little easier when they ask, 'Is it true that that positive signs are extraverted, that an elevated Neptune is musical, that adverse Mars transits indicate accidents . . .?' and so on (ibid.: 127). It seems, without being stated, that in each case, 'always' and/or 'necessarily' is assumed. So the test, before a single 'result', has already been set up in a particular way: the claims at stake must be systemic, abstract, nomothetic ones. But this would rule out just the kind of contextual, situated, embodied and embedded interventions of which astrology as divination consists. That impression is strengthened when they ask rhetorically whether a birthchart's factors have any 'real intrinsic meanings' (ibid.: 140). 'Intrinsic' here means clearly factors which do not depend on, let alone being constituted *by*, context, and the imprimatur of 'real' is conferred on them alone.

A closely related scientific criticism – and agreed by at least one leading astrologer (Elwell 1987; see Phillipson 2001: 183) – sees astrologers' 'dramatic disagreement on fundamentals' (Phillipson 2000: 157) as a profound problem, and points to the lack of 'progress' in deciding that. But as usual, objectivist assumptions have been smuggled into the discussion. Regarding 'progress', what if astrology is more like art than science? Do we spurn Renaissance painting because it has been superseded by, say, abstract expressionism? There may be progress of a sort here, but it is not the sort that is going anywhere in particular, and can therefore be judged by its final destination. And what if what is 'fundamental' responds to, and thus changes in relation to, context? Typically, the objectivist assumes that his definition of 'fundamental' – something that is always and everywhere the same, regardless of the situation – is the only possible one. But in life as it is lived, including astrological practice (and, for that matter, scientific practice: a point which apologists for scientism find even more offensive, if possible, than astrology), it is not just permissable but unavoidable that what is fundamental changes, in the precise actual situation concerned, without being any the less fundamental for that (see Smith 1988, 1997).

The kind of context that matters most in this case, as the researchers initally seem to recognize, is the ritual of preparing and interpreting the relevant astrological map, either for oneself or for another, in the divinatory situation nowadays usually called (in the latter case) a 'consultation'. However, since the astrologer and/or the client brings a complex set of values, assumptions, problems and strategies to *every* such situation, there is no such thing as its repetition; and since it is impossible to ascertain algorithmically which of all those factors is or are ever important, that point is true not just trivially but substantively.

The researchers' objectivist/realist bias becomes crystal clear when they state that 'The issue is whether the astrology ritual works better than a control ritual, e.g. by providing new information or by improving self-esteem' (Phillipson 2000: 143). 'The' astrological ritual – as if its practice was always the same in every important respect – is bad enough, but the oxymoron 'control ritual' would be laughable if it did not reveal such a gross misunderstanding of the phenomenon supposedly being analysed. As Roy A. Rappaport (1999: 37–8; cf. 169) points out, 'Ritual is not simply one of a number of more or less equivalent ways in which the material . . . may be expressed, presented, maintained or established . . . The manner of "saying" and "doing" is intrinsic to what is being said and done.' It follows that after what is unique in each ritual has been subtracted in order to leave what is in common, the remainder is no longer ritual but its empty husk.[5] Once this has been done, the fetish of 'replication' becomes quite irrelevant – 'As if', to quote Wittgenstein (1953: 265), 'someone were to buy several copies of the morning paper to assure himself that what it said was true'.[6]

After all this, to be told that the spirit of science is 'genuinely open-minded', and that 'As scientific researchers, our worldviews . . . are only tentative', rather fails to reassure (Phillipson 2000: 126, 150). Indeed, it seems to leave only the alternatives of remarkably unself-critical näiveté, bordering on sheer ignorance, or else hypocrisy. Scientists' world-views are no more or less tentative than anyone else's, since the very criteria that scientific research depend on depend for their efficacy on *assuming* the truth and importance of ideas and values for which no scientific support can be adduced without begging the question (and so on, in a potentially infinite regress). And in the case of these researchers, it is clear that an 'open mind' extends only to the phenomena to be subjected to scientific scrutiny, not to the nature of that scrutiny itself.[7]

'Subjective' vs 'Objective' Astrology

The same unadmitted bias continues in the researchers' treatment of 'subjective' vs 'objective' astrology. Taking these in order, 'In subjective astrology only subjective values matter. The correctness of a particular statement, or of a chart reading, or even of the chart itself, is of no direct concern' (Phillipson 2000: 129). But in practice there is only *perceived* correctness; even scientific correctness requires its apprehension as such by scientists. As Lakoff and Johnson (1999: 106) rhetorically ask, 'If it's not a truth for us, how can we make sense of its being a truth at all?' So how could correctness, of any kind, have nothing to do with subjectivity? Conversely, does subjectivity have no concern with correctness? That would seem to be contradicted by the researchers' own unavoidably subjective pursuit of 'truth'. Nor is it true of astrologers or their clients, no matter how 'subjective' they may be. Most practising astrologers know the truth of the poet Michael Longley's observation that "when you capture something with precision, you also release its mysterious aura. You don't get the mystery without the precision'.[8]

With subjective astrology, apparently, research would 'examine its effects on people rather than its content'. But how could these be unrelated? Again, 'the experiences of astrologers and their clients are themselves fascinating, whether or not they prove to be astrological' (Phillipson 2000: 164, 165). But an astrologer just *is* someone who practices astrology, and the experiences of their clients just *are* ones of astrology. A radical separation of the two depends entirely on an unargued, and highly dubious, rationalist-realist assumption that there is something called astrology 'out there' which can be separated from astrologers, and vice versa.[9]

The researchers continue that 'In objective astrology our subjective values do not matter . . . What matters are issues like: Are the statements of astrology true?' (ibid.: 129). Once again we find the same naive realism, not only as if 'truth' was entirely straightforward and unproblematic, but as if science, a thoroughly human practice and tradition – or objectivity, a human attitude and ideal – or truth, a human judgement – were possible without subjectivity (commitments, views, assumptions and values, not to mention ideas). And note the assumption under-pinning their whole approach: that of a radical distinction between 'objective' and 'subjective'. There are good reasons to doubt that such a crude divide, while analytic-ally possible, is either defensible or useful as a way to understand *any* human activity.

Perhaps the researchers were aware that their results are vulnerable to a critique of the assumptions on which they depend, because an aside pre-emptively damns questions about 'the nature of truth, reality, perception, language, and so on' as 'a smokescreen of speculation . . . Talk yes, actual progress no' (ibid.: 152). Unfortu-nately, it is necessary to point out the obvious: that the meaning and value of 'actual progress' in this context is not itself in the least obvious or simple, and that it cannot be determined without just such a discussion. It seems these researchers have already decided what actually constitutes 'actual progress', and tried to place it safely off-limits.

The fundamental point at stake doesn't seem particularly difficult, but it bears repeating: human beings don't live in an entirely objective world, since without subjective awareness of and interaction with a world, it effectively doesn't exist for them. Nor, conversely, can human subjectivity exist in a void; it requires a world to sustain it and be aware of. Every human activity necessarily partakes of both, and none is *either* purely subjective or objective. That, it should hardly be necessary to add, includes both astrology and science. The enterprise of 'explaining' astrology will be addressed below; here let us just note the irony, given the researchers' concern with 'progress', that they don't seem to have noticed how, even within scientific discourse, things have moved on somewhat since Cartesian dualism – for example, in systems, autopoietic, chaos and dissipative structure theories – in ways that recognize the point just made.[10]

With such a badly skewed starting-point, it is not surprising to find further confusion in its adumbration. Qualitative tests of astrology are rejected as non-rigorous (which seems to mean much the same thing as 'subjective'), being 'more open to creative interpretation, which amounts to the same thing' (Phillipson 2000: 131). The contrast drawn here is between metaphoric interpretation on the one hand and scientific rigour on the other. The logic seems to be that openness to interpretation = lack of rigour, and rigour = unamenability to interpretation; so complete rigour = no possibility of interpretation at all. But nothing, including the most rigorous scientific datum, interprets itself. As with every other human cognitive and communicative endeavour, 'Metaphorical thought is what makes abstract scientific theorising possible' (Lakoff and Johnson 1999: 128).[11]

It is embarrassing to have to make another such elementary point. On the other hand, it is instructive as to the kind of intellectual standards that prevail where criticism of astrology is concerned. The researchers also have plenty of company in practising, while denying, metaphoricity. Stephen Hawkings's mystical-megalomaniac fantasy about knowing the mind of God through physics and Dawkins's' 'selfish gene' – positing not only a gene as capable of acting selfishly but people as doing so for that reason – are only two of the more egregious examples. What makes them egregious, however, is not just the particular metaphors that are so clumsy and inappropriate, but the intellectual dishonesty (politely but efficiently exposed by Midgley 1992, 2001) of pretending that they are not metaphorical at all.

Although we do not need to explore them here in order to make our case, even the statistical analyses which the researchers' showcase depend crucially on assumptions and interpretations which are open to question in both principle and application.[12] This makes their citation as conclusively damning evidence against the reality of astrology as such all the more purely ideological (for example by Kelly et al. 1990, Kelly 1997).

Furthermore, despite the researchers' tendentious opposition between 'objective truth' and 'subjective experience', there are only different kinds of experience, and therefore truths. The canons of 'objective' science are therefore not more rigorous than those of 'subjective' humanities or the arts; they are simply different. And the same is true of astrology. The researchers comment that the difference between astrologers and themselves is that they (the latter) 'are more careful and rigorous' (Phillipson 2000: 127). Again, not so: astrologers and researchers are engaged in different enterprises. The former are attempting to answer questions astrologically, while the latter are attempting to answer a second-order question along the lines of 'Is astrology true?' Both parties are in pursuit of the truth in their own domains, and may be *equally* rigorous *or* sloppy in relation to that goal.

The researchers continue that 'Astrology seems unlikely to feel right unless astrologers and clients share a belief in [the truth of] objective astrology. Otherwise why bother with accurate charts?' (ibid.: 156). But this is to conflate 'true' with 'objective', as they do throughout, and without even the possibility of any 'scientific' support that doesn't involve already assuming the truth (or value) of science. The astrologer's work would be impossible without a notion of truth that is ultimately as demanding and precise, and potentially possesses as much integrity in his or her own sphere, as the corresponding notion for scientists in theirs. And the attempt to work with the appropriate kind of accurate data is as much, and as important, a requirement for astrologers as it is for scientific experimentation. But – and this is not to denigrate either pursuit – it is a *ritual* requirement.

Another crucial point concerns the researchers' assumption that just because astrological discourse consists, in part, of statements about the world or its states which therefore qualify as 'objective', it can, at least to that extent, be scientifically tested. But is that necessarily true? Suppose, in keeping with our construal of astrology so far, that someone has followed 'the advice of the stars' and taken one course of action as opposed to another. Is there any way at all he or she could go back to the point in his or her life preceding that course of action, and compare the outcome of following the advice of the oracle with that of ignoring it or doing the opposite? Of course not.[13] Yet this is the paradigmatic situation for those involved with the practice of astrology. And there is equally no way it can be 'scientifically tested' without first being turned into something very different, namely a second-order, artificial experimental situation, in which it becomes meaningful to speak of 'control rituals' and the like.

'Does Astrology Work?'

At this point, let us follow the researchers' own advice and 'consider what "it [astrology] works" actually means'. In their opinion, 'It means that *all non-astrological influences leading to the same result have been ruled out*' (Phillipson 2000: 132; italics in original). The researchers cite a long list of 'cognitive errors' which supposedly not only explain astrological truth but explain it away, i.e. there is supposedly nothing astrological left: for example, the Barnum effect (reading specifics into generalities), the Dr Fox effect (using impressive but meaningless jargon), cognitive dissonance (actually an unpleasant sense of conflict between experience and belief, but what they mean is explaining away the former in order to preserve the latter), hindsight bias (rearranging experience retrospectively), stacking the deck (asking only confirming questions), safety in complexity, and misattribution (mistakenly identifying causes).

But as already noted, astrology just *is* the experience of its truth – of it 'working' – in practice. To redescribe that, for everyone, as entirely something else is not to understand astrology, but to replace it with something else, in keeping with a very different agenda. And the latter is quite clear, because what actually distinguishes the modern psychological armoury, *as applied* by researchers to astrology, from the medieval theological apparatus used by Holy Mother Church to defend herself and save our souls from heresy? Or the armoury of 'cognitive errors' from St Augustine's demons?

Furthermore, how can 'astrological' and 'non-astrological' or 'control' factors possibly be cleanly separated and compared? Since every astrological situation is whole and unique, it is non-repeatable, and therefore non-comparable, *in the sense the researchers assume*. In practice, of course, similarities as well as differences

– 101 –

can be noted, and doing so is an essential part of learning astrology, or anything else; but nothing warrants their further extrapolation to universality or necessity, which is just the move that the 'scientific' critique of astrology depends upon. In an earlier metaphor, we suggested that the scientific claims of successful research amount to saying that the operation was a success, although the patient died; but it is more that astrology, as a lived and living experience, must already be dead, and must have been replaced by someone else (albeit of the same name) before this kind of operation can be performed at all.

The researchers rightly refer to the central experience of astrology 'working', although they do so only to de- and re-construct it as 'not (really) working'. But what does 'It works', taken seriously, actually mean in practice? Let us see.

- The '*it*' refers to the *whole astrological situation*, not just certain marks on a piece of paper which, by themselves, mean nothing until and unless they are interpreted in the context of, and in relation to, that situation. And that situation never repeats itself. (Even if the same question, linguistically speaking, is asked by the same person of the same astrologer, the initial situation has been radically altered by its 'repetition'.)
- The '*works*' of 'it works' means nothing more nor less than that 'person x in situation y experienced the truth of a perception or statement', where astrology was integral to situation y. So if the astrology is not present – even if, *per impossibile*, everything else is 'the same' – it constitutes a radically different situation.

Furthermore,

- To argue that '*astrology works*', as a realist astrologer might (and often does) because of experiences that it *did* work, is a further step with grave difficulties. Aside from the Humean point that no finite number of such experiences can support it, if astrology is divinatory it can still 'work' and be 'true' in a valid and meaningful way that owes nothing to a realist/objectivist sense of those words, which requires it to work always and everywhere – in the words of that marvellous scientific escape-clause, *ceteris paribus* ('other things being equal'). To quote Heaton (1990: 18) again, 'Astrology predicts, but you cannot predict when it is going to predict.' And being unavoidable, this is no failing!
- So to argue that '*astrology doesn't work*' – in the manner of a realist critic (or equally realist disillusioned ex-astrologer) – is another further step which is equally unsupported, for the same reasons.

Finally, to argue that astrology *seemed* to but *actually* 'didn't work' – that is, that a person experienced astrology working but was 'actually' or 'really' wrong (mistaken, deluded, etc.) – is another further step which is an essential part of the strategy of scientific critics. But what does such a claim mean in practice? It amounts to saying: 'person **r** (the researcher) in situation **s** (one to which examining the truth or otherwise of astrology is integral) has the experience that person **x** in situation **y** was wrong'. But persons **r** and **x** are very different, with different agenda generating different criteria; as are situations **s** and **y**. So what is happening here is an attempt to appropriate **x/y** and replace it with **r/s**. And this attempt proceeds by trying to convince an audience (which may include **x**) of the counter-truth of **r/s**, using rhetoric and persuasion (centred on showing the truth of **s**) in order to induce a similar experience that will replace **y**.

Now the exercise of explanatory redescription is not in itself wrong or harmful, of course. To repeat the distinction already made, it can illumine – indeed, it helps to create – our understanding of the primary phenomenon. Not so appropriation, however: the attempt to exclude all other explanations, and indeed eliminate the phenonenon as such. And why such a concerted programme, riding on a wider scientistic groundswell, if not in order to eliminate this atavistic enchantment, which has somehow (like many 'pagan superstitions') stubbornly survived the scientific revolution, and bring about Enlightenment? That, at any rate, is how the modernist magicians see themselves: a noble, even heroic image. The actual terminus of that programme is surely even clearer now that it was when Horkheimer and Adorno (1994: 3) laid it bare in 1944: 'the fully enlightened earth radiates disaster triumphant'. But this a question of values which cannot itself be decided scientifically.

It has been necessary to go into the subject of astrology and science in some detail because it is such a common contemporary misunderstanding that astrology is either scientifically/rationally true or false; and if the latter, then it must be delusory, fraudulent or superstitious. Thus most of the power/knowledge struggles over its nature have been concerned with this issue, and it has been assumed that to show astrological knowledge to be scientifically false settles the issue.

In fact, competent observers of modern science confirm that it is not able to do this kind of job. The historian of science John Henry (2002: 49–50), underlining that conclusion in his discipline, adds that

> sociologists of science have repeatedly shown that scientists who might, in principle, live up to the demands of this [experimental] method, in practice do not do so (even though they may retrospectively claim to have done so). Philosophers of science, moreover, have repeatedly been forced to acknowledge the impossibility of demarcating science from non-science in terms of a characteristic methodology.

And the philosopher of science A.F. Chalmers (1982: 166) concurs:

> there is no general category 'science' and no concept of truth which is up to the task of characterizing science as a search for truth. Each area of knowledge is to be judged on

its merits by investigating its aims and the extent to which it is able to fulfill them. Further, judgements concerning aims will themselves be relative to the social situation.[14]

Yet the ready recourse to science as ultimate arbiter of truth or reality persists (also noted by Phillipson 2000: 124), feeding off the scientistic assumption (not difficult to perceive in the above researchers' nostrums, and articulated by Dawkins) that non-scientific knowledge is inferior, if not unreal. In this approach, as Scott (1998: 305) puts it, 'Knowledge that arrives in any other form than through the techniques and instruments of formal scientific procedure does not deserve to be taken seriously. The imperial pretense of scientific modernism admits knowledge only if it arrives through the aperture that the experimental method has constructed for its admission.' This is an extreme view, certainly; but it is also a worryingly common one.

As we have suggested, recognizing the contingency of realist/objectivist pre-suppositions (pre-eminent in scientism) frees us to realize what an impoverished set of alternatives for human discourse they leave us with. And we have argued that astrology – at least in one crucial dimension, or one crucial kind of it – is not like that at all. That suggests that truth in this case (along with many others), while not a kind of propositional knowledge dealing with universal or necessary truth, is nonetheless integral to astrology as such. But in that case, what kind of truth, or perhaps more neutrally, knowledge, are we talking about?

Metis

Extremely schematically, the paradigm for knowledge in subsequent Western intellectual and cultural life was initiated by Plato who, after Socrates, set *episteme* – truth, by which he meant certain theoretical knowledge of abstract universals – over against *doxa*, or vulgar opinion. Only the former was granted the status of true knowledge. Aristotle, recognizing that this severe dichotomy failed to exhaust the nature of human intelligence, added the intermediary idea of *phronesis*: practical intelligence, as manifested in a craft or skill. This was considered to be a second-best kind of knowledge, not of universal and therefore necessary truth but local skills, nontransferable to other domains and with an irreducibly tacit component. And there the matter largely rested, successively refined but substantively accepted by subsequent philosophers. The superiority of propositional knowledge (often to the point of identifying it with knowledge as such) continued through Christian thought and Descartes, Locke and Hobbes to Kant, and remains the dominant view, suitably rephrased, in the sciences, both natural and social.

Recently, however, another kind of intelligence has been suggested: *metis*, or cunning wisdom. More a 'mode of action' or attitude of mind' than a concept, and therefore rarely articulated, it had hitherto escaped the purview of the history of ideas. It is characterized by suppleness of thought and action, the ability to see through and disregard conventions, to embrace paradox, and to respond quickly and appropriately to changing circumstances and particulars. Even compared with *phronesis*, *metis* is both intellectually and morally ambiguous. It 'operates with a peculiar twist, the unexpressed premise that both reality and language cannot be understood (or manipulated) in straightforward "rational" terms but must be approached by subtlety, indirection, and even cunning' (Raphals 1992: 5).

Metis was the daughter of the Titan Oceanus – animistic god of the great 'river' encircling the Earth – and the Titaness Tethys, themselves children of Uranus (Heaven) and Gaea (Earth). Zeus swallowed Metis, his first wife, while she was pregnant with Athena, who was then born from Zeus' head. She continued to advise Zeus from within. Athena, the goddess of strategy, was the patron of Odysseus: the best-known 'Western' exemplar, together with Penelope – although the virtues extolled by Machiavelli are also characteristically metic – and in 'Eastern' discourse, Monkey, but also Kuan Yin (the Bodhisattva of compassion). Detienne and Vernant (1978) reveal it as a consistent semantic field for more than ten centuries in the Greek world, and its cross-cultural presence has been carefully confirmed by Raphals (1992), who points to a remarkably precise Chinese equivalent, *zhi mou*, or wily wisdom, as exemplified by the Taoist sage. (*Zhi* is just as much a problem for Confucian moralism as *metis* is for Platonic and Christian truth.) It is also recognizable in Buddhist discourse as *upaya*, or 'skilful means'.

In contrast, Socrates, as developed by Plato, sought to make *tekhne* – an application of *episteme* – foundational: a science characterized by Aristotle in terms of measurement, universal applicability, teachability, and amenability to explanation. But as Raphals (1992: 227) points out, 'These four qualities are precisely those that *metis* eludes.' Its realm is one 'of shifting particulars that can be apprehended and described only indirectly and with skill and cunning'.

It would seem to follow that if metic truth is not unitary, universal and abstract but multiple, perspectival and particular, then it is also not passive, waiting to be apprehended by the heroic initiate, but *active*. It would make sense in this context that agency cannot be anthropocentrically reserved for human beings alone, as it is in modernist monism. And that further implies a real relationship between knower and known (that is, one in which the knowing can affect *both* parties). Perhaps this is how we may begin to make sense of Weber's extraordinary and tantalizing definition of truth: 'only that which *wants* to be valid for all those who *want* the truth' (quoted in Scaff 1989: 118, italics in original).

Scott (1998: 340) also draws a strong contrast between *metis* and *episteme* in that

Universalist claims seem inherent in the way in which rationalist knowledge is pursued . . . there seems to be no door in this epistemic edifice through which metis or practical knowledge could enter on its own terms. It is this imperialism that is troubling. As Pascal wrote, the great failure of rationalism is 'not its recognition of technical knowledge, but its failure to recognise any other'. By contrast, *metis* does not put all its eggs in one basket; it makes no claim to universality and in this sense is pluralistic.[15]

It is our contention that metic intelligence is the 'natural' mode of divination, and therefore an appropriate way to approach its understanding. Or, to put the same thing a different way, *metis* is the mode of being appropriate to negotiating an enchanted world. In a way that suggests that it is an instance of *metis*, divination too proceeds by way of the openly metaphoric (rather than propositional) development of symbolic images, often proceeding by indirection and intuitively (rather than rationally in the sense of *episteme*), in response to a situated inquiry, not so much influenced as constituted by its context, in which a strategic element, constellated around the inquirer's desire, coexists with constantly and unpredictably shifting particulars (not an eternal realm of universal truth).

In divination, an answer to the inquiry is elicited through a ritual whose point – and to this extent, it is indeed purposive – is precisely to allow contingency to take a form relevant to the exigencies of that moment (and not a form that is necessarily true, or for that matter good, in their Socratic senses). Hence the ubiquity of 'randomization' in divinatory ritual: the fall of the coins, the hand of cards drawn, the unpremeditated disposition of the planets at the moment a question is asked. The divinatory moment, when it metically takes such form and 'speaks', is one of enchantment: that is, a realization that the world *is* enchanted. And although *metis* shares with wonder a recognition of ontological and existential contingency, and therefore profound humility, it also admits the inalienable human attribute of purpose, of trying to plot and keep to a particular course; it thus corrects any tendency on the part of wonder to excessively transcendental otherworldliness.

To put it another way, divination is always ritually aleatory just because chance is the opposite of purpose and instrumentality, and its mode of being – like that of wonder – entails an opening up of the 'common sense' of narrow and limited purposive consciousness to what Bateson (1972: 434) called 'the whole systemic structure', the 'recognition of and guidance by a knowledge of [which]' is, he suggested, wisdom. And that coheres with what Morrison and others have noticed about divination historically and anthropologically: its central concern is not knowledge (factual, let alone scientific) but *wisdom* (ethical, spiritual and pragmatic). It remains only to add that not only any moment chosen for a divinatory purpose but the moment of birth itself, so considered, is aleatory – contingent, 'random' – in just the same way . . . which doesn't necessarily thereby render it arbitrary, insignificant or meaningless; far from it.

Notes

1. We shall use the 1996 version of his 1995 article.
2. Samuel Parker, FRS and Bishop of Oxford; see Curry 1989: 49.
3. The *Guardian* regularly features the same sort of columns, usually by Francis Wheen, Pat Kane or Catherine Bennett.
4. With thanks for his kind permission to do so. For a recent and thorough summary of scientific research into astrology from a 'sceptical' point of view, see Stein 1996. It is worth recording that in the spring of 2003, the leading 'researcher', Geoffrey Dean, was elected as a CSICOP Fellow.
5. Cf. Marie-Louise von Franz (1980: 26) on Rhine, the doyen of scientific research into parapsychology: 'he was foolish enough to believe that if he wanted to sell parapsychological phenomena to the scientific world then he must prove them statistically or with the concept of probability and – what a fool – he ended up by that in enemy territory . . . He tries to prove with the very means which eliminates the single case something which is only valid in the single case.'
6. With thanks to Mike Harding for this marvellous quotation.
7. Cf. Harding 2000: just such an exercise, which provoked a furious reaction from Dean et al. And since part of our import is that no argumentation is purely disinterested, it is not out of place here to note briefly two of Dean's chief rhetorical strategies. One is to tendentiously 'summarize' his opponents' arguments and then deal entirely with the resulting creation. The other is to engage in apparently endless reply and counter-reply, while conceding nothing, to the point where his opponents sensibly decide that the the process has become fruitless and decline to continue – whereupon Dean claims victory.
8. From an interview in the *Irish Times* (11 January 1992).
9. Also, as Brockbank (2002: 15) observes, 'the accuracy tests of Dean et al. imply a definition of astrology which excludes an astrologer whereas, in nearly every case, the astrology that is actually being practised requires an astrologer'.
10. For example Varela et al. (1991). A good recent discussion is Capra 1997. (See also the section in the next chapter on 'Explaining Divination'.)
11. On metaphor, see also Midgley 2001; Hesse 1980: 111–24; Ortony 1993 [1979]; Lakoff and Johnson 1980, 1999; Barfield 1967, 1977: 11–142, 1973 [1928], 1979: 36–64.
12. See the analysis by Geoffrey Cornelius in the second edition of his 1994. (See also Lehman 1994 for a good discussion of scientific double standards, abuse of 'scientific method', etc. in astrological research.)
13. This was what Milan Kundera referred to as 'the unbearable lightness of being'.

14. We would like to add, in case there is any doubt, that Henry and Chalmers are not fringe or extremist commentators but respected mainstream scholars. It is for that reason we have chosen not to quote, say, Fuller 1997, despite his acuity.
15. Unfortunately, Scott's analysis is undermined by his conflation of *metis* and *phronesis*, and much of what he ascribes to the former applies only to the latter.

–9–

Divination Today

The Big Picture

It is time to review where we have been so far. As we have shown, the history of astrology, both 'internally' and 'externally', strongly suggests the overall development Weber called 'disenchantment'. And this notwithstanding its complexity, nor the fact that at any one time in that history there are coexisting countermovements; nor the absence of a teleological and thus 'necessary' movement toward some sort of predetermined goal. From its origins as plural and local divination – that is, a dialogue with fate or the gods when 'concrete magic' was not yet undivided into spiritual or subjective and material or objective – astrology underwent a lengthy and uneven process of progressively more rationalization, abstraction and naturalization, initially Platonic but predominantly Aristotelian/Ptolemaic, into a single 'Machine of Destiny', until the 'natural' part was absorbed by the still more efficient modern Megamachine, whereupon what remained was redescribed (whether positively or disparagingly) as 'supernatural'. Overall, this process has entailed a significant impoverishment of symbolism, and consequently its potential for enchantment, whose hallmark is existential wonder.

Among the ironies involved is the extent to which astrologers themselves have helped to bring about this situation. As susceptible as anyone else to the seductions of the universalist (latterly modernist) promise of power, they have cast astrology as a misunderstood and unjustly unrecognized science, dealing with knowledge of an astrally determined future: a caricature at best, and an outright betrayal at worst. Of New Age gurus we might perhaps expect it; but even among those who seek to return to traditional astrology are some who maintain, without a trace of irony, that it offers a perfect system which can potentially be applied with guaranteed success. To do so requires ignoring Lilly's (1985 [1647]: B, 397) own insistent advice: '. . . the more holy thou art, and more near to God, the purer judgement thou shalt give'; 'Discretion, together with Art . . .'; This emphasis on discretion, i.e. wisdom, in the practice of judicial astrology – the kind that requires judgement – is exactly the opposite of *episteme* and system. On the contrary, it is metic, and allows for enchantment.

By the same token, Lilly (ibid.: 192) also advised the astrologer that 'you must know how to vary your Rules . . . wherein principally consist the masterpiece of the Art.' This too is a metic kind of knowledge, one that isn't, and *cannot* be, *in* the rules, that is, exhaustively specified propositionally. As Wittgenstein pointed out, one forever lacks a rule for how to interpret a rule, because such a meta-rule would require another one stating how to apply it, and so on in an infinite regress (see Holtzman and Leich 1981).

As for the question, 'Why practise astrology?' Bateson's (1979: 209) intuition should be heeded: 'I do not believe that the original purpose of the rain dance was to make "it" rain. I suspect that that is a degenerate misunderstanding of a much more profound religious need; to affirm membership in what we may call the ecological tautology, the eternal verities of life and environment.' Given the weight of literal-minded materialist misunderstanding, Bateson is obliged to overemphasize the spiritual component of concrete magic here; a rain ceremony affirming such membership does not by any means rule out the arrival of otherwise unforeseen rain, or other such practical and precise consequences. But the point he was trying to make stands. No more is the primary purpose of astrology to predict the future. Its proper role is the same affirmation of citizenship in a living world – the recognition of which is an experience of enchantment – in the course of addressing a particular and personal question. (In fact, the more general, casual or disinterested the divinatory question, the less likely is the answer to either inform or enchant; as the poet said, no precision, no mystery.)

Of course, to say this is to invite contempt from both sides of the great divide. The materialists will accuse us of being unacceptably metaphysical, while the supernaturalists – led by the ghost of Plato, and his many heirs[1] – will grumble at our introducing petty personal concerns into issues of spiritual truth. Actually, Dawkins objects equally strongly to such muddying the clear waters of material truth, thus showing yet again the continuity of modern science with theism.

William James is another philosopher from whom we can still learn much; indeed, his insights, arrived at quite independently, are often indistinguishable from those of Weber (see for example James 1956). And James's (1958: 377–8) discussion of this point cannot be bettered:

> To describe the world with all the various feelings of the individual pinch of destiny . . . left out from the description – they being as describable as anything else – would be something like offering a printed bill of fare as the equivalent for a solid meal . . . The individual's religion may be egotistic, and those private realities which it keeps in touch with may be narrow enough; but at any rate it always remains infinitely less hollow and abstract, as far as it goes, than a science which prides itself on taking no account of anything private at all . . . I think, therefore, that however particular questions connected with our individual destinies may be answered, it is only by acknowledging them as genuine questions, and living in the sphere of thought which they open up, that we become profound. But to live thus is to be religious . . .

We are concerned here with a specific form of religious life, of course: divination, and its leading 'Western' form, astrology. And it seems that against all the odds, and despite all the contempt, corruption and confusion (among astrologers as well as their opponents), its true potential survives. As Kane (1994: 238) observes, "The gods have not been silenced; in fact, they have been driven underground.'[2] 'Concrete magic' is not simply an archaic or atavistic state of mind/world long since happily outgrown (or, for that matter, tragically lost); although ancient indeed, it is a way of being in the world that is still present, and alive. And although it cannot be commanded or be relied upon, enchantment can still emerge, and surprise and change us, whenever it is honoured and invited.

In fact, it has a very contemporary urgency: in the context of a global programme of disenchantment, an integral part of the capital-state-science nexus, such apparently insubstantial moments take on a new significance and potential. True, they cannot themselves be marshalled into a counter-programme – not without contributing to the creation of merely another monist monster – but they can indirectly sustain a life, shared as well as private, of enchantment that is itself resistance and alternative (see Curry 1999).

We are therefore not advocating a literal-minded return to some primal undifferentiated state of mind or way of life. That would hardly be a promising strategy, let alone a metic one. But there is no good reason not to attempt an intelligent recovery of certain insights, priorities and practices – those of sanity and, inseparably, sanctity – too many of us have been unwise enough to abandon. As David Abram (1996: 270) has observed, 'It is surely not a matter of "going back", but of coming full circle.' And many of those share with divinatory astrology an embedded, embodied and ecological pluralism, including a post-secular spiritual (but not supernatural) dimension.

It also follows from this understanding of astrology as divination that its practice – in common with all other human practices – can be neither entirely 'objective' nor 'subjective'; or rather, that it is necessarily both. An act of divination necessarily requires *both* an enquirer with a question ('subject') *and* a world of which that subject partakes, including the cosmos that is essential to astrology in particular ('objects'). It entails a 'subjective' participation in an 'objectively' embodied and embedded way. So, for example, it is not surprising (in theory: always a surprise in practice) that astrological symbolism refuses to confine itself to either just the 'objective' world or the 'subjective' self, including the map of the birth of its putative subject.[3] As Hyde (1992) has pointed out, and as any reasonably competent astrologer will have experienced, it can equally speak, very pointedly, to and about the interpreter, and/or the circumstances in which it is being interpreted, regardless of 'whose' map it is. As a corollary, there is a considerable difference between the merely thematic kind of astrology that often passes for its practice today, in which the subject is acquainted in a more-or-less general way with the psychological or archetypal 'themes' in his or her life, and the kind of metic precision that is possible with a really skilled astrologer.[4]

Abram is very perceptive on the trap inherent in privileging either objectivity or subjectivity. Writing of the dominant kind of scientific discourse on the one hand and most of the 'New Age' kind on the other, he points out (1996: 66–7) that

> by prioritizing one or the other, both of these views perpetuate the distinction between human 'subjects' and natural 'objects', and hence neither threatens the common conception of sensible nature as a purely passive dimension suitable for human manipulation and use. While both of these views are unstable, each bolsters the other; by bouncing from one to the other – from scientific determinism to spiritual idealism and back again – contemporary discourse easily avoids the possibility that both the perceiving being and the perceived being are of the same stuff, that the perceiver and the perceived are interdependent and in some sense even reversible aspects of a common animate nature, or Flesh, that is at once both sensible and sensitive.

Or as Bateson (Bateson and Bateson 1987: 51, 59) earlier put it, 'These two species of superstition, these rival epistemologies, the supernatural and the mechanical, feed each other . . . And both are nonsense.'

Ironically, then, to the extent that astrology is incorporated into a 'New Age' world-view, it becomes embroiled in this sterile dualism which simply feeds the fantasy of a single Truth, to be accomplished by finally successfully absorbing its symbiotic twin (idealist or materialist). Since (re-)enchantment depends, as Weber pointed out, on a spiritual plurality of the kind that divination entails, astrology then loses its ability to re-enchant. And that is precisely what makes it so valuable now. The subject-object split, made famous by Descartes but based on centuries of Christian spirit/matter dualism (itself strongly influenced in this respect by Platonic philosophy), is fundamental to the strategy of disenchantment. Astrology has the potential to resist that, and to remind us of the sectarian and senseless way that distinction has been turned by science into an article of faith, and turned so destructively on many other fields of life.[5] Enchantment, in contrast, is an experience of the world as intrinsically meaningful, significant, and whole in a way that is fundamentally mysterious, and that includes oneself. In divination, an answer to a question which rings mysteriously but precisely true for those concerned is just such an experience.

Two reminders might be necessary here. First, the fact that this kind of truth is very different from the second-order experience of truth in an objectivist sense in no way disqualifies it, unless one subscribes to objectivist assumptions. Conversely, the experience of enchantment does not make it true in an objectivist sense; nor does it need to be.[6] Second, the centrality of spiritual wonder does not at all rule out the answer's pragmatic usefulness. Instrumental*ism* and utilitarian*ism* are the attempt to turn usefulness, which is integral to being alive, into the dominant value of a virtual religion – a very different matter. To view pragmatic and spiritual value as mutually exclusive is simply to accept that convention without question, and to forget Weber's point about concrete magic. While it seems that Weber himself was ultimately pessimistic about recovering such a sensibility, it is not necessary to be an optimist to hold that 'coming full circle' is both desirable and at least possibile, individually and even, to some extent, collectively.

Insofar as astrology still partakes of divination, then, enchantment is still at its heart; and as such, it is not to be fully explained in any fully calculable, rational or material and therefore masterable way. As we have seen, plurality and mystery are integral to such experiences, and their integrity can only be sustained by wonder and its correlates (as developed by Hepburn [1984]): humility and respect for otherness. They cannot be mastered through the application of a system – i.e. disenchanted – without becoming something very different (see Curry 1999 and Kane 1994: 150). They also cannot be captured (alive) by any physicalist metaphor, such as, say, the physical distances of the planets from the Earth; these have no relevance except insofar as they are interpreted *symbolically* and incorporated, as we have already said, ritually. In Hyde's phrase, astrology is 'a poetics of the cosmos' (Company of Astrologers seminar, 8 July 2001).

To put it another way, astrological divination is fundamentally and therefore, in its own terms, rightly unconcerned with the question of 'How?' The domain of wonder is irreducibly one that 'It is so!'[7] So to explore the former question is to engage in a different enterprise. That is perfectly legitimate, of course. Not so the attempt to reduce the latter domain entirely to the former, however; such an act of imperialism can only 'succeed' in not only misunderstanding and misrepresenting its subject, but in destroying it in the instances it stumbles upon. But such effects are, of course, far from accidental. 'The war against mystery and magic was for modernity the war of liberation leading to the declaration of reason's independence . . . [The] world had to be de-spiritualised, de-animated: denied the capacity of the subject' (Bauman 1992: x). It is here that astrology, rightly understood and practiced, has something to contribute to a healthy and hopeful re-enchantment of the world.

A fundamental dilemma is thus posed for astrologers, in that success as defined by the mainstream entails failure as enchantment, and therefore loss of the only way they can offer a critique of (let alone alternative to) mainstream culture; but success in terms of enchantment results in their marginalization and rejection by the mainstream, along with loss of the power, influence and respectability that the latter can offer. Some attempt to escape this difficult choice by pursuing the path, central to the entertainment industry, of glamour: enchantment for profit. But glamour, being will-driven, is only enchantment's simulacrum; the real thing has fled or died, so the price of escape that way – pretence as a way of life, best maintained by permanent self-delusion – is high. Our own view is, to coin a phrase, what does it profit a discourse to gain the world but lose its soul? This is the unworldly choice, of course, but what kind of a world does the other course offer?

'Explaining' Divination

It follows from everything that has been said so far that the enterprise of explaining astrology must be carefully qualified from the outset by what is meant by 'explaining'. For example, insofar as astrology is divination, it cannot be treated as if it was putatively, potentially or actually science (in the modern sense). Insofar as it is a participatory experience, it cannot be treated as if the contribution of that particular astrologer in that particular situation in relation to that/those particular question(s) could be taken for granted, or averaged out. Insofar as it is a ritual, it cannot be compared to a 'control ritual'. Insofar as it is metic, i.e. tactical and/or strategic, it cannot survive being treated as *episteme*, i.e. as algorhythmic, universal or strictly propositional knowledge.[8] Insofar as it is enchantment, it cannot be expected to survive putatively total rational explanation.

In other words, if it is a firm *desideratum* to take astrology seriously as such, those approaches, which are guaranteed to destroy it (within their ambit), must be rejected. But does that leave us with nothing to say? Only if one subscribes to what Bernard Williams (1985: 18) aptly called 'a rationalistic conception of rationality', which confuses reasons with Reason (see Smith 1997: 41), and offers a false choice: either everything can, at least in principle, be fully explained, or nothing can at all. Such mystification is essential to the ideology of scientism, and its programme of disenchantment. As such, that programme is uniquely inappropriate to something like astrology – but at the same time, astrology represents a challenge it is unable to resist trying to master and thus eliminate. (Hence the whiff of hypocrisy, whether conscious or not, in such researchers' occasional claims to 'really' have the interests of astrology at heart.)

The trouble is that scientism has such a firm grip now on the very idea of explanation and what constitutes it. Perhaps, then, we should leave it to them, and say that respecting astrology, what *is* a defensible intellectual goal, in which reason plays is an indispensible part, is *understanding* it: a better understanding, and therefore deeper appreciation, of the phenomenon, as it exists in the experience of those participating in it – something that includes those who are 'studying' it. (Wittgenstein still has much to teach us here.)

This was the goal of the pioneering anthropologist Lucien Lévy-Bruhl. Notwithstanding that he was never forgiven by the intellectual community for imputing a lack of logic to the 'primitive mind' – something he soon retracted – Lévy-Bruhl's concept of 'mystical participation' is very close to that of divination, and his late attempts to get to grips with it are a model of intellectual integrity. His starting-point was a recognition that participation is not representation or cognitive knowledge, and 'to try to apply this scheme to participation is to do it violence and to distort it.' Rather, 'from the affective point of view which predominates in the complex where participation is included . . . something felt as real is definitely real, whether it is possible or not.' And in seeking to understand mystical participation, he advised against 'taking for granted that things are given first and that afterwards they enter into participations . . . Participation enters into the very constitution of these things. Without participation, they would not be *given* in experience: they would not exist'. He concluded that 'participation is not "explained" – it cannot be and ought not to be, it has no need of legitimation; but one sees its necessary place in the human mind – and as a result its role in religion, in metaphysics, in art and even in the conception of the whole of nature' (Lévy-Bruhl 1975: 1, 5–6, 192, 179–80).

An approach of this kind would also realize and accept that examining astrology in different contexts and with different questions in mind will result in different understandings, which do not necessarily either cancel each other out or have to eventuate in one great and all-inclusive meta-understanding (the notorious 'view from nowhere'). It accepts that all understanding is necessarily limited, incomplete and provisional – but nonetheless potentially valuable, interesting or helpful. By the same token, since it can never be final or complete, it always needs renewing, both individually and collectively – a fact which entails a salutary humility. And if such an enterprise amounts more to wisdom than to what the mainstream is pleased to call knowledge, so much the worse for the latter. It is at least in very good company: the arts and humanities, for a start, along with those social sciences with a phenomenological and/or hermeneutic approach. (It is no coincidence that Weber was a pioneer of the latter.)

On this subject, we shall give the last word to the eminent Indologist Heinrich Zimmer (1948: 1–3), writing on the closely related subject of myth:

> The dilettante – Italian *dilettante* (present participle of the verb dilettare, 'to take delight in') – is one who takes delight in something . . . The moment we abandon this dilettante attitude toward the images of folklore and myth and begin to feel certain about their proper interpretation (as professional comprehenders, handling the tool of an infallible method), we deprive ourselves of the quickening contact, the dæmonic and inspiring assault that is the effect of their intrinsic virtue. We forfeit our proper humility and open-mindedness before the unknown, and refuse to be instructed . . . What they demand of us is not the monologue of the coroner's report, but the dialogue of a living conversation.

And what do the deadening compendia of so-called 'negative results' by the scientific researchers constitute, if not a coroner's report?

In the case of understanding astrology as divination, however, there is another and more specific obstacle, with strong historical roots. It is apparently a simple stipulation (in contrast to the crude reductionism of the scientific researchers) to take it seriously, in its own right, *ab initio*. But the experience of divination was very early and severely banned within Christian discourse, and it remains in exile. Whatever the tacit compromises in practice, this made it extremely difficult to theorize in a way that allows it to exist. And the same is all the more true within the modern scientific discourse that succeeded and partially supplanted Christianity. Both theistic and secular monisms (including their respective internal dualisms) rule out of court the reality of the relational, and therefore plural (which is both objective and subjective, and therefore solely neither) and soulful (which is both spiritual and material, and therefore solely neither) even before enquiry can begin.

Given these difficulties, we can appreciate C.G. Jung's remark (1950: xxxix) that '[the] less one thinks about the theory of the *I Ching*, the more soundly one sleeps'. It is also no coincidence that some of the best general discussions of divination are still either pagan – such as that of the neo-Platonic philosopher Iamblichus (*c*.250–*c*.338) – or non-Western, such as that of Chu Hsi (1130–1200), the neo-Confucian philosopher. Since there is no good reason to assume that all passage of time necessarily constitutes progress, there is no shame in returning to these sources in order to recover their wisdom, before trying to move beyond them. It is also good to be reminded of how long debates which may appear uniquely contemporary have been going on.

Plotinus, for example, objected in principle to the very idea that the planets cause things to happen: '. . . countless myriads of living beings are born and continue to be: to minister continuously to every separate one of these; to make them famous, rich, poor, lascivious . . . What kind of life is this for the stars, how could they possibly handle a task so huge?' (Plotinus 1991: 80 quoted in Phillipson 2002). Cicero (1923: 537) concurred, seeing the divine as an 'excellent and eternal Being' that would, or could, have no traffic with petty human concerns. And it is not difficult to translate such a view into Dawkins's apparently secular reverence for the heavens, and outrage at astrologers.

Iamblichus (1999: 81), in response to the similar doubts of Plotinus's follower Porphyry, explains 'that the Gods, employing many instruments as media, send indications to men; and that they also use the ministrant aid of demons and souls, and the whole of nature, and of everything in the world . . . For [divination] does not draw down the intellect of more excellent natures to sublunary concerns and to us, but this intellect being established in itself, converts to itself signs and the whole of divination, and discovers that these proceed from it' (cf. Shaw 1995).

Compare a neo-Confucian understanding of divination, according to which the tutelary spirit (*shen*) guiding divination is 'not a personal spirit but a daemonic power or intelligence which is active within the operations of heaven and earth, and which emanates from the person of the sage' (Graham 1957: 111–12). There is a distinct resonance with the classical *daemones*, before they were demonized by

Christianity. But even this definition was too arbitrary for Chu Hsi, the great philosopher of the classic Chinese divinatory text, the *I Ching*, who criticized the popular notion of divination as the work of *kuei* and *shen* (ghosts and spirits), as distinct from *ch'i*, the psycho-physical substrate of all things: '*Kuei* and *shen* are merely *ch'i*. That which bends and stretches back and forth is *ch'i*. Within heaven-and-earth there is nothing that is not *ch'i*. The *ch'i* of mankind and the *ch'i* of heaven-and-earth are always in contact, with no gap, but human beings themselves cannot see it. When the human mind moves, it must pass through *ch'i* and mutually stimulate and penetrate this bending and stretching back and forth. In such cases as divination . . . when there is movement there must be a response' (Smith et al. 1990: 202). Or as another neo-Confucian, Chou Tun-I (1017–1073), put it, the spirit (by which divination works) is that which, 'when acted upon, immediately penetrates all things' (Chan 1963: 467). That definition coheres perfectly with the nature of divination as requiring participation in order to become real (see Cornelius 1994: 143–4).

Ways Forward

We suspect that an attempt nowadays to produce a 'comprehensive' theory of divination would be likely to view it as, broadly speaking, a means of allowing access to the unconscious mind (whether as knowledge that one 'has' without normally being aware of it, or as knowledge that is trans- or super-personal of which one is normally unaware). But such a move could not, in itself, bypass the constraints of participation, *metis* and so on; and it brings its own potential problems. Too much psychological theory simply reproduces the ancestral split in terms of an 'inner' subjective mind and an 'outer' objective world, both equally reified, whose interrelations are then mystified. One also suspects that the use of the word 'unconscious' is being made to do a lot of work making something feel secular, safe and already understood that is actually none of these things. That in turn makes it more amenable to abstract system-building of the kind William James (1977 [1908]: 32) called 'vicious intellectualism', which treats a name 'as excluding from the fact named what the name's definition fails positively to include'.

But the dire intellectual situation of divination and related phenomena in contemporary Western thought is slowly changing for the better. Recent advances in pluralist and 'relativist' thought, several of which have already been touched on here, definitely permit new hope. We have already drawn upon Weber and his heirs in contemporary critical theory, the humane pragmatism and pluralism of his near-contemporary William James, and the efforts of Lévy-Bruhl, among others. One could also mention the rich new possibilities opened up by the pioneering systems theory of Gregory Bateson and its further development by Maturana and Varela (capably described by Capra); Merleau-Ponty's phenomenology, as articulated, for example, by Abram; the importance, recently rediscovered (by intellectuals), of local knowledge (see Geertz 1993); the post-critical philosophy inspired by Michael Polanyi's concept of 'tacit knowledge'; and the influence of the idea of 'forms of life' of the later Wittgenstein in philosophy. We have already described anthropology, which is intertwined with many of these approaches, as the single most promising so-called social science vis-à-vis astrology; but the potential of history and the humanities too, especially literary theory, cannot be discounted.

The burgeoning of science studies is encouraging, especially the kind developed by Bruno Latour (see also Smith 1997, 1988; Labinger and Collins 2002). He points out that both realism and relativism agree that reference to an absolute, universal (and therefore disenchanting) yardstick is essential, only differing in that the former hold that it is attainable, with it full knowledge; and the latter that it isn't, and therefore no knowledge. What Latour calls relationism, in contrast, is all about relations: practices, instruments, documents and translations. This focus is based on the realization that a Culture bracketed off from Nature is an impossible artefact, as is the reverse. 'There are only natures-cultures, and these offer the only possible basis for comparison.' Natures-cultures, subject-objects, local-globals – these are the appropriate *focii* of analysis. And they are constituted by networks, which themselves 'are simultaneously real, like nature; narrated, like discourse; and collective, like society' (Latour 1993: 104, 6). There are no essences, then, but a process: one which partakes of all of these, and which produces both humans and nonhumans – a distinction which is therefore not fundamental. This resonates promisingly with the experience of divination, in which a process of interpretation is not produced *by* humans but takes place in a way that unites and transcends, or subverts, the modernist divide between the human/cultural (e.g. the astrologer) and the nonhuman/natural (e.g. the planets). It should also remind us of the point made earlier about truth as active and even, albeit in a nonhuman way, sentient or intelligent (see also Viveiros de Castro 1998). Finally – and this is where Latour shows the way when Weberian pessimism cannot – he reminds us that (in the words of one his titles) we have never *been* modern, in the way the modernists would have us believe. This realization points to how (in ways that remain to be articulated) enchantment has survived.

Analytical psychology and its 'post-Jungianism' offshoots also have something to offer here. Tantalizingly, Jung (1966: 56, 55) realized that 'astrology represents the sum of all the psychological knowledge of antiquity', and that in the experience of 'the divinatory power of the *I Ching* . . . we have here an Archimedean point from which our Western attitude of mind could be lifted off its foundations'; but he apparently failed to connect the two. The principal such foundation is, of course, just the subject/object split instituted by monist rationalism-realism, and the attendant disenchantment – just what not only the *I Ching* but also astrology, properly understood, has the potential not only to reveal but in practice to undermine. And the schools of depth-psychological astrology (developed by Liz Greene) and archetypal psychology (whose chief exponent has been James Hillman) facilitate such a recognition through their emphasis on metaphor, in particular that of myth, as the irreducible language of psychic reality. The emphasis on soul as where we actually live – embodied, embedded, inherently relational, contingent, messy and incomplete – as distinct from the impossible dreams of either pure spirit or pure matter – is a healing one (see for example Greene 1984; Hillman 1983, 1997). But that will also depend on a willingness, as already discussed, to leave behind Jung's own psychological monism behind.

Finally, the slow mutual absorption and adaptation between Buddhism and the West is starting to bring to our awareness the oldest and almost certainly most sophisticated critique of essentialism, whether spiritual or material, of all: that of the philosopher Nagarjuna (second and third centuries), based on the concepts of *anatman* (nonself), *sunyata* (emptiness) and *pratitya samutpada* (co-dependent origination) (see Radha 1981). Undoubtedly such an awareness would, at the least, help make possible a more profound understanding of divination.

The liberating and fruitful potential of all this, however, depends on the extent to which particular intellectual practitioners, whatever the name and provenance of their discipline, are able to shake off its and their own scientistic, secularist and anthropocentric prejudices; and the latter run deep. As Charles Darwin once noted, 'Great is the power of steady misrepresentation'; and few subjects have been so long and consistently misrepresented, in keeping with those prejudices, as divination, astrological or otherwise. Change will not occur overnight, and it will encounter serious resistance along the way.

The Judder Effect

In a brilliant paper, Eduardo Viveiros de Castro (1998) has contrasted the radically different cosmo-philosophical premises of 'Western' and Amerindian thought. Not its least benefit is to reveal the sheer contingency of our most matter-of-fact, common-sense assumptions.

Viveiros de Castro discusses what constitutes a threateningly uncanny situation for an Amerindian. This invites the question, what is the corresponding situation (although not an exact structural equivalent) which we in the 'West' find disturbing, disorienting, 'spooky': in short, what the astrologer Pat Blackett, together with Maggie Hyde (2001) – describing the sort of unpleasant jar/shudder that can shake someone who experiences astrology and other forms of divination actually working – has called 'the Judder Effect'? It seems to us that it is something like this: an encounter between a 'normal', sensible, educated person and something which is normally simply a physical object or set of objects – a piece of paper, mapping the positions of the planets (themselves reassuringly 'physical'); a book opened to a page determined by the throw of more objects called coins; a spread of cards – which, however, then reveals itself as a subjectivity which 'speaks' to him or her.

Lévy-Bruhl (1975: 56) pointed out the usual 'solution':

> before the unintelligibility, at least, relative, of the mystical world, where the most extraordinary and inexplicable transformations occur, where the irregularity of pheno-mena appears as natural as their regularity, our mind experiences discomfort, confusion and perplexity: what is a world which is not rational and intelligible? And it gets out of it by saying: it is a world which is not real (imaginary, arbitrary, fabulous, like fairy stories) . . .[9]

This is the easy way out that Jung, to his eternal credit and our benefit, never took. In fact, he wrestled with this issue, framed as 'synchronicity', his entire working life, and never satisfactorily resolved it. In a letter to a colleague in 1957, he remarked that 'I well understand that you prefer to emphasize . . . the psycho-logical angle, but I must say that I am equally interested, at times even more so, in the metaphysical aspect of the phenomena, and in the question: how does it come that even inanimate objects are capable of behaving as if they were acquainted with my thoughts?' (Jung 1976: 344, and see Hyde 1992; Main 1997).

Now, someone who has such an experience is characteristically in a strange and delicate position. On the one hand, he has learned to consider himself, too, as essentially an objective physical body in spacetime: in short, an 'it'. But there is a ghost in the machine: his body is apparently inhabited by a subjective self, even though the authorities reassure him that this too will soon be explicable as merely the epiphenomenal effect of a brain. On the other hand, however, he has almost certainly absorbed the lesson that human beings have been telling themselves, in varying forms, for the past several millennia: that they alone are subjects, in the company solely of other humans and disembodied spirits. (Science has banished the latter, of course, en route to attempting to get rid of human subjectivity too.)

The world-view of most people in the 'West' today is a peculiar and unstable muddle of these two positions. But what concerns us here is that in *either* case, our hypothetical person is vulnerable to being overwhelmed by what both of them rule out of court: the experience of objects turning out to be also subjects, for example the planets, coins, book or cards knowing and communicating something – and not just anything, either, but something intimately personal. In the process of that shared knowing, he becomes a subject too, but not in the customarily accepted way; rather, one in a world of nonhuman subjects (and therefore also perspectives). And it's too late to resist, because in the moment of recognizing and responding (however involuntarily) to the shared subjectivity of the hitherto safely objective world, it has *already happened*; so subsequent resistance can only take the form of denial and damage limitation. All in all, to the extent this person, either by tempera-ment or training, subscribes to the dominant or hegemonic ideology – and not surprisingly, a big part of educational institutionalization involves inculcating just that – such an experience is a deeply uncomfortable one.

Of course, even if this is a fair description of one aspect of that ideology, it would be reductionist and patronizing to suggest that it is true of virtually every-one. It is certainly possible to learn to tolerate and appreciate the experience described above, and there are even those for whom it is a precious reminder of living in a world which, despite everything that has been done to it, is still enchanted.

The same polarity is reflected in another notorious part of Cartesian ideology, namely the fiction (so convenient for the food and pharmaceutical industries) that other animals too are really just objects: organic machines, in effect. To the extent this idea has been accepted, directly encountering nonhuman animal subjectivity, as distinct from sentimentality about animals, can also be unsettling. For others, however, that encounter too is a major source of cheer and relief in a relentlessly objectivized world.

Let us be quite clear: we are not suggesting, as a careless or hostile reader might suppose, that stellar matter, paper or coins can think (in just the way we think, that is). Rather they, like us, participate in what Bateson called 'the larger interactive system' which is itself intelligence, and pervades everything, as Iamblichus and Chu Hsi also recognized, in appropriate ways and extents. (Which is why, being the basis of understanding, it is not fully or finally understandable, let alone specifiable.) How could the appropriate response to this possibly be to predict 'the' future, or in Bateson's example, to 'make "it" rain'?

This brings us back to the observation (by Morrison, among others) regarding ancient divination: its point was not to foretell but to reveal a truth in and of the present, in a way that affirms shared membership in an inexhaustibly mysterious world. Nor is this attitude confined to the past; in Lama Chime Radha's contribu-tion on Tibetan Buddhist divination to the same collection, *Oracles and Divination*, his awareness (alone among the other scholars) of working within a *living* tradition is striking, and lends additional weight to his affirmation (1981: 24) that '[the] search is not merely for a way of foretelling specific events, but for the expression of an underlying world order, embracing both natural and supernatural realities'.

In cases of potential metaphysical dissonance in the presence of divination, who then is our 'Western' shaman? There doesn't seem to be a precise professional equivalent, but certainly there is a basic requirement for negotiating, let alone enjoying, such liminal changes of perspective, namely what Keats (1995: 49) called 'negative capability': that is, 'capable of being in uncertainties, mysteries, doubts, without any irritable reaching after fact and reason'. (Contrast scientism: an 'irritable reaching after fact and reason' turned into an entire world-view.) That ability, in turn, is central to the cunning wisdom of *metis*, so anyone who can think or act metically would not be so unsettled. And certain professions, at their best, involve using metic intelligence to help others not so skilled: counsellors, psychotherapists and psychoanalysts, spiritual (although not necessarily religious) advisors . . . and astrologers.

Astrology as Ecology

As has been suggested (after Weber), the contemporary hegemony of scientism is only the latest, albeit most powerful, phase of disenchantment. Its coincidence with ecological crisis, overwhelmingly human-caused, is also significant. The millennia-long emphasis on, and conflation of, the transcendental, the real, the objective and the true has now perhaps reached its apogee; and in this context, the voices of sanity are those reminding us that all our values and experiences 'are essentially the result of a cooperation of man and non-human nature: the universe would not contain them, were it not for our perceptual-creative efforts, and were it not equally for the contribution of the non-human world that both sustains and sets limits to our lives . . . There is no wholly-other paradise from which we are excluded; the only transcendence that can be real to us is an "immanent" one' (Hepburn 1984: 181–2). More pointedly, as Kane (1994: 50) puts it, 'all the work that various peoples have done – all the work that peoples must do – to live with the Earth on the Earth's terms is pre-empted by the dream of transcendence'.

That dream has affected astrology too – and not surprisingly, since its province, after all, embraces the cosmic. But the problem corresponds to the extent that the cosmic *alone* is defined as its concern, and the attempt made to eliminate the crucial element of human participation. Since that element was obviously irreducibly integral to divination, divinatory astrology – paradigmatically horary astrology – earned the opprobrium of ambitious astrologers as much as anyone else, if not more so: 'the vilest rubbish imaginable', and 'the curse of the science and the ruin of the astrologer', in the Theosophist astrologer Alan Leo's words, and in those of his bitter opponent, the 'scientific' astrologer A.J. Pearce, 'absurd and unwarrantable'.[10] Ptolemy's Aristotelian system, so influential for so long, arguably succeeded in preserving the astrological tradition as such in a hostile milieu (no small feat); but it also unwittingly prepared the way for the even more ruthless systematization of modern science, which has no need of astrology whatsoever. So astrologers need reminding that any pretences on their part to systematic or objective (let alone scientific) truth, as distinct from divinatory (but not therefore merely 'subjective') truth, only legitimizes the authority of those who would like to see them jailed for fraud.

As a route to short-term power and status, however, the transcendental/objectivist strategy has been so successful (in its own terms) that it presents a constant temptation; and the accompanying mindset can be very hard to shake, when it has become an entrenched mental habit. For example, in an obvious, almost banal sense, the planets and stars are natural objects. However, the meaning of 'natural' is itself not self-evident but historically contingent, having resulted from a lengthy and complex process of intellectual struggle. In terms of the modern scientific sense of 'natural', the heavenly bodies have by now been so thoroughly naturalized as purely material and lifeless bodies moving mechanically through space – in other words, disenchanted – that it is difficult to recapture the sense in which they have been 'natural' for most of astrology's history: a sense that does not preclude the spiritual.

Divination both facilitates and (to work) requires a recovery of that unity. Kane (1994: 37, 41, 39) usefully points to 'the knowledge of pattern' – also very much Bateson's concern – as 'the beginning of every practical wisdom.' And 'Nature is full of these patterns (information theorists call them "redundancies") which invite practical divination.' But this is no mere primitive proto-science, because such wisdom is not abstract but metic; it is intimately related to place; and its ultimate repository is myth. To quote Lama Radha (1981: 25) again:

> As one works with the symbolism and penetrates more deeply into its meaning, one learns by its aid to arrive at an integrated view of the world, to see the one in the many, the highest in the lowest, the infinitely great in what is infintesimally small, and to recognise behind all phenomena the unifying Emptiness which is void of all self-qualities and yet the creative source of all existence and relativities. In doing so one develops an intuitive insight into the workings of the world of nature, which reflect these universal principles, and that insight is the basis of the art of divination.

There is another blind-spot to which astrologers also seem prone. A horoscope for anyone or anything on Earth involves, by definition, by a division of space proceeding from the intersection of the celestial equator (extending out from the Earth's equator) and the ecliptic (the path the Earth travels around the Sun); to put it another way, it is a map of the heavens in relation to a particular place on Earth as well as moment of time. In other words, *without* the Earth there could be no astrology, at least as we know it. Yet this fact is heavily obscured both by the attention paid to the cosmic alone, and by an exclusive focus on 'objective' time.

The needed correction is to realize that what astrology offers, uniquely in its way – and this is its specificity with respect to enchantment – is wonder at partaking of an intrinisically meaningful place and moment on Earth that specifically *includes* the cosmos, especially the phenomenological cosmos (Sun and Moon, visible planets and stars), but also oneself, right down to the precise issue or concern that initiated the inquiry. It is thus an experience at once chthonic, cosmic and intimately personal: 'drawing down the Moon' indeed! As the neo-Confucian philosopher

Chang Tsai put it, 'Heaven is my father and Earth is my mother, and even such a small creature as I find an intimate place in their midst.'

He continues, 'Therefore that which fills the universe I regard as my body, and that which directs the universe I consider as my nature' (Chan 1963: 497). The recovery of such a sensibility, whether personal or collective, amounts to a recovery of sanity from the cosmic psychodrama of alienated modernity as famously voiced by Pascal: 'Le silence éternel de ces espaces infinis m'effrais.' Certainly, as Russell Hoban (1992: 139) put it, 'we've tried making both things and people *It*, and we've seen the results'. Anything that makes it possible to experience the cosmos as a *Thou*, as astrology potentially does, should therefore be welcomed, and at least given a chance.

In this context, it is encouraging that divinatory astrology is ecological in the broadest and truest sense: it partakes of an inexhaustible and therefore ultimately mysterious network of relationships and interdependencies; you are necessarily *in* it and *of* it. And this 'it' is – ultimately not just is like, but *is* – the Earth itself, a wild and, in effect, infinitely multiplicitous place. By contrast, science as scientism is inherently anti-ecological; the putative view is *of* the Earth, and 'it' is reduced to whatever will stay still, so to speak, because as Blake saw, it is already dead: hence the animate 'as inanimate' (cf. Abram 1996).

Notice that this place includes the cosmos, *not* the other way around. Significantly, Dawkins's scientism would have us believe the contrary: following the Abrahamic off-planet God, the naturalized cosmos includes the place as merely an aspect of space; and since the former is so vast, 'here' recedes into absolute insignificance . . . thus preparing the way for the ultimate scientific triumph, which is also its ultimate hypocrisy, of truth as the view from nowhere. An astrological map is one *of* the sky-space at a particular time; but that is only a ritual prerequisite to its heart: an experience of a place (not space) and moment (not time) that is animate, sacred, intelligent and whole. It includes 'subject', 'object', 'spiritual', 'material', 'person', 'Earth', 'cosmos' and indefinitely more besides. So not the least of astrology's potential services is to remind us that our home ('eco') has a cosmic dimension; and conversely, that the cosmos can, after all, be home.

Notes

1. But not, significantly, Iamblichus.
2. Cf. Hoban 1992: 138 – 'Why cannot any god die? Because gods do not replace one another.'

3. Cf. Greene (1984: 271), who argues that the connection between the soul and fate is mythic, and 'Myths, as we have seen, cross the boundaries between "inner" and "outer", and manifest on both levels.'

4. Cornelius (2001) has conceptualized this contrast in terms of 'speculative' and 'realized' interpretation.

5. See Scott 1998, for some of its effects in the twentieth century.

6. Cf. Barbara Herrnstein Smith's (1988: 156) point that even though the 'relativist' hears his own point that 'truth' is not merely a function of 'truth-value' as a negative one, 'the realist will hear it as equivalent to a positive and positively appalling point, namely that just someone's finding something good enough to believe is enough to *make* it "true" *in the realist/objectivist sense*'.

7. A point also made by Wittgenstein concerning the fact that the world *is*.

8. Cf. what the superb hypnotherapist Milton Erikson is supposed to have said about the NLP programme based on his work: 'They think they have me in a nutshell, but all they have is the shell.'

9. He continued, 'the philosopher can be tempted (and history shows that he has been and that he has usually succumbed to the temptation) to consider this rationality of the world which our science establishes and verifies, as reasonable in itself, as carrying in itself the reason of its legitimacy . . . [But] this intelligibility of the sensible world, ordered and ruled by science, is itself for ever unintelligible'.

10. From *Modern Astrology* (1896) 2(7): 434–7; quoted in Curry 1992: 165. (The second part of the quotation is actually entirely in the upper case.)

-10-

Minding the Heavens

The astronomy of the solar system and the nightly risings and settings of the stars were understood better by these [Mesolithic] ancestors of modern Europeans than by anyone else up to the time of Kepler . . . we are dealing with an extremely sophisticated culture that is quite unlike our present one. This scares many people. (Robin Heath, in Phillipson 2000)

In *Unweaving the Rainbow*, Richard Dawkins takes to task those poets such as Keats and Blake who have denigrated the scientific project, and attempts to reconcile the human experience of wonder and awe in face of such visually striking phenomena as the rainbow with Newton's account in terms of a measurable spectrum of light-waves impacting the human eye and brain. But there is more to this than meets the eye – as it were. For one thing, Newton's division of the visual spectrum into seven colours has no basis in the very material reality he assumes and purports to explicate, but is founded in the mystical significance of the number 'seven', itself part of a much earlier, pre-scientific attempt by ancient thinkers to theorize the universe: a pre-existent proto-science through which humans in times long past interpreted to themselves the majestic pageant of Nature.

This book adopts a different strategy from that of Dawkins: for us, the scientific 'grand narrative' to which Dawkins and his like are committed has lost its credibility in the fragmentation of consciousness characteristic of the postmodern condition. Here the scientific project, for all its grandeur and austere beauty, is just one of a plurality of mythological narratives competing for our allegiance.[1] Theoretically, we take our cue from the phenomenological tradition in European philosophy which, since the early twentieth-century work of Edmund Husserl, has pursued an approach to knowledge diametrically opposite to the reductionist and objectivist goal of mainstream Western science. Instead of stripping away the sensuous, body-based perception in pursuit of Galilean abstraction, phenomenology moves in the contrary direction, seeking the primary, corporeal knowing that necessarily precedes all conceptual accretions, including that most elaborated and prestigious ideological construction that is post-Enlightenment science.

Husserl and his innovative expositor Maurice Merleau-Ponty are the thinkers who have most advanced our understanding of the necessarily *embodied* nature of human consciousness, the primacy of bodily perception in constituting our awareness of ourselves as beings-in-a-world, a world of which, as sentient, physical entities, we are inextricably a part.

This embodied consciousness, Husserl also insisted, was not confined within the individual but had a collective nature, arising from the fact that we, as body-based experiencing subjects, are from the beginning in relation with a plurality of other experiencing subjects. Husserl gave the name of 'intersubjectivity' to this plural world of human consciousness. Yet there is in this multiform consciousness always a relation of selfhood and otherness, inherent in the fact that, in the words of David Abram in his marvellous *The Spell of the Sensuous*:

> While one's own body is experienced, as it were, only from within, these other bodies are experienced from outside; one can vary one's distance from these bodies and can move around them, while this is impossible in relation to one's own body. (1996: 37)

Husserl also gave the German name *Lebenswelt*, or 'life-world', to the particular, culturally influenced form assumed by any local grouping of embodied inter-subjectivities, while insisting on the fundamental rootedness of all human – and non-human – life-worlds in and on the Earth. It was this insistence on the primacy, at the base of all life-worlds, of the all-mothering Earth that led Husserl to write of 'the overthrow of the Copernican Theory', affirming that 'the original ark, earth, does not move' (McCormick and Elliston 1981: 230). For such is indeed our phenomenal experience, of an absolutely stable, fixed earth beneath our feet, the still centre round which sun and moon and the whole starry firmament revolve. So solid is this experience of earthly stability that even hard-nosed astronomers routinely speak of the sun 'rising' and 'setting'.

So there is a parallelism, indeed a formal homology, between our experience of singular embodiment and the presence of other embodied subjectivities, and our awareness of being 'Earthed', as it were, in relation to the plurality of celestial objects. Moreover our bodies, that our current cultural formation causes us to envisage as isolated, bounded entities, are in fact open systems that complete themselves only in interchange with the immensely larger body of the environing earth. In Abram's words:

> The breathing, sensing body draws its sustenance and its very substance from the soils, plants, and elements that surround it; it continually contributes itself, in turn, to the air, to the composting earth, to the nourishment of insects and oak trees and squirrels, ceaselessly spreading out of itself as well as breathing the world into itself, so that it is very difficult to discern, at any moment, precisely where this living body begins and where it ends. (1996: 46–7)

This natural 'conversation', as it were, between our human bodies and the Earth-body of the planet is the underlying process that births, nourishes and inspires all that is mental, psychic and spiritual in our human nature. Our perception of world and universe is at the very beginning, as Merleau-Ponty has already assured us (Merleau-Ponty 1962), a product of our sensory engagement with Nature. Contrary to a millennial Western tradition running from Plato through Descartes:

> The human mind is not some otherworldly essence that comes to house itself inside our physiology. Rather, it is instilled and provoked by the sensorial field itself, induced by the tensions and participations between the human body and the animate earth. (Abram 1997: 262)

Abram shows how the development of phonetic writing in ancient Greece and the growth of our literate civilization has produced the illusion of being separate from the natural world of plants and animals, rivers and seas, winds and clouds and stars; and he also shows, drawing on the insights of phenomenology, how – beneath this literacy-induced illusion that has turned what once was alive and teeming with spirit and intelligence into a vast but mindless machine – our primary perception of the world as animate still remains at a subconscious level:

> Direct, prereflective perception is inherently synaesthetic, participatory, and animistic, disclosing the things and elements that surround us not as inert objects but as expressive subjects, entities, powers, potencies. (ibid., 130)

Abram argues that the advent of phonetic literacy has diverted our animistic consciousness from the world of nature to the written word, which now 'enchants' us in the way that the natural world once did. His argument is plausible and intuitively convincing, subversively using the very medium of the world's disen-chantment, the written word, to invite us back to the lost paradise.

An Ideological Revolution

Where does astrology fit into this deepening inquiry into human potential, into the nature of 'mind'? In our quest for understanding of what astrology precisely *is*, as Curry also frames the question, we most need to discover what this 'dialogue with divinity' posited by postmodern astrologers as the distinctive sign of their craft actually means. That is why we begin by turning, as Abram also does, to the evidence provided by sensitive ethnographers of pre-literate, 'tribal' cultures around the world. Tylor, one of the first to see that the evidence on such peoples' conscious-ness of their environment revealed a seemingly universal apprehension of human interaction with non-human intelligence, used the term 'animism' to denote this curious propensity of 'primitive' humankind. This evidence suggests that there is indeed, as the much maligned Lucien Lévy-Bruhl also suggested, a way of thinking among all these peoples, notwithstanding local, culture-specific variations, that marks them as qualitatively different from the rational inhabitants of urban industrial society. In times past this underlying, basic difference was taken to be a sign of intellectual inferiority, as Tylor assumed, and as the earlier Lévy-Bruhl seemed to imply with his term 'prelogical'.[2]

There is another highly relevant source of information on our topic, one that was not available to Merleau-Ponty and of which Abram seems unaware, and that is the wealth of data obtained comparatively recently by psychologists working with newly born human infants, beings of our own species as yet uninfluenced by the preconceptions of industrial civilization.

What has been discovered in this department of psychology amounts to an ideological revolution of the first magnitude, one as yet hardly acknowledged outside the boundaries of this sub-discipline, but which is of the first importance for the current inquiry. I say 'revolution' because what has been discovered threatens to demolish some of the most deeply ingrained assumptions of our culture on the supposed duality of body and mind, flesh and spirit, individual and society.

The hard laboratory evidence shows that the 'intersubjectivity' posited by Husserl and Merleau-Ponty is no socially induced state of mind in *Homo sapiens*, but is an innate, genetically programmed attribute of our species, present in infant consciousness from the very moment of birth, if not before. Until the paradigm-busting work of Edinburgh University psychologists Colwyn Trevarthen and T.G.R. Bower in the 1970s, it was assumed that the neonate (newborn) human mind was a *tabula rasa* fit to be moulded and imprinted by the environing society and culture, the world the newborn entered perceived by it as 'a blooming, buzzing confusion', in the famous phrase of William James. Merleau-Ponty himself subscribed to this now exploded view, speaking of neonate consciousness as 'the chaos in which I am submerged' (1964: 118).[3]

The Dialogical Animal

That simple picture of human consciousness was shattered by the observation that newly born infants regularly interacted with those around them, imitating their facial expressions with an immediacy that suggested the infant felt itself, in Bower's words, 'to be a member of the human race right from the start' (1977: 32). Bower goes on to consider the 'plain and incredible fact' that newborn babies engage in what he calls 'interactional synchrony', making miniscule bodily movements in exact imitation of the phonemic units of speech of any nearby human. This extraordinary 'dance' is almost imperceptible to ordinary vision, but became noticeable when high-speed cinematographic film of the infants was subjected to close analysis. 'This points to an astonishing ability to analyse the flow of sound in any language into its component parts', Bower comments, adding that '[t]he behavior also shows a predisposition to behave in a social manner, to *interact* with other humans, rather than simply to react to them' (ibid.: 33). And he concludes:

> . . . the data indicates that the newborn . . . thinks he [*sic*] is a human being and has a great many social responses directed towards other human beings. (ibid.: 27–8)

The implications of these findings, which are measurable and replicable in accordance with the exacting standards of modern science, are truly astounding. A few moments' thought should convince most people that the phenomenal world we inhabit is immensely richer than the tasteless, colourless, soundless and fleshless mechanism projected by modern science. But it takes something of a leap of faith for a modern urbanized human to accept the reality of Husserl's apprehension that we are all psychically connected, not only to one another, but also to the universe. 'It sounds a nice idea, and wouldn't it be great if it turned out to be true?', is the feeling Husserl's prime insight tends to evoke. Well, we now have solid evidence to support that daring hypothesis, in the revelation of what Trevarthen has called an 'innate intersubjectivity' (Trevarthen and Logotheti 1989) inscribed in our genetic constitution as human beings. We are born, it seems, with a drive to engage in dialogue with what is around us. How else to interpret the astonishing fact that infants only hours old respond to the phonemic units of meaning in any spoken language, a meaning they sense and respond to with their entire, albeit tiny, bodies? Yes, we Earthpeople (the root meaning of the word 'human') are designed to communicate, in the transitive sense of sharing with others, enjoying in common, as the *OED* has it. Yet even the innovative thought of Husserl's devoted disciple Maurice Merleau-Ponty failed to grasp the radical essentiality of the human propensity for dialogue. This fact emerges from an important recent contribution by two psychologists, Shaun Gallagher and Andrew Meltzoff (1996). Drawing on recent studies of infant perception and self-awareness, Gallagher and Meltzoff argue that a firmly defined sense of selfhood and otherness is innate in human beings and not, as Merleau-Ponty had assumed on the basis of then current theory, a product of a developmental process. Similarly, these authorities suggest, the newborn comes equipped with awareness of an articulated bodily schema, whereas Merleau-Ponty supposed such a corporeal sense to emerge during post-natal life. Most importantly, Gallagher and Meltzoff are able to conclude that the human infant emerges into the world with an already formulated sense of self, and, most crucially for the argument being developed here, of relation between self and other:

> The experiential connection between self and other is operative from birth, and is not, as Merleau-Ponty contends, a syncretic confusion. At the very least, for the newborn

infant there is a rudimentary differentiation between self and non-self, so that one's earliest experiences include a sense of self and of others. (1996: 229)

Participation with Divinity

This dialogical animal, who comes into the world dancing in response to language (cf. Bower 1975), the peculiar propensity for dialogue inscribed in its genes, what do its senses tell it about the world? That everything is instinct with life, spirit, intelligence, and is therefore open to conversation. The innate impulsion to dialogue with a multiverse of intelligent beings, starting with fellow humans and including every animal and plant, every rock and river and ocean; also the clouds in the sky, winds and storms and rain, and all the luminous inhabitants of the starry vault. For *this* animal, all that *is*, is in some sense alive.

This dialogical species is uniquely endowed with the power to put itself empathetically in the place of the other, to sense the other's very being, whether human, animal or divine. This power is our birthright, our natural heritage, our destiny, and it confers participation with divinity in the work of creation. To be sure, this precious heritage has been millennially denied and suppressed in urban European society, first by official Christianity and latterly by the new, dominating priesthood of scientific rationalism. Only in rural areas and in the preliterate 'tribal' cultures of the non-European world do such powers fleetingly survive, usually in secret.

All the evidence suggests that prehistoric human beings were abundantly in possession of the dialogical faculty, their insightful vision embracing the entire natural environment, earthly and celestial. As the modernist painter Joan Miró commented, referring to the marvellous Palaeolithic cave paintings of the Dordogne, especially Lascaux, 'la peinture est en décadence depuis l'âge des cavernes' ('painting has declined since the age of the caves') (Miró 1977).

How did our ancient ancestors speak to one another of this endless conversation with Nature? Certainly they composed stories, in which the various humanly perceived powers in the world, among them the heavenly bodies, appeared as actors. Those celestial entities we now call planets, each with its characteristic pattern of rhythmic movement across the over-arching vault, played prominent roles, as did the moon and the sun and the world-girdling constellations. Studies of storytelling in oral cultures during the last century have dispelled the false idea that such tales are little more than 'primitive' versions of written texts. Unlike the fixed, singularly authored products of literate culture, orally transmitted 'traditional' stories are both anonymous and collective. Ancestral creations of the group, they emerge into the present through the active, joint participation of the teller and his or her audience. There is a special immediacy and spontaneity in this act of collective creation and re-creation, summed up in the words of the folklorist Albert

Lord: 'For the oral poet the moment of composition is the performance . . . an oral poem is not composed *for* but *in* performance' (1960: 13).

Picture a group of humans sitting round a fire and gazing at one or other of the unchanging constellations decorating the night sky, while one of their number tells, or sings, its story. Imagine this scene occurring numberless times through hundreds of thousands, even millions, of years. Was this the making of what we now think of as the human mind? Imagine the meaningful shapes of the constellations triggering creativity in these beings, igniting the charged moment of dialogical communion with supra-human intelligence that is the essence of all art, all religion. The 'cosmic' myths that have come down to us from remote prehistory are the outcome of such moments of human communion with divinity.

And what is the 'divine'? Divinity is that which is supremely *other*, the highest object and inspiration of dialogue and dialogical knowing. Because our human ideas of hierarchy are meaningless on a cosmic scale and most likely did not exist anyway for *Homo sapiens* before history, a terrestrial animal and a celestial god or goddess could equally serve as emblems of divine otherness (remember Lascaux!). And of course the word 'zodiac', the belt of astrological signs through which the sun, moon and visible planets perform their annual apparent movements, literally means 'path of animals'.

Driven by the dialogical imperative to engage even with the intangible majesty of the starry heavens, humankind narrated the world into existence from the solid, nurturing ground of Mother Earth. Contemplating the multiplicitous wonders of the firmament above while simultaneously aware of the vast invisibility beneath, realm of the ancestors and spirit animals, *Homo sapiens* constructed its own mind as both mirror and moulder of a living, mindful universe.[4] All we now see and know issues from that age-long and unending creative dialogue, even the grand story of modern science, as Husserl insisted.

Notes

1. In the words of Zygmunt Bauman, 'Postmodernity is marked by a view of the human world as irreducibly and irrevocably pluralistic, split into a multitude of sovereign units and sites of authority, with no horizontal or vertical order, either in actuality or in potency . . . the postmodern worldview entails the dissipation of objectivity'. *Intimations of Postmodernity*, London: Routledge (1992), 35.
2. It should be remembered that Lévy-Bruhl eventually withdrew the term 'pre-logical', with its pejorative implications, in his posthumously published *Carnets*.

3. Curiously, Professor Susan Greenfield, a well-known neuroscientist with a doggedly materialist agenda, appears unaware of this research when she avows her belief in the exploded *tabula rasa* theory of neonate consciousness in her popularizing work *Journey to the Centers of the Mind* (1995). A similar misplaced adherence to outmoded theory seems to underly Professor Richard Dawkins's assumptions on children's alleged gullibility' and 'credulity' in *Unweaving the Rainbow* (1998), 138ff. For exactly contrary evidence and argument see Toren 1993.

4. Astrologer Bernadette Brady suggests that 'each human mind is its own starry sky – we do have our circumpolar stars, we do have the centre of our mind, and we seek it just like the Pole Star; we seek the place that everything else orbits around . . . inside here is exactly the same as outside there' (in Phillipson 2000: 16). A similar model of the human mind as a mirror of the celestial firmament was proposed by the Italian Renaissance philosopher Marsilio Ficino (see Moore 1982).

–11–

Conversing with the Stars

I know the names of the stars from north to south . . . I was in the firmament with
Mary Magdalene . . .

> Taliesin, shamanic bard of Wales, sixth century CE

To the minds of the lower races it seems that all nature is possessed, pervaded,
crowded, with spiritual beings.

> E.B. Tylor, *Primitive Culture*

We have considered in Chapter 10 how the unending conversation that is mythical
narrative has constructed the universe we experience today. Unsurprisingly, we
find a common pattern recurring in pre-scientific descriptions of the cosmos as
perceived in diverse cultures around the world. The basic architecture is usually
tripartite, consisting of an upper world identified with the sky, a middle world of
mundane reality, and an invisible lower world, sensed to exist beneath our feet. We
should notice here an underlying harmony, indeed a symmetry, between our bodily
architecture and the perceived form of the cosmos. What is most and peculiarly
apparent to members of our species, by reason of our uniquely upright, bipedal
posture, is the dividing line of the horizon, defining the contrasting spheres of
upper and lower visible worlds. That dividing line intersects the verticality of our
characteristic stationary and locomotive modes, our possession of naturally-based
axial coordinates defining a cosmic space that is the dwelling place of Mind, a
mind that is neither wholly human nor wholly non-human, being formed out of
continuing dialogue between human and Other. Directly contrary to the bleak
apprehension of mechanistic and reductionist science, for which, in the chilling
words of one of its most brilliant exponents, 'man . . . is alone in the universe's
unfeeling immensity' (Monod 1997: 180), the fundamental affinity of humankind
and cosmos has been conceptualized in strikingly similar terms by numerous
unrelated pre-scientific cultures and civilizations around the world. Thus, the Hopi
Native Americans of Arizona hold that:

> The living body of man and the living body of earth were constructed in the same way.
> Through each ran an axis, man's axis being the backbone, the vertebral column, which
> controlled the equilibrium of his movements and his functions. Along this axis were

several vibratory centers which echoed the primordial sound of life throughout the universe. (Waters 1963: 11)

The Dogon people of Mali in West Africa similarly speak of the energetic force said to pervade the universe as 'vibrations'. Humankind and universe are one, according to the Dogon, because everything is formed through the union of opposites, an idea expressed in the common African notion of cosmic twinship.[1] The related Bambara people, like the Hopi, see the vertebral column of the human body as 'the biological and ontological axis' of the human person. Opposed but complementary principles of masculinity and femininity are said to be diffused through the body of each person, to effect a balance (Dieterlen 1951).

The concept of the embodied human person as participating in a universal energy field is highly developed in the thought of classical India, where the pervasive energy principle is called *prana*. As with the Hopi, the spine is conceived as the axis of a set of vibrational centres or vortices, called *chakras*, and concerned with a wide range of psychic, corporeal and social modes by which human beings relate to the world and the universe (cf. Eliade 1958: 236–44). Ancient China developed an analogous cosmology, in which the embodied human person was seen as a subsystem linked to the grand system of the universe through participation in an all-pervasive energy flow called *ch'i*. This force assumed balanced and complementary positive and negative forms, called *Yin* and *Yang*. In the human body these forms were predominantly associated with the right and left sides, respectively (Mann 1973: 46). A remarkably similar doctrine is to be found in esoteric Judaism, where there is a close correspondence between the centres called *Sefiroth*, said to be aligned along the spinal axis, and the Sanskritic model of the *chakras*. The correspondence extends to the identification of lateral forces associated with the Kabbalistic *Sefiroth* and expressing male and female, positive and negative, energy charges. The latter are called respectively *Ida* (positive) and *Pingala* (negative) in the Sanskritic system, and *Hokhmah* (masculine or sun side) and *Binah* (feminine or moon side) in the Kabbalah (cf. Poncé 1973: 150–7). These ideas also resemble the Native American concepts of the positive *tonal*, associated with the right side of the body, and the negative *nagual*, associated with the left (cf. Castaneda 1974: 147 ff.) Where Hopi cosmology recognizes five energy vortices along the spinal axis, the Sanskritic and Kabbalistic systems both name seven; the Inka (Inca) adepts identify an additional two vortices, aligned with the spinal array but outside the body, relating the person to the cosmos (Villoldo 2000: 68).

A Layered Structure

These cosmic models from around the globe, put together by nameless theoreticians long before the death of God and disenchantment of the world, have an obvious affinity to one another. That is because they are conceptual constructs appropriate to our human physiology and ontology as a bipedal species possessing bodies distinguished by bilateral symmetry and sexual duality. For a civilization of super-intelligent moles, or octopi, the universe would no doubt appear, and be, radically different from the one we 'know'.

There is a further, and deeper, reason why these pre-scientific world-pictures seem so strangely, indeed hauntingly, familiar and reassuring to so many people today. For countless ages we as a species, and other beings who lived before us in linear time, participated in the creation of the living, conscious universe we still subliminally experience beneath the 'unfeeling immensity' of the soulless machine depicted by materialist and objectivist science. Moreover, as already mentioned, indigenous models of this pre-scientific universe around the world invariably depict it as having a layered structure, most commonly a tripartite division between upper, middle and lower worlds. These three – occasionally more – worlds are always pictured as linked together and accessible through a central channel or pillar, the *axis mundi* or world axis. In some cultures this mediating axis has the form of a ladder, a vine or rope or a chain of arrows, as in the Americas; of a sacred mountain, as in Hindu, Iranian and Babylonian cosmology; of the multi-semantic Rainbow Serpent as in Australia, of the central pole of the traditional tent as in Siberia. Often this central axis, cosmic analogue of the human vertebral column, is called the Tree of Life, as in the Judaic Kabbalah or the cosmic tree Ygdrassil of Norse mythology. In the words of anthropologist Joan Halifax:

> It is this tree with its life-giving waters that binds all realms together. The roots of the World Tree penetrate the depths of the Underworld. The body of the tree transects the Middle World. And the crown embraces the heavens. (1982: 21)

It was the gifted mythologist Mircea Eliade who was the first to notice and document the remarkable similarity between indigenous accounts of cosmic architecture worldwide. His classic study *Le shamanisme: techniques archaïques de l'extase* (1951)[2] is mainly focused on the no less remarkably similar character-istics and biographies of those expert navigators of the layered cosmos, now generally called *shamans* after the term used by the Evenks (Tungus) nomads of eastern Siberia. A *shaman* is a person of either sex with an accepted ability to ascend and descend the *axis mundi*, voyage in the normally invisible worlds of 'spirit', and return with knowledge and power beneficial to his or her local com-munity. As Eliade was the first to show, and as has since been abundantly confirmed through local case studies and first-person accounts, such exceptional individuals are to be found in every human group, and throughout history and pre-history.[3] Absurdly, not so long ago it was the received wisdom in anthropology that tribal shamans, when not simply charlatans, were victims of mental illness, notably schizophrenia (see Silverman 1967). Only recently has it been accepted that, so far from being pathological cases, genuine shamans are extraordinarily endowed with mental strength and resilience. Typically, a fully fledged shaman has come through horrendous psychic ordeals involving the virtual dissolution of his or her socially constructed personality and often including a near-death experience (NDE). The crucial difference between an initiated shaman and a schizophrenic is that the latter is the passive victim of overwhelming and unpredictable attacks by psychic forces, whereas the former voluntarily enters into and returns from the world of non-ordinary reality, engaging with spirit entities on a basis of equality (see Noll 1983). The topic of shamanism has developed into a major academic preoccupation in the past thirty years and has become the subject of a continuing flood of mass-circulation books of varying quality and credibility. Again, what is remarkable about these first-hand accounts is the basic commonality of the shamanic experience among ethnically and historically unrelated communities around the world. Anthropologist Barbara Myerhoff describes shamanic ecstasy among the Huichol Native Americans of northern Mexico in terms that, allowing for local cultural specifics, could as well apply to shamanic experience in general:

> In shaman-dominated religions, the special responsibility of the shaman is to return to *illud tempus*[4] on behalf of his people, to make his ecstatic journey through the assistance of animal tutelary spirits and bring back information of the other realms to ordinary mortals. As mediator, the shaman travels back and forth and, with exquisite balance, never becomes too closely tied to the mundane or to the supernatural. His soul leaves his body during trance states and by means of a magical flight he rejoins that which was once unified – man and animals, the living and the dead, man and the gods. The Huichol mara'akame [shaman] does more than this for his people; he takes the pilgrims themselves to *illud tempus* as deities during the peyote hunt, sharing with them all that existed before the world began . . . at the climactic moment of the peyote hunt he . . . becomes one with them as they become one with the deer, the maize, and the peyote. (1974: 253–4)

This remarkable passage from the work of the gifted American anthropologist not only epitomizes the essence of the shamanic experience worldwide, it also brings us to the heart of mythopaeic thought, for shamanism and myth-making are intimately related. Originally the same person was shaman and poet, creator of world-making narrative and transcender of time and space in experiential realization of cosmic interconnectedness. Taliessin, the sixth-century CE shamanic bard of Wales, was the last of an immensely long line reaching back to remotest human prehistory, but all true poets to this day are aware of the mystical source of their gift in the normally invisible world of spiritual powers, as the twentieth-century bard Robert Graves has famously argued (Graves 1961).

So what then is it about the shamanic experience that has made it the focus of so much scholarly and popular interest since the controversial works of Carlos

Castaneda in the late 1960s and 1970s? Alan Campbell, writing from his work with Amazonian forest people, suggests that in shamanism we are dealing not with an office, such as chiefship, but with a quality:

> if it [shamanism] is a quality rather than an office, then it admits of degrees. You can have a lot of it or a little of it . . . You are *either* a chief *or* you are not – that's an office – but you can be more or less shamanistic. (1989: 106)

Campbell's important insight can be taken further. What is essentially shamanic is not an office or social role but a relation between a human being and an 'other' which may be one or more fellow-humans or a non-human inhabitant of the same environment – an animal, a river, a plant, a rock or stone, a heavenly object – anything, in fact, perceived by the mythic consciousness as possessing will and mind. As far as humans are concerned, we suggest that the ability and power to enter into a relationship with the special quality of the shamanic is an enhanced instance of that unique faculty of the species which we have called 'dialogic', our innate species-ability to imaginatively and empathetically put ourselves 'in the place of' the other. That peculiar faculty is latent in some, patent in others. It can be developed by deliberate training, or – as the ethnographic evidence reveals – precipitated by life-changing events, often catastrophic. In the case of full-blown shamanism, we are seeing that dialogical faculty developed to the highest possible degree, admitting the shaman to an extraordinary 'conversation' of all-embracing, cosmic dimensions.

End of a Taboo

It is no 'mere' coincidence that the same post-1960s period that has seen an intense scholarly and popular preoccupation with 'shamanism' is also the period during which the phenomenon of 'consciousness', for long a taboo topic in psychology and social science, has burgeoned into a major cross-disciplinary issue (see Cohen and Rapport 1995).[5] Though foreshadowed by William James's *Varieties of Religious Experience* (1958 [1902]), for the greater part of last century the doctrine of Behaviourism, psychology's version of 'scientific' objectivism, dogmatically excluded subjective experience from its account of the human mind. During the same period the bizarre dogma of J.B. Watson, psychological behaviourism's founding father, that human beings have no innate 'instincts' (Watson 1931: 94), became received wisdom in social science: supposedly, we are born as Lockean blank slates, awaiting the formative impress of socio-cultural influences (cf. Midgley 1979). The readmission in the late 1960s of the long-tabooed concept of 'consciousness' was iconic of a seismic change in human self-awareness that continues to resonate through the compartmentalized domains of academia, from psychology and neurophysiology to philosophy and the social sciences; a change most strongly articulated in Arne Naess's 'Deep Ecology', with its rediscovery of the fundamental interconnectedness of *Homo sapiens* with all other life-forms, with the planet and the universe. Nearer home, the revolutionary theories of linguist Noam Chomsky successfully demolished the reigning stimulus-response model of infant language-learning, drawn from behaviourist psychology, by demonstrating our innate endowment with communicative competence, while Lévi-Straussian structuralism relocated the basis of human cognition from the isolated individual – the famous *Cogito* of Cartesian philosophy – to the network of relations between communicating persons. The previously absolute distinction between 'subjective' and 'objective' reality lost its force with the increasing sense that, in the words of physicist Fritjof Capra:

> the sharp Cartesian division between mind and matter, between the observer and the observed, can no longer be maintained. We can never speak about nature without, at the same time, speaking about ourselves. (Capra 1982: 77)

Analogously, in post-colonial, post-modern anthropology the controversial and immensely popular works of Castaneda, depicting the adventures of a 'gringo' ethnographer entering into the paranormal world of Native American 'sorcery', foreshadowed the dissolution of the conventional distinction between 'us' and 'them', anthropologist and anthropologized, and the development of what has come to be called 'experiential' anthropology. Here the classical period of field research in an alien culture becomes a moment when the anthropologist, already and inevitably socialized into the reductionist materialism of mainstream Western science, learns to experience subjectively, in his or her own person, the 'altered state' realities of trance and spirit communication. Unsurprisingly, it is to the radical philosophies of the various phenomenological schools – to Dilthey, Heidegger, Husserl, Merleau-Ponty and Abram – that these anthropologists have turned when seeking validation and explication of their paradigm-busting field data. The new 'experiential' explorations have also enabled us to positively reappraise the patient scholarly labours of philosopher Lucien Lévy-Bruhl, one of the most misunderstood and unjustly neglected figures in modern anthropology. On the face of it, the ideas of the French philosopher are doubly outrageous to present-day anthropological sensibilities. First, his persistent use of the now tabooed word 'primitive'; and second, in the face of anthropology's disciplinary investment in the postulate of ethnic difference, Lévy-Bruhl's insistence on the essential sameness of non-Western peoples' experience of the world. For our purposes here, what is important to notice is that the Lévy-Bruhlian *oeuvre* systematically complements, albeit in very different terms, the much more recent ethnographic data on shamanic consciousness, although this fact has gone unremarked by most anthropologists. One who does make the correlation, grounded in her own participatory field experience of ritual healing in rural Zambia, is Edith Turner. She writes that Lévy-Bruhl's first book, *Les fonctions mentales dans les sociétés inférieures* (1910), translated into English under the now naive-seeming title of *How Natives Think*, was for her the 'most important' work of early modern anthropology:

> I now saw that his 'law of participation', the discovery of the ambience of mystical meaning that surrounded the senses of 'primitives', went beyond partial categories such as 'sympathetic magic' and 'contagious magic' and included all senses and meaning in one world of ancient tradition in which everything had a 'soul' and human life was bathed in it while life lasted. (1992: 10–11)

In his groundbreaking 1910 volume, Lévy-Bruhl had already laid out the logically scandalous nature of 'primitive' thought in which, contrary to the principles of Aristotelian rationality central to Western civilization, 'phenomena can be, though in a way incomprehensible to us, both themselves and other than themselves'. He instances the case of the Bororo people of the Amazon forest who, according to their ethnographer Karl von den Steinen, asserted they were red *araras* (parakeets). This, Lévy-Bruhl explained, 'is not a name they give themselves, nor a relationship that they claim. What they desire to express by it is actual identity' (1926 [1910]: 76–7).

In her sympathetic gloss on Lévy-Bruhl, Edith Turner goes on to show how the French philosopher's at first exclusively cerebral account of 'primitive' mentality in terms of the 'collective representations' of Durkheim and Mauss, radically changed as his understanding developed and the misleading term 'prelogical' was abandoned in favour of *participation mystique*, a way of apprehending the world no longer restricted to a segment of humankind but a species prerogative. In Lévy-Bruhl's own words in his posthumously published *Notebooks*,

> there is not a primitive mentality distinguishable from the other by two characteristics which are peculiar to it (mystical and prelogical). There is a mystical mentality which is more marked and more easily observable among 'primitive peoples' than in our own societies, but it is present in every human mind. (1975: 101)

What Lévy-Bruhl was reaching for, as Edith Turner's insightful comments indicate, was a formulation that eluded the customarily opposed categories of 'rational' and 'emotional', while fusing them in a nameless state that combined both. In this extraordinary state the thinking-feeling subject, he said, communed with its object and participated in it, 'not only in the ideological, but also in the physical and mystical sense of the word' (1975: 362). Lévy-Bruhl was a veritable saint of scholarship, who spent a lifetime struggling to formulate in academic language a fundamental human experience directly opposed to the rationalistic grain of

Western civilization, and particularly that of his own socio-cultural background in France.

In fact, anthropology has coined a number of expressions in successive attempts to pin down the elusive nature of a phenomenon that, whether labelled 'shamanic ecstasy', 'spirit possession', 'mystical participation', 'altered state experience', 'trance' or 'dissociation', was until recently regarded as a condition affecting those *others* who were the proper objects of ethnographic inquiry, and from which the dispassionate scientific observers of institutional anthropology were necessarily exempt. The first fully qualified member of the profession to break ranks in this respect was Michael Harner, during field research among the Conibo Native Americans of the Peruvian Amazon in 1960–1. It was during this, his second field trip to the Amazon forests, that Harner was initiated into the way of the *paje*, or shaman, with the aid of the locally sacred drink made from the *ayahuasca* (*Banisteriopsis*) vine. This mind-altering experience changed Harner's life, leading him to abandon his secure and prestigious university post in New York City and embark on a new, missionizing career aimed at bringing ancient shamanic know-ledge preserved in existing 'tribal' societies to the urbanized peoples of the industrial world. Using the classic medium of drumming rather than psychotropic substances, Harner found it surprisingly easy to induce in urbanites with no previous acquaintance with shamanic 'journeying', paranormal experiences strikingly similar to those reported in tribal ethnographies (Harner 1990).[6]

In June 1961, about the same time that Harner was initiated into Amazonian shamanism, Carlos Castaneda, then a graduate student in anthropology at UCLA, was gathering information in rural Mexico on medicinal herbs, when he had a fateful encounter with a Yaqui Native American called Don Juan. That at least is the story, the contested verisimilitude of which has spawned a minor academic industry. Our own 'take' on this vexed issue is that regardless of whether Castaneda's narrative corresponds with historical and ethnographic 'fact', this man's visionary writings construct the authentic myth of post-colonial and postmodern anthropology, its mind-gripping power evidenced in the huge sales and worldwide popularity of Castaneda's works in the late 1960s and 1970s. The title of Castaneda's second volume on his extraordinary adventures with his Yaqui teacher, *A Separate Reality*, is iconic of that myth and its radical challenge to the dominant 'grand narrative' of mainstream science.

Altered States

While Harner and Castaneda helped to inspire a new movement in anthropology aimed at integrating the inner world of mind/spirit in its account of the human world, other developments within and without the discipline also fed into the 'consciousness' revolution of the past four decades. In anthropology Erika Bourguignon's landmark *Possession* (1976) established with chapter and verse the global incidence of what is called 'spirit possession' (note the inherent – and useful – ambiguity in this phrase: who 'possesses' whom?).[7] A few years earlier Roger W. Sperry's 'split brain' experiments had led Sperry and his collaborators to an understanding of the distinct and complementary kinds of awareness localized in the left and right cerebral hemispheres. A novel fusion of psychology and neuro-physiology confirmed the left brain as the principal location of linear, particulate, logical thought, temporal sense and language (known since Broca's pioneering discoveries in the late nineteenth century), and the for long poorly understood and undervalued right brain, as the prime source of 'holistic', poetic and mystical comprehension (cf. Ornstein 1972). These developments culminated in the psychological concept of 'altered states' of consciousness, and a new research agenda focused on the role and function of such 'altered states' in human mental, spiritual and social evolution. Through the later 1960s and 1970s it became apparent that, in the words of psychologist Charles C. Tart,

> Within Western culture we have strong negative attitudes towards ASCs [alternative states of consciousness]: there is the normal (good) state of consciousness and there are pathological changes in consciousness. (1969: 2)

Similarly, anthropologist Barbara Tedlock has noted the same civilization's historical devaluation of the altered-state experience of dreaming: for Aristotle, she reminds us, dreams were (inferior) copies of reality, rather than the alternative reality they are for many non-Western cultures (1987: 2). The appearance of A.M. Ludwig's term 'altered state of consciousness' in academic discourse (Tart 1969) marked a resurgence of social-scientific and philosophical interest in the nature of these long-tabooed states.[8] Novelist Aldous Huxley's account in *The Doors of Perception* (1994) of his mescaline-induced visionary experiences foreshadowed the emergence in the later 1960s in North America and Europe of an anti-establishment youth culture that celebrated the use of psychotropic substances to expand consciousness. The idea that a drive to experience 'altered states' was genetic in human beings and hence had a Darwinian 'survival value' for our species, became possible.

> ... the desire to alter consciousness periodically is an innate, normal drive analogous to hunger or the sexual drive ... we are dealing not with something socially or culturally based but rather with a biological characteristic of the species. (Weil 1972: 19)

The later twentieth century also saw the development of electronic technology that appears to mirror and confirm, at the level of materiality, the natural capacities of the human mind to experience forms of consciousness transcending ordinary, mundane awareness. In 1979 neurobiologist Barbara Lex brought together the differential functions of left and right cerebral hemispheres and electroencephalographic data on patterns of brain activity exhibited by subjects in a state of ritual trance. Lex described an elegant parallelism between participants' progress through a ritual process culminating in ecstatic trance and reported states of 'ineffable bliss', and a structured series of changes in electrical activity in the participants' brains, beginning with the left-brain dominance characteristic of ordinary, waking consciousness, proceeding through a shift to right-brain dominance associated with the dream-state, culminating in a novel, harmonious integration of left- and right-brain functions. Lex is at pains to make clear that this mental integration and harmony between particularistic and logical left-brain and holistic right-brain, subjectively reported as an extraordinary state in which 'logical paradoxes or the awareness of polar opposites as presented in myth appear simultaneously both as antinonomies and as unified wholes' (d'Aquili and Laughlin 1979: 177), involves not just the brain but the whole nervous system, thus the entire body (Lex 1979: 119). Her contention is taken an important step further in the later work of neuro-surgeon Antonio Damasio who, moving on from the isolated organism proposed by Lex, the physiological version of Descartes' lonely *Cogito*, insists that 'comprehensive understanding of the human mind requires an organismic perspective' focused on an integrated body fully interactive with a physical and social environment (1994: 252). Here we are close to Abram's perception, drawing particularly on the work of Merleau-Ponty, that

> the boundaries of a living body are open and indeterminate; more like membranes than barriers, they define a surface of metamorphosis and exchange. (Abram 1996: 46)

In certain states of consciousness, it is now apparent, this minded, interactive body is able to experience exchange and communion beyond its immediate social and physical environment, with ordinarily invisible cosmic powers.

A Human Universal

Anthropologist Philip M. Peek has taken up the neurobiologists' insights into the innate, genetic basis of our millennial human capacities to expand and transcend the world of ordinary consciousness, to investigate the process of ritual divination in Africa. Underlying a plethora of local variations, Peek identifies a basic pattern, which he suggests is also a human universal. All divination systems, African included,

> temporarily shift decision-making into a liminal realm by emphatically participating in opposing cognitive modes . . . it is just this opposition of modes that makes the divinatory enterprise unique and, ultimately, so effective. (1991: 193)

Peek instances the well-known Yoruba Ifa oracle as a classic example of the special bringing together of opposing cognitive modes characteristic of divination. The Ifa system comprises a vast and complex body of traditional knowledge in verse form:

> Yet the actual process of divination clearly operates in a contrary ('nonrational') mode. Why cast palm nuts to determine which verses to cite? Why not go directly to the verses themselves? And why with divination such as basket shaking and bone throwing, which appear so haphazard, do we find such careful 'ratiocinating' and exacting analysis of the cast configurations by the diviners? (ibid.)

Peek further draws our attention to the special nature of the dialogue between diviner and client when the holistic and pattern-cognizing 'right brain' knowledge of the professional diviner is brought into creative conjunction with the particulate and logical ('left brain') thinking of the client relating to his or her mundane problems. It is during this moment of impassioned communion that the shared consciousness of diviner and client is raised to a transcendent state in which genuine revelation and a joint appropriation of new knowledge can occur. In this 'unique synthesis of cognition modes' (Peek 1991: 203) we can also recognize d'Aquili and Laughlin's ritually-induced perception of logical antinomies as unified wholes; and Lévy-Bruhl's posthumous characterization of 'mystical participation' as a state of seemingly paradoxical 'duality-unity' (1975: 113–14).

What light do these convergent insights and evidences from anthropology, psychology, neurophysiology and philosophy throw on the epistemological status of present-day Western astrology? We have seen how ancient human awareness of connection with a cosmic environment seems to have begun with perception of synchrony between the female menstrual rhythm and the cyclical phases of the moon. This primal sense of cosmic harmony, remembered in Christian myth as the Garden of Eden, was finally sundered by the emergence of modern science on the basis of the Cartesian caesura between the (superior) mental-spiritual essence of 'man' and the (inferior) domain of material Nature. This fateful development, which led by a logical progression to the Nietschean 'death of God' and the Weberian 'disenchantment' of a world reduced by scientific cosmology to the status of a vast, soulless machine, was already prefigured five millennia ago in the cosmic dualism of Plato and Aristotle. Their exaltation of the ethereal Ideal over and above the contingency of matter and embodiment legitimated Christian cosmology; when the Christian world-view was finally eclipsed with the eighteenth-century European Enlightenment, a contrary metaphysic of reductionist material-ism seized the 'scientific' imagination and remains dominant to this day, with consequences of which we are only too well aware.

Sperry, whose pioneering research led to our present knowledge of the dual cognitive modalities of the human mind and brain, initially subscribed to the conventional scientific wisdom, according to which the material stuff of cerebral organization 'caused' the movement of thought. However, in his later years Sperry advanced a radically different theory, of a world shaped by both mental and material forces. As he and his colleague Polly Heniger explained what they called 'a true worldview paradigm shift' in neurophysiology,

> In the traditional atomistic or microdeterministic view of science, everything is determined from below upward . . . Brain states determine mental states, but not vice versa. In the new view, however, things are determined reciprocally, not only from lower levels upward, but also from above downward. (Sperry and Heniger 1994: 4)

And they add a vitally important corollary:

> . . . Furthermore, these upward and downward forms of determinism are not symmetric, but quite different in kind. Thus the two counter-flow control systems do not collide, conflict, or in any way counteract each other. (ibid.)

The somewhat jargonistic language should not be allowed to obscure the profundity of the ideas in play here. Sperry and Heniger are not presenting a modern version of the Zoroastrian cosmic struggle between the forces of darkness and light. They are moving beyond the Aristotelean linear logic and the axiom of the excluded middle ('either p or not p') that still dominates Western thought outside the esoteric zone of quantum physics[9] to sketch a theory of extraordinary subtlety. As subtle as the mystical participation tracked by Lévy-Bruhl in a world where humans can assume animal form, or be in more than one place simultaneously (both common shamanic practices), as subtle as the dialogical movement from the inveterate duality of speaker and interlocutor to the momentary oneness of communion, this is a world of multiple and incommensurate powers rather than uniform forces conforming to a mechanical logic: a world of flow rather than substance, of creative chaos rather than linear causality.

While forever dynamic and unfolding, this world is not without form. We have an innate ability to interact with and navigate in it. That is because the human body – the microcosm in mystical parlance – provides the template or model for the macrocosmic universe, just as, reciprocally, we humans reflect in our neurophysiology, the very architecture of the cosmos. For indeed we are made of higher and lower faculties, just as the over-arching heavens are perceived to surpass, in their unfathomable grandeur, the earth below. Yet our primal perception is also of a celestial space created by, brought forth by the all-mothering earth, as Husserl was the first modern to divine:

> Underneath the modern, scientific conception of space as a mathematically infinite and homogenous void, Husserl discloses the experienced spatiality of the *earth* itself . . . the earth itself is not 'in' space, since it is earth that, from the first, *provides* space. (Abram 1996: 42)

How to reconcile these opposed, equally primary, perceptions? As our consciousness moves from one worldmaking source to the other, we are made aware that the grandest instance of dialogue, our quintessential attribute, is the cosmic conversation of earth and heaven; and that we humans, Earth's children, we dialogical animals, are fashioned to participate in that cosmic dialogue, unto the very highest. For we are innately equipped to respond to the multiple voices, both earthly and celestial, that constitute our spiritual environment. The new understanding of human mental duality engendered by modern neurophysiology translates ancient intuitions of cosmic kinship into a language of neurones and synapses, networks and cybernetics. The cosmic dialogue of earth and heaven is replayed within the human skull as the complementarity of left and right cerebral hemispheres, the separation of things perceived by the left brain is complemented by the connection of all intuited by the right brain. The same duality of right and left is mirrored in our common experience of the sun's diurnal journey across the sky from east to west, directional markers loaded with symbolic significance by every human culture, and inscribed in the bilateral architecture of the body; and an analogous duality, linked with the cardinal directions north and south, associates these spatial aspects with corporeal front and back, before and behind.

If we now return to Sperry and Heniger's 'new paradigm' of non-conflictual, non-contradictory upward and downward causation, connections can be readily made between this model from neurophysiology and other recent insights and discoveries in the now vast field of consciousness studies, ranging from shamanic journeying and Lévy-Bruhlian 'mystical participation', through 'altered state' experiences in ritual trance and divination, to the phenomenology of perception (Husserl, Heidegger, Merleau-Ponty, Abram) and the philosophy of a participatory universe in which humans are co-creators with the divine. Seen in light of the Sperry-Heniger paradigm, the separation of things, including our own individual bodies, that constitutes mundane experience, and the privileged awareness of connection and wholeness achieved in moments of divinatory revelation, are not incompatible. In such special moments, as we have already noticed, each of the two apparently opposed 'truths' can be comprehended as implying and completing the other. Commenting on the implications of the Sperryan model of upward and downward causation, parapsychologist Dean Radin observes that '[we] are fully interconnected with all things, and we are isolated individuals. Both' (Radin 1997: 282).

Co-creation

Here, contrary to the alienated apprehensions of conventional science, we are proposing a fundamental harmony between the human species and the universe.

We see the essential defining attribute of that species as the dialogical process, with its unending alternation between the duality of speaker and interlocutor, their associated experience of unity in communion, and the celebrated dualities of mind and body, spirit and matter, divine and human, subjective and objective. In the words of philosopher Henryk Skolimowski, we are talking about human participation, as co-creators with divinity, in the work of world-making:

> Participatory philosophy . . . implies a rediscovery of participation . . . of creatively contributing to this world – and thereby shaping one's meaning and one's destiny in this world. (1994: 369)[10]

What relevance does such a conception of cosmic harmony as a process of human participation in the work of the gods have for our understanding of the astrological project in the postmodern Western world? Astrologer Geoffrey Cornelius, one of the principal advocates of a divinatory reading of his craft, criticizes what he sees as the conceptual incoherence of the majority of his colleagues, whom he sees as dominated by the reigning scientific paradigm of rationality and objectivity. In *The Moment of Astrology* (2003 [1994]), his major theoretical statement, Cornelius argues for the central role of *horary*, a long-neglected astrological method based on the client's horoscope at the moment of consultation, in the divinatory process. He draws on ideas from medieval Christian theology to illuminate his understanding of expansive changes in consciousness of both client and astrologer during consultation, describing a movement from the literal through allegory to metaphor and symbol. During this movement astrologer and client are able to become participants with divine agencies ('daemones') in a joint negotiation of the client's destiny.[11]

Our own anthropologically inspired account of the immemorially ancient human ritual of divination, this scientifically outlawed procedure that has been well dubbed 'ritual of rituals' by anthropologist Richard Werbner (Werbner 1983: 4), accords well enough with Cornelius's description. Our understanding of divination has a broader scope, however. First, because – as already outlined – we wish to recognize the practice of divination in the most basic sense as an innate human impulse and capacity. Second, in the particular case of astrology, our intention is to explain why the heavenly bodies have, since remote prehistory and no less today in the era of objective science triumphant, exerted and continue to exert such a mysteriously potent influence on the human imagination. Such an explanation must needs bring together our carnal architecture, our species-specific upright gait that naturally promotes a felt symbolic correspondence between our sensing and thinking upper parts and the ethereal celestial domain outspread above the solid earth at our feet; and must link the majestic spectacle of the planets and stars, and the constellations of stars, clothed as they all are in the time-binding, cosmically resonant stories of myth, with our primal, pre-linguistic sense of engagement in perpetual dialogue with a speaking environment. And then finally, where the complementarity of our mental grasp and play between awareness of particularity and separation and the mystical knowledge of connectedness and wholeness joins in the moment of divination – Cornelius's 'moment of astrology' – with the dialogical union in communion of above and below, heaven and earth. As Maggie Hyde, another leading exponent of the divinatory account of astrology, has observed:

> Unlike other diviners, astrologers divine with more than a stone, more than a coin, more than a pack of cards. Their act of divination spreads the heavens and assigns symbolic significance to the most awesome, untouchable and non-personal of objects, the planets and stars themselves. (1992: 77)

Precisely, and this equation and mutual reflection of heaven and earth, this bringing together in reciprocal implication of spirit and matter, a move that has been absolutely forbidden by monotheistic, transcendent religion, brings us into participation with an irreducible multiplicity of divine powers. It brings polytheism alive once more. It connects us with our prehuman, animal ancestry. It affords us conversation with the stars.

Notes

1. M. Griaule and G. Dieterlen in Forde 1954: 87–8. For Bambara, every man and woman has an opposite-sex twin who lives in the water or the sky and is half of one's total identity as a person (Dieterlen 1951: 56–60).
2. A revised and expanded version was published in English by Princeton University Press in 1964, under the title *Shamanism: Archaic Techniques of Ecstasy.* Eliade's work has been criticized for being both unduly restrictive in its definition of the shamanic role and partial in its use of sources, but remains the foundation of modern shamanic studies.
3. For a balanced recent survey of the topic see Hutton (2001).
4. 'That other time', a Latin expression employed by Eliade, referring to the common mythical motif of a paradisical world of harmony and peace before time proper began.
5. For the past seven years the Tucson campus of the University of Arizona has hosted an international, multi-disciplinary conference on Consciousness. This event brings together scientists and scholars from such diverse fields as neuroscience, psychology, philosophy, anthropology and aesthetics.

6. In another publication, Harner comments that the 'the ease and effectiveness of shamanic drumming [in inducing 'shamanic' experiences in modern urban dwellers] is almost embarrassing!' (in Nicholson 1987: 14). One of us (Willis) has been able to verify Harner's discovery, having led neo-shamanic groups in Edinburgh University since 1993, with similar results (see Willis 1994).

7. Few of the hundreds of studies of this phenomenon bother to note that the very concept of 'possession' is peculiarly 'Western' and rarely translates easily into 'tribal' languages. In Bantu African languages, for instance, the closest verbal forms to our 'possession' or 'ownership' mean 'the one who is identified with such-and-such a place' (as in the case of a king or chief). The same locution can denote 'identification' with a particular psychic agency or 'spirit'.

8. In 1902 William James, in his pioneering *Varieties of Religious Experience*, had offered a descriptive account of qualitative changes in consciousness.

9. See Cooper (1975) for an interesting comparison of the use of the idea of indeterminacy in 'primitive' thought and quantum physics. He suggests that both domains use a three-valued logic: truth, falsity, and indeterminate.

10. This is a view seemingly echoed by anthropologist Roy Rappaport who, in his monumental *Ritual and Religion in the Making of Humanity*, advocates a 'postmodern science . . . an order of epistemology and action in which both those who seek to understand the nature of meaning and its fabrication are reunited within a world which they do not merely observe, but in the creation of which they participate and which they strive to maintain' (1999: 457).

11. At a meeting in London in July 2001 of the Company of Astrologers, an association of British astrologers espousing the 'divinatory' reading of their profession, Maggie Hyde described the 'confusion and wow and flutter' that precedes the sudden vision of wholeness during a consultation, while Geoffrey Cornelius referred to his frequent 'state of amazement' at the multiple inter-connections often revealed by astrology (Willis, unpublished notes). In the introduction to this book (p. 11), Willis describes his experience of an apparent 'altered state' in a professional astrologer during a consultation.

Appendix

The subject of this brief appendix, for which Patrick Curry is responsible, may strike the general reader as excessively technical. It concerns the current scholarly consensus on the historical origins of divinatory astrology. The author is not an expert on this particular subject, and so writes under correction (not to say with trepidation); nonetheless, it is too important to let pass.

As an intial comment, let me remind the reader that the various kinds of astrology include natal (nativities), mundane (e.g. political), elections (choosing a propitious time to start an enterprise) and interrogations or horary (enquiring of the stars their will concerning an enterprise); and that *katarche* was the ritual act of enquiring of the gods (or fates) as to their will respecting a human enterprise, a practice that was already extant in Greece at the time of the transmission thereto of Babylonian astrology. The affinity between interrogations and *katarche* is obvious.

A major presence in this field is Professor David Pingree. In his influential entry on astrology in the *Dictionary of the History of Ideas* (1969), Pingree defines astrology as 'the study of the impact of the celestial bodies . . . upon the sublunar world' – a view which clearly *presupposes* a causal and specifically Aristotelian astrology. But Ptolemy's work was an intervention in, and not the starting-point of, the history of astrology; and to thus exclude Babylonian astrology as such seems arbitrary at best. It is true that 'Astrology so defined . . . is certainly not of Babylonian origin'; but the definition is surely wrong.

That impression is further strengthened by Pingree's formulation of the belief behind katarchic astrology as being 'that any act is influenced by the horoscope of its inception as is any individual by the horoscope of his birth'. That is true of elections, but there is a very significant difference between them and interrogations. In the former case it is the person who selects the moment and therefore its cosmic import; whereas in the latter the moment is chosen not as a propitious one but precisely without already knowing (or taking into account) its characteristics, in order to let the gods (*qua* celestial bodies) speak, and thereby say whether the time is propitious or not. That difference is why the Ptolemaic root-metaphor of a seed-moment, which Pingree has adopted, can be stretched to cover elections but *not* interrogations. It is also presumably why Ptolemy notoriously failed to include and discuss interrogations in his otherwise comprehensive re-statement of astrology.

Pingree's programme has recently found restatement in his book *From Astral Omens to Astrology* (1997), wherein he describes catarchic astrology as the kind undertaken 'to determine the best time for initiating actions' (p. 21) – again, plainly elections rather than interrogations – and argues that interrogational astrology developed in second–third-century India, only reaching Europe from there via Arabic translations from Sanskrit. Without denying such a transmission, it is highly implausible as a theory of the origin of katarchic astrology in Europe. For one thing, it requires us to believe that the above-mentioned affinity between *katarche* and interrogations – both being undeniably divinatory – was not equally obvious to the ancient Greeks, even when they named early horoscopic practices *katarche*!

Pingree's curious attitude to interrogations and katarchic astrology seems largely a consequence of his determination to adopt a rigidly Ptolemaic definition of astrology *tout court*, repeated in the later publication, in which he attempts, notwithstanding their incongruity, to include interrogations: 'All these types of astrology depend on the notion that the planets transmit motion (change) to the four elements . . . in the sublunar world', adding that '[this] theory is completely different from that of celestial omens, in which the gods . . . send messages concerning their intention . . . by means of celestial phenomena' (p. 21). There is certainly a difference; but the only way to define the one and not the other as astrology is by applying retrospectively, and therefore anachronistically, the Ptolemaic revision. Bouché-Leclerq, in his much earlier work *L'Astrologie Grecque* (1899), seems to have been much closer to the truth. He identified interrogations as an 'application' of *katarche* (p. 641), and remarked that 'la généthlialogie' – i.e., Ptolemaic natal astrology – 'tendant à supprimer le système de [*katarche*]' (p. 469). (For a contemporary account, which developes the same point of view in the course of a counter-Ptolemaic revolution, see Cornelius 2003.)

If one were to speculate as to the reasons for attempting to prosecute such a problematic point of view, it would be difficult not to suspect an attempt to 'clean up' astrology's origins in divination. After all, that was importantly Ptolemy's own stated intention: to give his subject a more rational and natural footing. He can therefore be recouped, however teleologically and patronizingly, as a 'scientist' *avant la lettre*. But such an enterprise will always be vulnerable to a still brighter, whiter version with no astrology (or anything like it) at all.

Bibliography

Abram, D. (1996), *The Spell of the Sensuous: Perception and Language in a More-Than-Human World*, New York: Random House.

Adorno, T.W. (1994), *The Stars Down to Earth and Other Essays on the Irrational in Culture*, London: Routledge.

Baigent, M. (1994), *From the Omens of Babylon: Astrology and Ancient Meso-potamia*, London: Arkana/Penguin.

Bakhtin, M. (1990), *The Dialogic Imagination*, Bloomington: Indiana University Press.

Barfield, O. (1967), *Speaker's Meaning*, Middletown: Wesleyan University Press.

—— (1973 [1928]), *Poetic Diction: A Study in Meaning*, Middletown: Wesleyan University Press.

—— (1977), *The Rediscovery of Meaning, and Other Essays*, Middletown: Wesleyan University Press.

—— (1979), *History, Guilt and Habit*, Middletown: Wesleyan University Press.

Barton, T. (1994), *Ancient Astrology*, London: Routledge.

Basedow, H. (1925), *The Australian Aboriginal*, Adelaide: F.W. Preece.

Bateson, G. (1972), *Steps to an Ecology of Mind*, New York: Ballantine.

—— (1979), *Mind and Nature: A Necessary Unity*, New York: Dutton.

Bateson, G. and Bateson, M.C. (1987), *Angels Fear: An Investigation into the Nature and Meaning of the Sacred*, London: Rider.

Bauman, Z. (1989), *Modernity and the Holocaust*, London: Verso.

—— (1992), *Intimations of Postmodernity*, London: Routledge.

Berlin, I. (1969), *Four Essays on Liberty*, Oxford: Oxford University Press.

—— (1998), *The Proper Study of Mankind: An Anthology of Essays*, ed. Henry Hardy, London: Pimlico.

Bouché-Leclerq, A. (1899), *L'Astrologie Grecque*, Paris: Ernest Leroux.

Bourguignon, E. (1976), *Possession*, San Francisco: Chandler and Sharp.

Bower, T.G.R. (1977), *Primer of Infant Development*, San Francisco: W.H. Freeman.

Briffault, R. (1927), *The Mothers: A Study of the Origins, Sentiments and Institutions*, London: George Allen and Unwin, 3 vols.

Brockbank, J. (2002), 'The Sceptical Attack of Dean et al. on Astrology', unpublished paper.

Brown, G.M. (1969), *An Orkney Tapestry*, London: Gollancz.

Buchler, I.R. and Maddock, K. (1978), *The Rainbow Serpent*, The Hague: Mouton.

Burke, P. (1978), *Popular Culture in Early Modern Europe*, London: Temple Smith.

Burtt, E.A. (1924), *The Metaphysical Foundations of Physical Science: A Historical and Critical Essay*, London: Routledge & Kegan Paul.

Calasso, R. (1993), *The Marriage of Cadmus and Harmony*, London: Jonathan Cape.

Campbell, A. (1989), *To Square with Genesis: Causal Statements and Shamanic Ideas in Wayãpí*, Edinburgh: Edinburgh University Press.

Campion, N. (1995), *The Great Year: Astrology, Millenarianism and History in the Western Tradition*, London: Penguin.

Capra, F. (1982), *The Turning Point: Science, Society and the Rising Culture*, London: Fontana.

—— (1997), *The Web of Life: A New Synthesis of Mind and Matter*, London: Flamingo/HarperCollins.

Castaneda, C. (1968), *The Teachings of Don Juan: A Yaqui Way of Knowledge*, Los Angeles: University of California Press.

—— (1971) *A Separate Reality: further conversations with Don Juan*, New York: Simon and Schuster.

—— (1974) *Tales of Power*, New York: Simon and Schuster.

Chalmers, A.F. (1982), *What is this Thing Called Science?* 2nd edn, Milton Keynes: Open University Press.

Chan, W.-T. (1963), *A Source Book in Chinese Philosophy*, Princeton: Princeton University Press.

Christino, K. (2002), *Foreseeing the Future: Evangeline Adams and Astrology in America*, Amherst: Onereed Publications.

Cicero (1923), *On Divination*, transl. W.A. Falconer, Cambridge, MA: Harvard University Press.

Clark, J. (1993), CSICOP, in J. Clark (ed.), *Encyclopedia of Strange and Unexplained Psychical Phenomena*, Detroit: Gale Research Inc.

Cohen, A. and Rapport, N. (eds) (1995), *Questions of Consciousness*, London: Routledge.

Cooter, R. (1981), Deploying Pseudoscience: Then and Now, in M.P. Hanen, J. Osler and R.G.Weyant (eds), *Science, Pseudo-science and Society*, Waterloo, Ontario: Wilfred Laurier University Press.

Cooper, D.E. (1975), 'Alternative Logic in "Primitive Thought"', *Man* (n.s.), 10: 238–56.

Cornelius, G. (1982), 'Astrology and Divination', unpublished paper.

—— (1984), 'The Moment of Astrology, Part III: Katarche', *Astrology* 58(1): 14–24.

—— (1985), 'A Modern Astrological Perspective', in William Lilly, *Christian Astrology*, London: Regulus.

—— (1998), 'Is Astrology Divination and Does it Matter?', *The Mountain Astro-loger*, October/November: 38–44.

—— (2001), 'The Illusion of Fate', *Bulletin* 25 of the Company of Astrologers, November 2001; see http://coa.hubcom.net.

—— (2003 [1994]), *The Moment of Astrology: Origins in Divination*, 2nd edn. London: Penguin/Arkana.

Culver, R.B. and Ianna, P.A. (1988), *Astrology: True or False? A Scientific Evalu-ation*, rev. edn, Buffalo: Prometheus Books.

Cumont, F. (1960), *Astrology and Religion among the Greeks and Romans*, New York: Dover.

Curry, P. (1982), 'Research on the Mars Effect', *Zetetic Scholar* 9: 33–54, 78–83.

—— (1983), 'An Aporia for Astrology', in M. Budd, P. Curry, G. Douglas and B. Jaye, *Radical Astrology*, London: the Radical Astrology Group.

—— (1985), 'Afterword', in W. Lilly, *Christian Astrology*, London: Regulus.

—— (ed.) (1987), *Astrology, Science and Society*, Woodbridge: Boydell.

—— (1989), *Prophecy and Power: Astrology in Early Modern England*, Cambridge: Polity Press.

—— (1991), 'Astrology in Early Modern England', in S. Pumfrey, P.L. Rossi and M. Slawinsky (eds), *Science, Culture and Popular Belief in Renaissance Europe*, Manchester: Manchester University Press.

—— (1992), *A Confusion of Prophets: Victorian and Edwardian Astrology*, London: Collins & Brown.

—— (1999a), 'Astrology: From Pagan to Postmodern?', *Astrological Journal* 36(1): 69–75.

—— (1999b), 'Magic *vs.* Enchantment', *Journal of Contemporary Religion* 9: 401–12.

—— (2000), 'Astrology on Trial, and its Historians: Reflections on the Histori-ography of Superstition', *Culture and Cosmos* 4(2): 47–56.

—— (2003), 'William Lilly', entry in the *New Dictionary of National Biography*, Oxford: Oxford University Press.

Damasio, A.R. (1994), *Descartes' Error: Emotion, Reason, and the Human Brain*, New York: Putnam.

Daniélou, A. (1984), *Shiva and Dyonysus: The Religion of Nature and Eros*, New York: Inner Traditions International.

D'Aquili, E. and Laughlin, C.D. (1979), 'Neurobiology of Myth and Ritual', in E. D'Aquili, C.D. Laughlin and J. McManus (eds), *The Spectrum of Ritual*, New York: Columbia University Press, 152–82.

D'Aquili, E., Laughlin, C.D. and McManus, J. (eds) (1979), *The Spectrum of Ritual*, New York: Columbia University Press.

Davidson, H.E. (1981), 'The Germanic World', in M. Loewe and C. Blacker (eds), *Oracles and Divination*, Boulder: Shambhala.

Bibliography

Davis, E. (1998), *Techgnosis: Myth, Magic and Mysticism in the Age of Information*, New York: Random House.

Dawkins, R. (1989), *The Selfish Gene*, Oxford: Oxford University Press.

—— (1995), 'The Real Romance in the Stars', *Independent on Sunday*, 31 December 1995; another version, only slightly emended, appeared in *The Astrological Journal*, May/June 1996, 38(3): 133–41.

—— (1998), *Unweaving the Rainbow*, London: Allen Lane.

Dean, G. (2000), 'Attribution: A Pervasive New Artifact in the Gauquelin Data', *Astrology under Scrutiny* 13: 1–87.

Dean, G. and Mather, A. (1977), *Recent Advances in Astrology*, Subiaco: Analogic.

Dennett, C. (1996), *Kinds of Minds: Towards an Understanding of Consciousness*, London: Weidenfeld & Nicolson.

Detienne, M. and Vernant, J.-P. (1978), *Cunning Intelligence in Greek Culture and Society*, transl. J. Lloyd, Atlantic Highlands, NJ: Humanities Press.

Dieterlen, G. (1951), *Essai sur la religion bambara*, Paris: Presses universitaires de France.

Dodds, E.R. (1951), *The Greeks and the Irrational*, Berkeley, CA: University of California Press.

Durant, J. and Bauer, M. (1997), 'British Public Perceptions of Astrology: An Approach from the Sociology of Knowledge', *Culture and Cosmos* 1(1): 55–71.

Eccles, B. (1996), 'The Radical Nature of Sun-Sign Astrology', *Astrological Journal* 38(5): 306–10.

Eliade, M. (1958), *Yoga*, New York: Bollingen.

—— (1964 [1951]), *Shamanism: Archaic Techniques of Ecstasy*, Princeton: Princeton University Press.

Elwell, D. (1987), *The Cosmic Loom*, London: Unwin Hyman.

Empson, W. (1935), *Some Versions of Pastoral*, London: Chatto & Windus.

—— (1987), *Argufying: Essays on Literature and Culture*, ed. J. Haffenden, London: Chatto & Windus.

Ertel, S. (2000–01), 'Tampering with Birth Dates', *Correlation* 19(2): 37–46.

—— (2001–02), 'Births of Priests', *Correlation* 20(1): 30–6.

—— (2002–03), 'Whence Midnight Avoidance?', *Correlation* 21(1): 35–9.

—— (2002), 'Superstitions Should Decline', *Correlation* 20(2): 39–48.

Evernden, N. (1992), *The Social Construction of Nature* (Baltimore: Johns Hopkins University Press.

Eysenck, H.J. and Nias, D.K.B. (1982), *Astrology: Science or Superstition?*, London: Penguin.

Feyerabend, P. (1978), *Science in a Free Society*, London: NLB.

—— (1987), *Farewell to Reason*, London: Verso.

—— (1995), *Killing Time*, Chicago: University of Chicago Press.

Ficino, M. (1981), *The Letters of Marsilio Ficino*, transl. the School of Economic Science, 3 vols, London: Shepheard-Walwyn.

Fontenrose, J. (1978), *The Delphic Oracle: Its Responses and Operations, with a Catalogue of Responses*, Berkeley: University of California Press.

Forde, C.D. (ed.) (1954), *African Worlds: Studies in the Cosmological Ideas and Values of African Peoples*, London: International African Institute.

Forman, P. (1997), 'Recent Science: Late-Modern and Post-Modern', in T. Söderqvist (ed.), *The Historiography of Contemporary Science and Technology*, Amsterdam: Harwood Academic.

Foucault, M. (1977), 'Nietschze, History, Genealogy', in D.F. Bouchard (ed.), *Michel Foucault: Language, Counter-Memory, Practice: Selected Essays and Interviews*, Ithaca, NY: Cornell University Press.

Fowler, W.W. (1911), *The Religious Experience of the Roman People from the Earliest Time to the Age of Augustus*, London: Macmillan.

Frazer, J.G. (1925), *The Golden Bough*, London: Macmillan.

Fuller, S. (1997), *Science*, Buckingham: Open University Press.

Gallagher, S. and Meltzoff, A. (1996), 'The Earliest Sense of Self and Others: Merleau-Ponty and Recent Developmental Studies', *Philosophical Psychology* 9(2): 213–36.

Garin, E. (1983), *Astrology in the Renaissance: The Zodiac of Life*, London: Routledge & Kegan Paul.

Gauchet, M. (1997), *The Disenchantment of the World: A Political History of Religion*, transl. Oscar Burge, Princeton: Princeton University Press.

Gauquelin, M. (1983), *The Truth about Astrology*, transl. S. Matthews, Oxford: Basil Blackwell.

—— (1988), *Written in the Stars*, Wellingborough: Aquarian.

Geertz, C. (1993), *Local Knowledge*, London: Fontana/HarperCollins.

Geneva, A. (1985), *Astrology and the Seventeenth-Century Mind: William Lilly and the Language of the Stars*, Manchester: Manchester University Press.

Gimbutas, M. (1982 [1974]), *The Goddesses and Gods of Old Europe 6500–3500 BC: Myths and Cult Images*, London: Thames & Hudson.

Godwin, J. (1994), *The Theosophical Enlightenment*, Albany, NY: State University of New York Press.

Gooch, S. (1995), *Cities of Dreams: When Women Ruled the Earth*, London: Aulis.

Grafton, A. (1999), *Cardanos Cosmos: The Worlds and Works of a Renaissance Astrologer*, Cambridge, MA: Harvard University Press.

Graham, A.C. (1957), *Two Chinese Philosophers*, London: Lund Humphries.

Graves, R. (1961), *The White Goddess: A Historical Grammar of Poetic Myth*, London: Faber & Faber.

Gray, J. (1995), *Isaiah Berlin*, London: HarperCollins.

Greene, L. (1984), *The Astrology of Fate*, York Beach, ME: Samuel Weiser.

Greenfield, S. (1995), *Journey to the Center of the Mind: Towards a Science of Consciousness*, New York: W.H. Freeman.

Grim, P. (ed.) (1990), *Philosophy of Science and the Occult*, Albany, NY: State University of New York Press.

Guinard, H.P., see http://cura.free.fr

Gurney, O.R. (1981), 'The Babylonians and Hittites', in M. Loewe and C. Blacker (eds), *Oracles and Divination*, Boulder: Shambhala.

Habermas, J. (1971), *Knowledge and Human Interests*, transl. J.J. Schapiro, Boston: Beacon.

Halifax, J. (1982), *Shaman: The Wounded Healer*, London: Thames & Hudson.

Hansen, G.P. (1992), *Journal of the American Society for Psychical Research* 86.

Harding, M. (2000), 'Prejudice in Astrological Research', *Correlation* 19(1): 17–33.

Hassan, I. (1992), 'Pluralism in Postmodern Perspective', in C. Jencks (ed.), *The Post-Modern Reader*, London: Academy Editions.

Heaton, J. (1990), *Metis: Divination, Psychotherapy and Cunning Intelligence*, London: Company of Astrologers.

Henry, J. (2002 [1997]), *The Scientific Revolution and the Origins of Modern Science*, 2nd edn, Basingstoke: Palgrave Macmillan.

Hepburn, R.W. (1984), *'Wonder' and Other Essays*, Edinburgh: Edinburgh University Press.

Hesse, M. (1980), *Revolutions and Reconstructions in the Philosophy of Science*, Brighton: Harvester.

de Heusch, L. (1982), *The Drunken King, or, The Origin of the State*, trans. R. Willis, Bloomington: Indiana University Press. Orig. French *Le noi ivre, on l'origine de l'Etat*, Paris: Gallimard, 1972.

Hillman, J. (1975), *Revisioning Psychology*, New York: Harper and Row.

—— (1981), 'Appendix – Psychology: Monotheistic or Polytheistic', in D.L. Miller (ed.), *The New Polytheism*, 2nd edn, Dallas: Springs.

—— (1983), *Archetypal Psychology: A Brief Account*, Dallas: Spring.

—— (1997), 'Heaven Retains within its Sphere Half of all Bodies and Maladies', http://www.springpub.com/astro.htm

Hoban, R. (1992), *The Moment Under the Moment*, London: Jonathan Cape.

Holtzman, S.H. and Leich, C.M. (eds) (1981), *Wittgenstein: To Follow a Rule*, London: Routledge.

Horkheimer, M. and Adorno, T.W. (1994), *Dialectic of Enlightenment*, trans. J. Cumming, New York: Continuum.

Howe, E. (1984), *Astrology and the Third Reich*, Wellingborough: Aquarian; first publ. 1967 as *Urania's Children*.

Hutton, R. (2001), *Shamans: Siberian spirituality and the Western Imagination*, London: Hambledon.

Huxley, A. (1994 [1954]), *The Doors of Perception*, London: Flamingo.

Hyde, M. (1992), *Jung and Astrology*, London: Aquarian/Thorsons.

—— (2001), 'The Judder Effect: Astrology and Alternative Reality', *Astrological Journal* 43(5): 48–53.

Iamblichus (1999), *Iamblichus on the Mysteries*, trans. T. Taylor, Frome: The Prometheus Trust.

James, W. (1956), *The Will to Believe and Other Essays in Popular Philosophy*, New York: Dover.

—— (1958 [1902]), *The Varieties of Religious Experience*, New York: Mentor/ New American library.

—— (1977 [1908]), *A Pluralistic Universe*, Cambridge, MA: Harvard University Press.

Jonas, H. (1982), *The Phenomenon of Life: Toward a Philosophical Biology*, Chicago: University of Chicago Press.

Jung, C.G. (1950), 'Foreword', in *The I Ching or Book of Changes*, transl. Richard Wilhelm and Cary F. Baynes, Princeton: Princeton University Press.

—— (1966), *The Spirit in Man, Art, and Literature*, vol. 15 of the *CW*, New York: Bollingen/Pantheon.

—— (1976), *Letters 2*: 1951–1961, sel. and ed. G. Adler with A. Jaffé, trans. R.F.C. Hull, London: Routledge & Kegan Paul.

—— (1987), *Synchronicity: An Acausal Connecting Principle*, London: Ark.

Kane, S. (1994), *Wisdom of the Mythtellers*, Peterborough, Ontario: Broadview Press.

Keats, J. (1995), *The Sayings of John Keats*, ed. J.L.C. Peerless, London: Duckworth.

Kelly, I.W. (1997), 'Modern Astrology: A Critique', *Psychological Reports* 81: 1035–66.

Kelly, I.W., Dean, G. and Saklofske, D.H. (1990), 'Astrology: A Critical Review', in P. Grim (ed.), *Philosophy of Science and the Occult*, New York: State University of New York Press.

Kontos, A. (1994), 'The World Disenchanted, and the Return of Gods and Demons', in A. Horowitz and T. Maley (eds), *The Barbarism of Reason: Max Weber and the Twilight of Reason*, Toronto: University of Toronto Press.

Krupp, E.C. (1991), *Beyond the Blue Horizon*, New York: HarperCollins.

Labinger, J.A. and Collins, H. (2002), *The One Culture? A Conversation about Science*, Chicago: University of Chicago Press.

Laclau, E. (1990), *New Reflections on the Revolution of Our Time*, London: Verso.

Laclau, E. and Mouffe, C. (2001 [1985]), *Hegemony and Socialist Strategy: Towards a Radical Democratic Politics*, 2nd edn, London: Verso.

Lakoff, G. and Johnson, M. (1980), *Metaphors We Live By*, Chicago: University of Chicago Press.

—— and —— (1999), *Philosophy in the Flesh: The Embodied Mind and its Challenge to Western Thought*, New York: Basic.

Lambek, M. (ed.) (2002), *A Reader in the Anthropology of Religion*, Oxford: Blackwell.

Lash, J. (1999), *Quest for the Zodiac: The Cosmic Code Beyond Astrology*, Lough-borough: Thoth.

Latour, B. (1993), *We Have Never Been Modern*, trans. C. Porter, Hemel Hempstead: Harvester Wheatsheaf.

Laughlin, C.D. (1997), 'The Evolution of Cyborg Consciousness', *Anthropology of Consciousness*, 8(4): 144–59.

Lehman, J.L. (1994), 'Tiptoeing Through the Method: An Historical Review of Empiricism in Astrology 1990–91', *Astrological Journal* 36(1): 60–8.

Lévi-Strauss, C. (1964), *Le Cru et le cuit*, Paris: Plon.

—— (1978), *Origin of Table Manners*, London: Cape.

—— (1981), *The Naked Man*, London: Cape.

Lévy-Bruhl, L. (1926 [1910]), *How Natives Think*, London: Allen & Unwin.

—— (1975), *The Notebooks on Primitive Mentality*, trans. P. Rivière, Oxford: Basil Blackwell.

Lex, B. (1979), 'The Neurobiology of Ritual Trance', in E. d'Aquili, C.D. Laughlin and J. McManus (eds), *The Spectrum of Ritual*, New York: Columbia University Press.

Lienhardt, G. (1961), *Divinity and Experience: The Religion of the Dinka*, Oxford: Clarendon.

Lilly, W. (1985 [1647]), *Christian Astrology*, London: Regulus.

Lloyd, G.E.R. (1979), *Magic, Reason and Experience: Studies in the Origins and Development of Greek Science*, Cambridge: Cambridge University Press.

Loewe, M. and Blacker, C. (eds) (1981), *Oracles and Divination*, Boulder: Shambhala.

Long, A.A. (1982), 'Astrology: Arguments Pro and Contra', in J. Barnes, J. Brunschweig, M. Burnyeat and M. Schofield, *Science and Speculation: Studies in Hellenic Theory and Practice*, Cambridge: Cambridge University Press.

Lord, A.B. (1960), *The Singer of Tales*, Cambridge, MA: Harvard University Press.

Lyotard, F. (1988), 'An Interview with François Lyotard', in W. van Reijen and D. Veerman, *Theory, Culture and Society* 5(2–3): 277–309.

Machiavelli, N. (1970), *The Discourses*, ed. B. Crick, London: Penguin.

MacNeice, L. (1964), *Astrology*, ed. D. Hill, London: Aldus Books.

Macpherson, C.B. (1962), *The Political Theory of Possessive Individualism: Hobbes to Locke*, Oxford: Oxford University Press.

Main, R. (1997), *Jung on Synchronicity and the Paranormal*, London: Routledge.

Mann, F. (1973), *Acupuncture*, New York: Vintage.

Mars, G. (1982), *Cheats at Work: An Anthology of Workplace Crime*, London: Allen & Unwin.

Marshack, A. (1972), *The Roots of Civilization: The Cognitive Beginnings of Man's First Art, Symbol and Notation*, London: Weidenfeld and Nicolson.

Maturana, H. and Varela, F. (1987), *The Tree of Knowledge*, Boston: Shambhala.

Bibliography

Maurer, E.M. and Roberts, A.F. (1985), *The Rising of a New Moon: A Century of Tabwa Art*, Ann Arbor: University of Michigan Press.

Mayo, J. (1971), *Teach Yourself Astrology*, London: Sevenoaks.

McCormick, P. and Elliston, F.A. (eds) (1981), *Husserl: Shorter Works*, Brighton: Harvester.

McDonough, M. (2002), www.astrobank.com/AstrologicalResearch.htm.

Merleau-Ponty, M. (1962), *Phenomenology of Perception*, London: Routledge.

—— (1964) *The Primacy of Perception*, Evanston: Northwestern University Press.

Midgley, M. (1979), *Beast and Man: The Roots of Human Nature*, Hassocks: Harvester.

—— (1992), *Science as Salvation: A Modern Myth and its Meaning*, London: Routledge.

—— (2001), *Science and Poetry*, London: Routledge.

Miró, J. (1977), *Ceci est la couleur de mes rêves*, Paris: Éditions du Seuil.

Monod, J. (1997), *Chance and Necessity: On the Natural Philosophy of Modern Biology*, London: Penguin.

Moore, T. (1982), *The Planets Within: Marcilio Ficino's Astrological Psychology*, Lewisburg: Bucknell University Press.

Morrison, J.S. (1981), 'The Classical World', in M. Loewe and C. Blacker (eds), *Oracles and Divination*, Boulder: Shambhala.

Myerhoff, B. (1974), *Peyote Hunt: the Sacred Journey of the Huichol Indians*, Ithaca: Cornell University Press.

Naipaul, V.S. (1998), *Beyond Belief: Islamic Excursions Among the Converted Peoples*, London: Little, Brown & Co.

Nicholson, S. (ed.) (1987), *Shamanism: an Expanded View of Reality,* Wheaton, IL: Theosophical Publishing House.

Noble, V. (1991), *Shakti Woman: the new female shamanism*, New York: Harper-Collins.

Noll, R. (1983), 'Shamanism and Schizophrenia', *American Ethnologist* 10: 443–59.

North, J.D. (1986), 'Celestial Influence: the Major Premiss of Astrology', in P. Zambelli (ed.), *Astrologi hallucinati: Stars and the End of the World in Luther's Time*, Berlin: Walter de Gruyter.

Ornstein, R. (1972), *The Psychology of Consciousness*, San Francisco: W.H. Freeman.

Ortony, A. (ed.) (1993 [1979]), *Metaphor and Thought*, 2nd edn, Cambridge: Cambridge University Press.

Parker, J. (2002), text of the 2002 Charles Carter Memorial Lecture, *Astrological Journal*, September/October.

Peek, P.M. (ed.) (1991), *African Divination Systems: Ways of Knowing,* Bloomington: Indiana University Press.

Phillipson, G. (2000), *Astrology in the Year Zero*, London: Flare.

—— (2002), 'Astrology and the Anatomy of Doubt', *Mercury Direct*, insert in *Mountain Astrologer* 104: 2–12.

Pinch, T.J. and Collins, H.M. (1984), 'Private Science and Public Knowledge: The CSICOP and its Use of the Literature, *Social Studies of Science* 14: 521–46.

Pingree, D. (1969), 'Astrology', in P.P. Weiner, *Dictionary of the History of Ideas*, New York: Charles Scribners Sons.

—— (1997), *From Astral Omens to Astrology: From Babylon to Bikaner*, Rome: Istituto Italiano per Africa Oriente.

Plotinus (1991), *The Enneads*, London: Penguin.

Polanyi, M. (1958), *Tacit Knowledge: Towards a Post-Critical Philosophy*, London: Routledge & Kegan Paul.

Poncé, C. (1973), *Kabbalah*, San Francisco: Straight Arrow.

Ptolemy (1940), *Tetrabiblos*, transl. F.E. Robbins Falconer, Cambridge, MA: Harvard University Press.

Radha, L.C. (1981), 'Tibet', in M. Loewe and C. Blacker (eds), *Oracles and Divination*, Boulder: Shambhala.

Radin, D. (1997), *The Conscious Universe: The Scientific Truth of Psychic Phenomena*, New York: HarperEdge.

Raphals, L. (1992), *Knowing Words: Wisdom and Cunning in the Classical Traditions of China and Greece*, Ithaca: Cornell University Press.

Rappaport, R.A. (1999), *Ritual and Religion in the Making of Humanity*, Cambridge: Cambridge University Press.

Rawlins, D. (1981), 'Starbaby', *Fate* 34(10): 67–99.

Ridder-Patrick, J. (1991), *A Handbook of Medical Astrology*, London: Arkana.

Roberts, A.F. (1980), 'Heroic Beasts, Beastly Heroes: Principles of Cosmology and Chiefship among the Lakeside BaTabwa of Zaire', PhD dissertation, Chicago: University of Chicago.

—— (1986), 'Duality in Tabwa Art', *African Arts*, 19(4): 26–35, 86–7.

Samuels, A. (1985), *Jung and the Post-Jungians*, London: Routledge & Kegan Paul.

de Santillana, G., and von Dechend, H. (1969), *Hamlet's Mill: An Essay on Myth and the Frame of Time*, Boston: Shambhala.

Sasportas, H. (1985), *The Twelve Houses: An Introduction to the Houses in Astrological Interpretation*, London: Aquarian.

Scaff, L.A. (1989), *Fleeing the Iron Cage: Culture, Politics and Modernity in the Thought of Max Weber*, Berkeley: University of California Press.

Scarborough, M. (1994), *Myth and Modernity: Postcritical Reflections*, Albany, NY: State University of New York Press.

Schaffer, S. (1987), 'Newton's Comets and the Transformation of Astrology', in P. Curry (ed.) *Astrology, Science and Society*, Woodbridge: Boydell.

Schoffeleers, J.M. (1992), *River of Blood: The Genesis of a Martyr Cult in Southern Malawi, c.AD 1600*, Madison: University of Wisconsin Press.

Bibliography

Scott, J.C. (1998), *Seeing Like a State: How Certain Schemes to Improve the Human Condition Have Failed*, New Haven: Yale University Press.

Shaw, G. (1995), *Theurgy and the Soul: The Neoplatonism of Iamblichus*, University Park, PA: Pennsylvania State University Press.

Shumaker, W. (1972), *The Occult Sciences in the Renaissance: A Study in Intellectual Patterns*, Berkeley, CA: University of California Press.

Shuttle, P. and Redgrove, P. (1978), *The Wise Wound: Menstruation and Everywoman*, London: Gollancz.

Silverman, J. (1967), 'Shamans and Acute Schizophrenia', *American Anthropologist* 69: 21–31.

Sjöö, M. and Mor, B. (1987), *The Great Cosmic Mother: Rediscovering the Religion of the Earth*, New York: HarperCollins.

Skolimowski, H. (1994), *The Participatory Mind: A New Theory of Knowledge and the Universe*, London: Arkana Penguin.

Smith, B.H. (1988), *Contingencies of Value: Alternative Perspectives for Critical Theory*, Cambridge, MA: Harvard University Press.

—— (1997), *Belief and Resistance: Dynamics of Contemporary Intellectual Controversy*, Cambridge, MA: Harvard University Press.

Smith, K., Jr., Bol, P.K., Adler, J.A. and Wyatt, D.J. (1990), *Sung Dynasty Uses of the I Ching*, Princeton: Princeton University Press.

Soyinka, W. (2002), 'Faiths that Preach Tolerance', *Guardian*, 4 May.

Spencer, N. (2000), *True as the Stars Above. Adventures in Modern Astrology*, London: Gollancz.

Sperry, R.W. and Heniger, P. (1994), 'Consciousness and the Cognitive Revolution: A True Worldview Paradigm Shift', *Anthropology of Consciousness*, 5(3): 3–7.

Stein, G. (ed.) (1996), *The Encyclopedia of the Paranormal*, Amherst: Prometheus Books, Astrology.

Stone, A. (1989), *Wyrd. Fate and Destiny in North European Paganism*, London: the author.

Tart, C.T. (ed.) (1969), *Altered States of Consciousness: A Book of Readings*, New York: Wiley.

Tedlock, B. (1987), *Dreaming: Anthropological and Psychological Interpretations*, Cambridge: Cambridge University Press.

Tester, J. (1987), *A History of Western Astrology*, Woodbridge: Boydell.

Thomas, K. (1973 [1971]), *Religion and the Decline of Magic*, Harmondsworth: Penguin.

Thompson, W.I. (1981), *The Time Falling Bodies Take to Light: Mythology, Sexuality, and the Origins of Culture*, London: Rider/Hutchinson.

Tolkien, J.R.R. (1988 [1964]), 'On Fairy-Stories', in *Tree and Leaf*, London: Unwin Hyman.

Toren, C. (1993), 'Making History: The Significance of Childhood Cognition for a Comparative Anthropology of Mind', *Man* (n.s.), 28: 461–78.

Toulmin, S. (1990), *Cosmopolis: The Hidden Agenda of Modernity*, Chicago: Chicago University Press.

Trevarthen, C. and Logotheti, K. (1989), 'Child in Society, and Society in Children: the Nature of Basic Trust', in S. Howell and R. Willis, *Societies at Peace,* London: Routledge.

Turner, E. (1992), *Experiencing Ritual: A New Interpretation of African Healing*, Philadelphia: University of Pennsylvania Press.

Tylor, E.B. (1871), *Primitive Culture*, 2 vols, London: John Murray.

Urton, G. (1981), *At the Crossroads of the Earth and Sky: An Andean Cosmology,* Austin: University of Texas Press.

Varela, F.J., Thompson, E. and Rosch, E. (1991), *The Embodied Mind: Cognitive Science and Human Experience*, Cambridge, MA: MIT Press.

Villoldo, A. (2000), *Shaman Healer Sage: How to Heal Yourself and Others with the Energy Medicine of the Americas,* London: Bantam.

Viveiros de Castro, E. (1998), 'The Transformation of Objects into Subjects in Amerindian Cosmologies', paper given in December 1998 at the University of Manchester; published in 1998 (in a slightly different version) as 'Cosmological Deixsis and Amerindian Perspectivism', *Journal of the Royal Anthropological Institute* 4: 469–88; reprinted in M. Lambek (ed.) (2002), *A Reader in the Anthropology of Religion*, Oxford: Blackwell.

von Franz, M.-L. (1980), *On Divination and Synchronicity: The Psychology of Meaningful Chance*, Toronto: Inner City Books.

Voss, A. (2000), 'The Astrology of Marsilio Ficino: Divination or Science?', *Culture and Cosmos* 4(2): 29–45.

Wallace, P. and Wallace, N. (1977), *Killing Me Softly: The Destruction of a Heritage*, Melbourne: Nelson.

Wallace-Murphy, T. and Hopkins, M. (1999), *Rosslyn: Guardian of the Secrets of the Holy Grail*, Shaftesbury: Element.

Waters, F. (1963), *Book of the Hopi: the First Revelation of the Hopi's Historical and Religious World-view of Life*, New York: Ballantyne.

Watson, J.B. (1931), *Behaviorism*, London: Kegan Paul, Trench, Trubner.

Weber, M. (1958 [1904–5]), *The Protestant Ethic and the Spirit of Capitalism*, New York: Charles Scribner & Sons.

—— (1991), *From Max Weber: Essays in Sociology*, ed. H.H. Gerth and C. Mills Wright, London: Routledge.

Webster, C. (1982), *From Paracelsus to Newton: Magic and the Making of Modern Science*, Cambridge: Cambridge University Press.

Weil, A. (1972), *The Natural Mind: A New Way of Looking at Drugs and the Higher Consciousness*, Boston: Houghton Mifflin.

Werbner, R. (1983), *Ritual Passage, Sacred Journey: The Process of Organization of Religious Movement*, Washington: Smithsonian Institution Press.

Bibliography

Williams, B. (1985), *Ethics and the Limits of Philosophy*, London: Fontana.
Willis, R. (1994), 'New Shamanism', *Anthropology Today,* December: 16–18.
—— (1999), *Some Spirits Heal, Others Only Dance: A Journey into Human Selfhood in an African Village*, Oxford: Berg.
Wittgenstein, L. (1953), *Philosophical Investigations*, ed. G.E.M. Anscombe and R. Rhees, Oxford: Blackwell.
Zimmer, H. (1948), *The King and the Corpse: Tales of the Soul's Conquest of Evil*, Princeton: Princeton University Press.
Zoller, R. (1982), 'Aristotelianism and Hermeticism in Medieval Astrology', *Geocosmic Research Monographs* 3: 24–8.

Index

Aborigines, Dreamtime 39–40
Abram, David 2, 111, 112, 128–9, 144
Adorno, Theodor 4, 79, 86, 93
Africa
  cosmic identities 29–32
  origin myths 42–3
  sky-earth connections 33–4
alchemy 8
altered states, consciousness 142–4
animals, subjectivity 121
animism 15–16, 129–30
anthropology
  and civilization 17–18
  experiential 140
Apollo 59
Aquinas, St Thomas 50, 70–1, 80
archaeology
  masculinist bias 18–22
  prehistoric civilizations 17–18
Aristotelian astrology 69–71
Aristotle 56, 104
Arroyo, Stephen 72
astrologers 109–10
astrology
  and science 52, 60–3, 71–2, 88, 92–106
  as divination 23–4, 58–60, 66–7, 109–14,
    148–9
  as ecology 122–4
  critics of 4, 16, 52, 93–6
  definition 1, 52–3
  history of 3, 16–23, 49–52, 109, 151–2
  modern attitudes 60–3
  research 90–1, 96–104
  schools of 65–75
Atkins, Peter 82, 83
augurium 49, 59
augury, Romans 57
Augustine, St 50
aurispicium 49, 59
Australia, celestial myths 39–40
axis, universal 135–7
axis mundi 137

Bachofen, J.J. 20
Bacon, Francis 76n4, 82
Bakhtin, Mikhail 1
Bambara people 136, 149n1
Bateson, Gregory 76n5, 80–1, 83, 106, 110, 112,
  117, 121
bâtons de commandement 19
Bauman, Zygmunt 133n1
behaviourism 139
Berlin, Isaiah 76n6, 79, 96
biblical stories 37n10
Blackett, Pat 119

body-based symbolism 29, 36nn8–9
Bohm, David 83
Bororo people 42–3, 141
Bouché-Leclerq, A. 60, 152
Bourguignon, Erika 143
Bower, T.G.R. 130–1
Brady, Bernadette 134n4
brain, duality 143, 144, 147
Breuil, Abbé 19
Briffault, Robert 20–1
Brockbank, James 107n9
Brown, George MacKay 4

Calasso, Roberto 68–9
Campbell, Alan 139
Campbell, Joseph 44
Capra, Fritjof 140
Castaneda, Carlos 140, 142
chakras 136
Chalmers, A.F. 103–4, 108n14
Chang Tsai 124
chaos theory 10, 14n8
China
  cosmic energy 136
  rivers 28
Chinniah, Charmaine 9–10
Chomsky, Noam 140
Chou Tun-I 117
Christianity
  and astrology 50, 60, 93
  pagan origins 28, 36n6
Chuang Tsu 87
Chu Hsi 116, 117
Cicero 59–60, 116
civilization, development of 17–18
Company of Astrologers 12, 150n11
'concrete magic' 13, 60–1, 74, 81, 111
consciousness
  altered states 142–4
  embodied 127–8
  infants 130–2, 134n3
  study of 139–40, 147, 149n5
  see also mind
constellations
  lunar 26
  views of 94–5
Copernicus 9, 14n7
Cornelius, Geoffrey 12, 23, 55, 59, 148, 150n11
cosmic models 135–7
CSICOP (Committee for the Scientific
  Investigation of Claims of the Paranormal) 96

daemones 68, 116–17, 148
Damasio, Antonio 144
Daniélou, Alain 28

Index

Darwin, Charles 119
Davidson, H.E. 55, 56
Dawkins, Richard
on astrology 6, 88, 93–6
scientism 82, 110, 124
'selfish gene' 100
Unweaving the Rainbow 93–4, 127, 134n3
Dean, Geoffrey 72, 107n7
de Heusch, Luc 29–31
Delphic Oracle 57, 59
Dennett, Daniel 16
de Santillana, Giorgio 18, 21, 44–7
Descartes, René 82
destiny *see* fate
dialogical imperative 2, 133
dialogue
human 130–2
with divinity 1–3, 11, 28–9, 132–3
disenchantment
and science 81–4
Weber's thesis 77–81
see also enchantment
divination
and astrology 23–4, 58–60, 66–7, 109–14,
148–9
discourse 11, 55–8
explaining 114–17
future of 117–19
ritual of 106, 148, 150n11
Dodds, E.R. 57
Dogon people 136
doxa 104
dreaming 15
Dreamtime 39–40
drumming, shamanic 142, 150n6
dualisms
brain 143, 144, 147
positive/negative 78, 136
sky/earth 32–5
Dürer, Albrecht 36n4

earth, and sky 28, 33–5
ecology, and astrology 122–4
Egypt 22, 27
Eliade, Mircea 44, 137, 149n2
embodied consciousness 127–8
Empson, William 78
enchantment 86–8, 112–13
see also disenchantment
episteme 104, 105–6, 114
Erikson, Milton 125n8
Europe, divinatory discourse 56–7
Eysenck, Hans 6

fate 55–8, 74–5
Feyerabend, Paul 79, 81, 90–1
Ficino, Marsilio 67, 134n4
Fipa people 15, 24
fire, myths of 33
foretelling, of fate 55–6
Foucault, Michel 77, 79, 85
Fowler, J.Warde 57
Franklin, Benjamin 51
Frazer, J.G. 41

Galileo 82
Gallagher, Shaun 131

Gauquelin, Michel and Françoise 6–8, 14n5, 72
Geller, Uri 7
gendered identity
moon 23, 31–2, 35–6n1
planets 23
see also women
Geneva, Ann 53
Gibson, William 14n9
Gilgamesh, myths 46–7, 47n5, 48n6
Gimbutas, Marija 21
global commonalities, myths 41–2, 44–7
Goddess culture 21
Gooch, Stan 25, 27, 41
Gould, Stephen Jay 83
Graves, Robert 138
Greeks
astrology 49, 59–60
divination 57
myths 41–2
Greene, Liz 62, 72, 73, 125n3
Greenfield, Susan 134n3

Halifax, Joan 137
Harner, Michael 142
Hawking, Stephen 82, 100
Heaton, John 63
Heniger, Polly 146, 147
Henry, John 5–9, 103, 108n14
Hepburn, Ronald 87
Hermetic astrology *see* neo-Platonic astrology
Hillman, James 75
Hipparchus 45
Hoban, Russell 124
Ho, Maewan 83
Homer 69
Hopi Native Americans 135–6
horary astrology 67, 148
Horkheimer, Max 79, 86, 93
horoscopos 49
Huichol Native Americans 138
humans, and universe 135–6, 147–9
hunter myths 43–4
Husserl, Edmund 2, 127–8, 131, 146
Huxley, Aldous 143
Hyde, Maggie 12, 111, 113, 119, 149, 150n11

Iamblichus 67, 116
Iceland, divination 56
I Ching 116, 117, 118
illud tempus 138, 149n4
Inca cosmology 26–7, 28
India
astrology 50
cosmic energy 136
rivers 28
infants, consciousness 130–2, 134n3
intersubjectivity 2, 128, 130
Israel, Beth Alpha zodiac 27

James, William 69, 79, 110, 117, 130, 139,
150n8
Jeans, James, *The Mysterious Universe* 5
Johnson, Mark 85, 98
Judaism, cosmic energy 136
Judder Effect 119–22
Jung, C.G. 44, 73, 116, 118, 120
Jupiter, gendered identity 23

Index

Kane, Sean   111, 122
katarche   49, 59, 151–2
Kepler, Johannes   8, 9, 14n6
Kontos, Alkis   84, 86–7
Kungkarangkalpa myth   40

Laclau, Ernesto   82
Lakoff, George   85, 98
Lash, John   25, 26
Latour, Bruno   118
Laughlin, Charles   8–9
Laussel Venus   20, 30, 36n2
Lebenswelt (life-world)   128
Leo, Alan   51, 72, 74–5, 122
Lévi-Strauss, Claude   32–3, 34–5, 41, 44
Lévy-Bruhl, Lucien   114–15, 120, 129–30, 133n2, 140–2
Lex, Barbara   144
Lilly, William   53, 61, 67, 109–10
Lloyd, G.E.R.   57
Lodmund the Old   56
Longley, Michael   98
Lord, Albert   132–3
Lovelock, James   83
Ludwig, A.M.   143
lunar zodiac
 constellations   26
 South America   26–7
Lyotard, François   84

Machiavelli, Niccolo   57
MacNeice, Louis   80
magic   76n4, 87
Margulis, Lynn   83
Mars
 effect on personality   6
 gendered identity   23
Marshack, Alexander   17, 18–20, 25
Marx, Karl   85
masculinist bias, archaeological studies   18–22
Matako people, myths   43
Mellaart, Andrew   21
Meltzoff, Andrew   131
menstrual cycle   19, 23, 26, 36n5
Merleau-Ponty, Maurice   2, 85, 118, 127, 129, 130, 131
Mesopotamia, astrology of   3, 17, 22, 25, 58–9
metis   13, 104–6, 121–2
Midgley, Mary   81–2
Milky Way   27, 28, 39, 47n1
Mill, John Stuart   79
mind
 as universe   133, 134n4
 see also consciousness
Miró, Joan   132
modern period, disenchantment   77–81
monism   78–81
moon
 and female cycles   19, 25, 26–7, 36n5
 gendered identity   23, 31–2, 35–6n1
 influence of   8, 19–20
 prehistoric observations of   17, 25–6
 see also lunar zodiac
Mor, Barbara   21
Morrison, J.S.   52, 57, 91
Mouffe, Chantal   82

Mound Builder culture   27
Mtumbi the Aardvark   31–2, 43–4
Müller, Max   44
Mumford, Lewis   80
Mungaleza   31
Myerhoff, Barbara   138
myths
 Australia   39–40
 definition   125n3
 global commonalities   41–2, 44–7
 hunter   43–4
 making of   132–3
 origin of stars   42–4
 sky-earth relations   32–5

Naess, Arne   140
Nagarjuna   119
near-death experience   138
'neo-astrology'   7
Neolothic period   18, 25–6, 45
neo-Platonic astrology   50, 67–9
Neptune, gendered identity   23
neurophysiology   144, 146, 147
'New Age' astrology   112
Noble, Vicki   19
North America, sky-earth mythology   35
Nyiru, myth of   40

objectivity, astrology   98–101, 111–12
omens, divination   58–60
Orion
 myths   41–2, 43–4, 46, 47
 and the Pleiades   40, 41
Other, dialogue with   1–2, 135, 139

Palaeolithic period   17, 18–21, 45
participation   114–15
Partridge, John   51
Pearce, A.J.   122
Peek, Philip M.   144–5
personality traits, and planetary positions   6–7
phenomenology   2, 127
Phillipson, Garry   96
phronesis   104
Pico della Mirandola   76n4
Pingree, David   151–2
planets
 as influence   70
 gendered identity   23
 and personality traits   6–7
 see also under individual planets
Plato   56, 69, 104
 see also neo-Platonic astrology
Pleiades, and Orion   40, 41–2
Plotinus   67, 116
pluralism   75
Plutarch   1, 68
Pluto, gendered identity   23
Polanyi, Michael   86, 118
popular astrology   65–6
Porphyry   67
possession, by spirits   143, 150n7
postmodern astrology   23–4
postmodernity   133n1
precession of the equinoxes   45
prehistoric civilizations   17–22, 25–6, 132–3

prelogical 130, 133n2
'primitive' societies
mentality 15–16, 114, 141
see also prehistoric civilizations
psychological astrology 72–5
Ptolemaic astrology 69–71, 151–2
Ptolemy 22, 49, 59–60, 70

Quechua cosmology 26–7, 28, 36n7

Radha, Lama Chime 121, 123
Radin, Dean 147
rainbow, analysis of 127
Rappaport, Roy 62, 97, 150n10
Raven myth 41–2
reflections, earth and sky 28, 33–5
relationism 118
religion
monotheism 78
see also Christianity
research, scientific 90–1, 96–104
Rhudhyar, Dane 72
Ridder-Patrick, Jane 10–11
ritual, divination 106, 148, 150n11
Roberts, Allen 29, 31, 43–4
Romans
astrology 49
divination 57, 59–60
Rose, Stephen 83

Sasportas, Howard 74
Saturn
effect on personality 6
gendered identity 23
influence on author 10, 11
Scarborough, Milton 80, 86
schizophrenia 138
Schoffeleers, Matthew 33
science
and astrology 52, 60–3, 71–2, 88, 93–106
and postmodernity 127
and religion 78–9
as disenchantment 81–4
research into astrology 90–1, 96–104
scientism 4, 81–3, 114, 121, 124
Scott, James C. 77, 79, 83, 104, 105–6, 108n16
seasons, cycle of 31
'seed moment' 65, 70, 73
Sefiroth 136
serpent, symbol of 21–2
shamanism 137–9, 142, 150n6
Sjöö, Monica 21
Skolimowski, Henryk 148
sky, and earth 28, 32–5
Smith, Barbara Herrnstein 79, 125n6
Snaketamer figure 26, 36n4
Socrates 105
South America
lunar zodiac 26–7
origin myths 42–3
sky-earth mythology 34–5
space science, and astrology 8–9
Sperry, Roger W. 143, 146, 147
spine, as axis 135–6

spirit possession 143, 150n7
Stone, Alby 55–6
subjectivity, astrology 98–101, 111–12
Sun
as symbol of self 73
visibility 25
superstition 51, 91
Sutcliffe, Thomas 96
Swift, Jonathan 51
synchronicity 120
system, the 84–6

Tabwa people 29–30, 31–2, 36nn8–9, 43–4
Taliessin 138
Tart, Charles C. 143
Taurus, myths 47
Tedlock, Barbara 143
Teller, Edward 83
Theosophy 51, 72
Thomas, Keith 50
Thompson, William Irwin 18, 19, 20, 24, 47
Thorstein 56
Tolkien, J.R.R. 87
Travers, P.L. 62
Tree of Life 137
Trevarthen, Colwyn 130, 131
truth 112, 125n6
Turner, Edith 141
Tylor, E.B. 15, 129–30

underworld 36n7
universe, human models of 135–7
Uranus
gendered identity 23
influence on author 10, 11
Urton, Gary 26–7, 28

Varela, Francisco 83
Venus, gendered identity 23
Virgo, concept of 36n3
Viveiros de Castro, Eduardo 119
von Dechend, Hertha 21, 44–7
von Franz, Marie-Louise 107n5

Wallace, Phyl and Noel 40
Watson, James 2
Watson, J.B. 139
Weber, Max 13, 55, 60, 75, 77–81, 113
Weinberg, Steven 95
Wells, H.G., War of the Worlds 5
Werbner, Richard 148
Williams, Bernard 114
Wittgenstein, Ludwig 110
Wolpert, Lewis 82
women
and lunar cycles 19, 23, 26–7, 36n5
prehistoric 19–22, 24

Yin and Yang 136
Yoruba, Ifa oracle 145

Zimmer, Heinrich 115
zodiac
lunar 26–8
solar 26